St. George's School

Sapientia Utriusque Vitæ Lumen

Presented by

Miss Doris Stretton
and
Mr. Gerald Stretton

October, 1986

The Dance Theatre of Jean Cocteau

Theater and Dramatic Studies, No. 33

Oscar G. Brockett, Series Editor

Leslie Waggener Professor of Fine Arts
and Professor of Drama
The University of Texas at Austin

Bernard Beckerman, Series Editor, 1980-1983

Brander Matthews Professor of Dramatic Literature
Columbia University in the City of New York

Other Titles in This Series

The Dance Theatre of Jean Cocteau

by
Frank W.D. Ries

UMI RESEARCH PRESS
Ann Arbor, Michigan

Produced and distributed by
UMI Research Press
an imprint of
University Microfilms International
A Xerox Information Resources Company
Ann Arbor, Michigan 48106

Library of Congress Cataloging in Publication Data

Ries, Frank W. D. (Frank William David), 1950-
The dance theatre of Jean Cocteau.

(Theater and dramatic studies ; no. 33)
Bibliography: p.
Includes index.
1. Ballet. 2. Cocteau, Jean, 1889-1963.
3. Dancing—Reviews. I. Title. II. Series.
GV1787.R54 1986   792.8'2   85-19078
ISBN 0-8357-1711-9 (alk. paper)

For my parents, with love and thanks

Orphée, 1944
Roland Petit, the choreographer, posed behind a
Cocteau drawing as Cocteau himself adjusts the
headpiece to be worn for the ballet, with Janine Charrat
to the right.
Photograph by Serge Lido.
(Courtesy of the Stravinsky-Diaghilev Foundation)

Contents

Figures

Preface

The world has always looked askance at a jack-of-all-trades—how can you be good in one field while expending energy in many directions? And if you want to be accepted by the cognoscenti you should specialize even further and concentrate on a narrow range within a given discipline. Jean Cocteau spent his career working in as many areas as possible, guided, he said, by his muses. He even invented a tenth muse for cinema when he began to direct and produce films. Much has been written about Cocteau in biographical terms as well as in specialized studies. Writers continue to be divided about his worth. His defenders call him the first true multimedia artist who was ahead of his time in his concepts and his creations; his detractors see him as a publicity seeker whose works were frequently trivial or merely sensational. Twenty years after his death Cocteau is still being reassessed and reevaluated. He continues to defy classification or, at least, no two critics seem to be able to agree on how to classify him.

Despite the various studies devoted to Cocteau's writings, poems, plays, films, designs, drawings, and theories there has never been an in-depth study devoted to his work within the dance world except for cursory overviews of his involvement with the Ballets Russes. There may be many reasons for this apparent neglect, mostly to do with Cocteau's exact relationship to dance. Terpsichore was the most reluctant of Cocteau's many muses since he himself was not a trained dancer and had to depend on others, usually the choreographer, to visualize his ideas. This, however, did not stop Cocteau from working and creating dances, just as his inability to compose music did not stop him from writing critiques of musicians and making himself the mentor for "Les Six." Even after his death, his plays, poems, designs, even his life story, have been the inspiration for theatrical dance presentations.

This book is mainly a discussion and analysis of Cocteau's work in ballet, his theories and writings on dance, and his influence on the dance world in general. Each particular ballet Cocteau was involved with (in whatever capacity) is discussed against the current activity in the dance world and, where important, in terms of Cocteau's personal involvement. The important revivals, if any, are explored immediately after the analysis of the original production. Although the ballets are looked at within the context of Cocteau's life, this book has no intention of being a biography of the poet nor a discussion of his other varied activities, unless they are directly connected with his work in dance.

After surveying all Cocteau's dance works one discovers that his major concern was the expansion of the thematic material for dance composition within the ballet idiom. Cocteau continually looked for new means for theatrical stimulation, following Diaghilev's dictum to "astonish" his audiences. Some historians have dismissed his approach as a continual search for the last word in fashion which later succumbed to pretense. For these critics his influence on dance would probably be seen as peripheral at best. Yet is this judgment really fair? Cocteau's self-evaluations often get in the way of the works he was involved with and it is always necessary to separate the two areas before making any conclusions. While many of Cocteau's dance contributions may not seem important at first, they were frequently inspirational for others in terms of the expansion of form and even technique. He was fascinated with the incorporation of everything from music hall numbers to acrobatics within the confines of classical ballet. Surprisingly, Cocteau did not work with any of the modern dance experimentalists but confined himself and his concepts primarily to ballet companies. Cocteau was fascinated with the challenge of working his revolution from within, rather than without, such as Isadora Duncan had done. He studiously avoided calling any of his dance works "ballets" and devised various terms of classification, usually different for each composition. This was his own vision of dance as theatre. His ideas may not seem radical today, because much of what he did has been adopted and assimilated by contemporary choreographers and designers. This does not, however, diminish their importance within the context of dance or theatre history.

Frank W. D. Ries

Santa Barbara, California

Acknowledgments

In a work of this length it is inevitable that many people and institutions be thanked. I am indebted to Selma Jeanne Cohen for her supervision and advice on a paper I delivered in her Russian Ballet seminar held in Chicago in 1975 (from which this present work evolved), and Oscar Brockett for his recommendations during the early stages of research. Parmenia Migel Ekstrom was extremely generous with the sources of the Stravinsky-Diaghilev Foundation and in allowing the material to be used in this book. The late Georges Auric, the late Sir Anton Dolin, Nicolas Beriosoff, the late Valentine Gross Hugo, the late Leonide Massine, the late Darius Milhaud, and Marina Svetlova were all extremely tolerant of my continual inquiries and I am also grateful to David Leonard of Dance Books, Ltd., and Norman Crider of the Ballet Shop in New York for supplying me with rare programs, books, and other items which were not readily available anywhere else.

Cocteau's writing style, idiomatic at best, is always difficult to convey in English. I am grateful to those translators, credited in the text, who have published translations of his works that I was able to use. Not all of his works, however, were translated and, although I have done a majority of the translations, I am grateful to Kenneth Griffiths for his generous help and time in translating the German text of the reviews for *La Dame à la licorne*, to Nadine Stafford Greybill for her recommendations on the early chapters (especially chapter 4), and Mrs. Ekstrom and Mme. Svetlova for going over the French to English text for both the footnotes and appendix.

Institutions and libraries which have been helpful for the research include the Dance Collection of the New York Public Library and Museum for the Performing Arts at Lincoln Center; the Music Library at Indiana University, Bloomington; the University Library, Cambridge, England; the British Museum, London; the Theatre Museum, Stockholm; the Bibliothèque de l'Opéra, Bibliothèque nationale and Bibliothèque de l'Arsenal in Paris; the Bayerische Staatstheater, Munich; and Sotheby Park Bernet, Monaco. I am also grateful to Marie-Françoise Christout in Paris for suggestions and Dr. Milo Keynes and the late Sir Geoffrey Keynes in England for advice and contacts that put me in reach of valuable primary materials.

In the later stages of the work Walter Meserve was untiring in his attention to detail and helped me clarify my presentation of the material. The comments and criticisms of Eugene Bristow, Sam Smiley, Richard Lorber, M. Henderson, and Rona Sande were also welcome, while the hospitality of Marcus Bugler in New York, M. et Mme. David Long in Paris, and Dr. Stephen Wyatt in London allowed me to have extended stays during important stages of research. I must also thank Martin Silver of the Music Library at the University of California, Santa Barbara, for checking certain dates and facts, and Edward F. Underhay for patience and advice during the last stages of writing and rewriting. If I have inadvertently forgotten to thank anyone for their help I ask their forgiveness. Despite all these marvelous contributions I must be held entirely responsible for the contents of this book.

The author is grateful to the following for permission to quote from copyrighted material: Alfred A. Knopf, Inc., for sections of *Notes Without Music*, by Darius Milhaud, translated by Donald Evans, edited by Rollo H. Meyers, copyright 1953; and John Murray, Publishers, for sections from *Dancing for Diaghilev*, by Lydia Sokolova, edited by Richard Buckle, copyright 1960.

1

Le Prince du Frivole

Poetry always causes a scandal. It is a stroke of luck that nobody notices it.
—Jean Cocteau, *Beauty Secrets*

Everything Jean Cocteau did he defined in terms of *poésie*—poetry. His autobiographical writings, rich in poetic style, are also rich in poetic license, but they are important in their documentation of what Cocteau felt was influential in his life. He was born on the fifth of July, 1889, Place Sully, at Maisons-Lafitte near Seine-et-Osie, a suburb of Paris where the racecourse brought the fashionable crowds on weekends from the city. Perhaps it was the view of the chic and famous that first excited the boy, who would always remain a Parisian in temperament, style, and taste throughout his life—whether it be his lifelong disregard for languages other than French (he only learned a smattering of English and German), or the wearing and giving of Cartier's Trinity or "Three Gold" rolling rings to his successive lovers and protégés.[1] The style Cocteau affected was not a reaction to a poverty-stricken childhood, since he was brought up in fairly well-to-do circumstances, and his family encouraged his study of the arts, especially painting. Home life, however, did not instill discipline. His teachers reported that he showed aptitude and intelligence, but his classwork suffered because he tended to do only what interested him.

Cocteau's father committed suicide in April 1899, under circumstances which have never been fully explained; Cocteau makes very few references to him (or fathers in general) in any of his writings and his mother remained the dominant figure in his life and frequently his work. The few memories Cocteau does have of both his parents has to do with their avid theatre-going, and he remembered himself as a child watching "my mother and father leaving for the theatre and from then on I have suffered from the fever of crimson and gold."[2] This fever developed into a fascination not only for what happened on the stage but also for what happened behind the stage and in the audience. When he was too young to be taken to the theatre, he would watch his mother in the ritual of preparation: "I was the audience for my mother's toilette."[3] He would follow her actions in the mirror and imagine how she would look in her theatre box, what she would see, how she would applaud. He too wanted to embark on "the red river" of the theatre carpets and know "the forbidden great gold rooms." Consoling himself with his mother's discarded programs, he would mentally recreate the performance from what he read and visually recreate them with his brother in the toy theatre they built together. He waited impatiently to enter the magical world itself. When he was finally taken to the theatre, it was not to an opera or a classical tragedy, but, in consideration of his youth, a "spectacle," a form of mixed entertainment very popular before the war, vestiges of which are still found in the British pantomime.

> Every curtain that rises takes me back to that solemn moment when, as the curtain of the Châtelet [Theatre] rose on 'Round the World in Eighty Days, the chasms of darkness and of light became one, separated by the footlights. These footlights set the bottom of the wall of painted canvas aglow. As the flimsy wall did not touch the boards one obtained a glimpse of coming and going [like flames leaping] out of a furnace.[4]

This "coming and going" would always fascinate Cocteau, and he was always analyzing the perspective in performance from the spectator's seat in the auditorium with the very different view obtained from backstage in the wings. He wanted to get as close to the workings as possible; he was a moth drawn to this particular flame. "The theatre is a furnace. Whoever does not suspect this is consumed in the long run or else burns out at once. It damps one's zeal. It attacks by fire and water."[5] Cocteau developed an empathy for performers and would suffer and cry, laugh and shout along with them. In terms of dance, feats of technique or great pantomimic characterizations would alike leave him breathless: "delicious moments of suffering that I would not exchange for anything."[6]

The theatrical spectacles excited the young Cocteau, but the circus influenced him even more and would play an important part in his work in ballet; it can be found in Parade, Le Boeuf sur le toit, Le Train bleu, Les Mariés de la Tour Eiffel. The smell of the circus, the delicious combination of the everyday and the magical tingled his nerves. "Horse manure, tanbark, stables, sweat, expectations, excitement," all was a "golden dung-dust" which was heaped upon the spectators and created an illusion of glamour in the circus ring.[7]

There were the acrobats with their daredevil tricks of lightning-fast jumps and somersaults with easy, graceful landings—the contrast within the purity of movement. There was the little horse that galloped across the stage with the entr'acte sign on its back—the reality of the imaginary horse Cocteau would concoct in 1917 for Parade. There were the clowns with their slapstick humor and the nautical pantomime, the traditional grand finale of the French circus. In 1904, five years after Cocteau's first view of circus life, "Americain rhythm" entered the Nouveau-Cirque with the strutting finery of the cakewalk, which made "everything else turn pale and flee."[8] This was Cocteau's first introduction to American jazz and its roots in Negro spirituals and dances. These elements would prove very influental on the group of musicians he would encourage in the 1920s, "Les Six." Negro dancers were imported from America and Cocteau watched, fascinated with their dance technique. One of the top performing pairs were M. et Mme. Elks, whom Cocteau described in some detail:

> They danced: skinny, crooked, beribboned, glittering with sequins, spangled with gaudy lights, hats raked over their eyes, their ears, knees higher than their thrust-out chins, hands twirling flexible canes, wrenching their gestures from themselves and hammering the artificial floor with taps on their patent leather shoes. They danced, they glided, they reared, they kicked, they broke themselves in two, three, four, then they stood up again, they bowed. . . . And behind them the whole city, the whole of Europe, began dancing.[9]

This dance frenzy swept Europe as new forms were tried on the ballroom floor: the tango, the rhumba, the cakewalk, the turkey-trot. Exhibition dancers such as Vernon and Irene Castle showed society how to dance the newest fads.[10]

Cocteau, meanwhile, was trying to give his life some purpose. Only fifteen in 1904, but precocious for his age, he would continually run away from school and continued to have a difficult time disciplining himself to study. He spent the time away from classes writing poetry and going to the theatre. These theatrical visits enabled him to meet Edouard de Max (1869–1925), an actor of great flamboyance and style who was then appearing at the Odéon. Offstage Max wore eyeshadow and jewels and onstage his deportment tended to be effeminate, but he was extremely popular with Parisian audiences, especially when he played Nero in Racine's tragedy *Britannicus*. Max was very impressed with the young Cocteau's work on paper—so much so that he hired the Theatre Femina for the afternoon of 4 April 1908, and, before a fashionable, invited audience, with a number of other actors, he read Cocteau's fledgling poems. It was a very chic debut for a not quite nineteen-year-old boy, who also proved to be charming to everyone who met him. The society Cocteau was introduced to was dominated by homosexuals who would naturally be taken by his youth and attractiveness, but that did not lessen their perception of the young boy's talent. Marcel Proust (1871–1922), then in the midst of writing his *A la recherche du temps perdu*, thought him "remarkably gifted and intelligent," and predicted he would have a remarkable career, if he would only discipline himself.[11] At this point, however, Cocteau was too busy enjoying the new friends, parties, social engagements, and soirées to worry about discipline. He met such people as Eugénie, last Empress of the French, who gave him posies since she could no longer award medals, and society nicknamed him *le Prince du Frivole* since he was so urbane, so witty, so highspirited, and something of a dandy. At the time he found the nickname flattering, but later discovered its distracting qualities as people were reluctant to take him seriously.

Paris in the decade before the war was a mecca for artists of all nationalities and philosophies and it was this Paris that Cocteau was only now beginning to discover. It was the period of "isms" when humor became a method and style, when dreams became part of an artistic reality, when work was shaped by ambiguity and open to equivocal interpretations. Felicien Fagus, critic for the *Gazette d'Art*, commented in a review of Pablo Picasso's (1881–1973) paintings in 1901 that "the image of Paris as a good-time city, the home of fashion, fun and refined feelings was fading. A change was in the air."[12] No longer did artists have to display their works at official salon shows to gain acceptance and the youthful rebels of Montmartre and Montparnasse pitted themselves against massive displays of traditional art, such as the Sculpture Hall in the Grand Palais during the Exposition de Paris in 1900, by opening a "Salon des Indépendents," or in private showings, as Picasso did. There was a change in the social habits of the artists involved, as well. No longer did they frequent the houses of the famous and aristocratic, who had once been their patrons, but they gathered in cafes such as the Café au Lapin or the Moulin Rouge where every new idea could be heatedly debated, accepted, or rejected.

In music, Claude Debussy (1862–1918) and Maurice Ravel (1875–1937) were experimenting with tonal colors and structural harmonies that would soon challenge the facile and melodious compositions of Jules Massenet (1842–1912) and Charles Gounod (1818–1893). In drama, however, France continued to follow the tradition set down by Eugène Scribe (1791–1861) and Alexandre Dumas, *fils* (1824–1895), with such playwrights as Paul Hervieu (1857–1915), who wrote dramas of ideas, while Georges Feydeau (1862–1921) penned witty farces set in exaggerated situations. However, this is hindsight analysis, for drama at this time was just as highly respected as her sister arts of music, painting, sculpture and opera and all were considered important and innovative in varying degrees. This was not so with dance and in this period one usually meant ballet when referring to dance in its theatrical connotations.

The technique of the ballet dancer had been handed down from the courts of Italy and codified by the dancing masters of Louis XIV, who made the art respectable and, for a time, more important than opera or theatre. Ballet was aristocratic in bearing and manner and during the seventeenth century had dealt mostly with subjects of myths intertwined with compliments to the ruler which, by the eighteenth century, had evolved into pastorals in Trianon-styled settings.

After the French Revolution the technique of ballet began to evolve in a new direction with the emphasis gradually being placed more and more on the ballerina, who was learning how to pose on the points of her toes in her heel-less dancing shoes. Eventually darning gave some support to the ends of her slippers and roles began to emphasize the female dancer as sylph, ondine, or sprite, floating through misty glades or enchanted forests. During the Romantic period the ballerina dominated the dance stages of Europe and the Paris Opéra produced such masterpieces as *La Sylphide* (1832) and *Giselle* (1841) to showcase the dancer-actress as star.

By this period, however, the intelligentsia were deriding ballet as a middle-class entertainment and involvement was allowed only in the most surreptitious manner. Théophile Gautier (1811–1872), the great Romantic poet who praised the dance in so many of his reviews, was discouraged from putting his name on the scenario of *Giselle*. Even Eugène Scribe, though he allowed his name to be associated with his boulevard plays, wrote most of his ballet scenarii anonymously. By the end of the nineteenth century, ballet had decayed to such an extent in Paris that men's roles were played *en travesti* by women and dancing was relegated to the third act of an opera or operetta or in the revival of a tried favorite such as *La Farandole* (1883/1885). When something innovative was tried, like the ballet *Namouna* (1882), it seemed out of place at the Paris Opéra and quickly disappeared.[13]

Some of the *literati* at the turn of the century considered dance as having greater potential than was revealed in the brief divertissements inserted into theatrical presentations. Stéphane Mallarmé (1842–1898) thought dance could be inspirational, though he still felt it was a predominantly female art. He idealized woman into "the dancer" and felt only the performer could show the dance since "dancing alone, because of its evolutions, together with mime, seem to me to necessitate a real space on stage."[14] For Mallarmé the abstract dance was personified by Loïe Fuller (1862–1928), though she was not a dancer in the classical sense and had never received any dance training. Fuller was an American who began in touring shows and revues but did not really make a name for herself until she appeared in Paris at the Folies-Bergère in 1892. For the Exposition in 1900 a special theatre was erected for her where she could experiment with new lighting effects on the swirling draperies which she wore and which she would twist and turn to create butterflies, a blooming flower, wind storms, or leaping fire. Cocteau saw her at the 1900 Exposition and wrote about her thirty-five years later in his *Portraits-souvenirs*:

> I retain a single lively, flamboyant image from that confusing, dusty Exposition: Loïe Fuller. . . . Is it at all possible to forget this woman who invented the dance of her epoch? A fat American girl, who was ugly and wore glasses [off stage], standing on a special trapdoor-lens [illuminated from below], maneuvering waves of supple voile with poles, and somber, active, invisible, like the bee in the flower, the arm spun around her like countless orchids of light and [billowing waves of] fabric that wind, ascend, flare, swish, turn, float, change form, like pottery in the hands of the potter. . . . "[15]

Fuller inspired many French writers and artists and helped spark some to hope dance did have possibilities beyond the pink tulle of the corps de ballet of the Paris Opéra. It was Isadora Duncan (1878–1927), however, who had an even greater influence in the dance world.

Duncan, like Fuller, was also an American who had difficulty establishing herself in the United States and decided to try Europe. After only a few ballet classes, which she considered too restrictive, she created her own dance style and philosophy which she felt should begin with inner expressiveness. She abandoned tights and the tutu for a loose Greek-style drapery and bare feet. She toured Europe with increasing success, even going to Russia in 1905, and established Paris as her center of residence, though she had schools which she supervised not only in the French capital but also Berlin and, later, Moscow. Cocteau did not meet Isadora until 1912 in Nice, but she left a profound impression on him. "Isadora!" he exclaimed, "How much I remember this admirable and dignified woman. I would like to paraphrase Nietzsche and Wilde: 'She becomes the best because she is the dance.'"[16] Cocteau thought her a little mad, but the more fascinating for it. For him she was a dancer who could perform magnificently under any circumstances, whether she was accompanied by an orchestra in Cologne or by a phonograph recording in a small drawing room in Nice. Cocteau saw her as Jocaste, victim of fate. When he later wrote his play, La Machine infernale, his retelling of the Oedipus myth, he had his Jocaste strangle herself with a red scarf, just as Isadora had been strangled by her red scarf when it caught in the spokes of the wheel of her car in 1927. The parallel was intentional: "To the end she was brave and obstinate as ever."[17] The color red would later take on symbolic meaning for Cocteau when depicting his women on stage, as red was used for the female garb in such ballets as Le Jeune homme et la mort, Phèdre, and La Dame à la licorne.

While Fuller and Duncan were inspirational for many artists, they could only have a limited influence on the technical aspects of dance. They were solo performers who depended on their personalities and style to carry their ideas across to audiences and training was of secondary consideration in their work—perhaps in reaction to the world of ballet where training was of primary concern. Duncan did try to set up schools and a technique in later years but most of the schools collapsed soon after her death because of the lack of an organized, systematic approach. Ballet, where the individual was subordinate to the group in the learning of an approved pattern of steps and movements, had potential for development if it did not become too rigid in the following of a formula approach. This is what had happened to late nineteenth-century ballet in France: it had lost its expressiveness in the pursuit of a formalism set by a previous (Romantic) aesthetic. Ballet, however, can be vitalized by transplantation since it is not so dependent on a particular personality and as long as essential basics of technique and tradition are preserved in its new geographical environment. Italy had transferred dance to France during the Renaissance where it had been transformed without losing its essential focus on training and discipline. The same had happened when choreographers and dancing masters spread French styles and techniques across the map of Europe during the eighteenth and nineteenth centuries.

Now Russia, which had accepted and revitalized balletic form, gave it back to the West through the presentation of the Ballets Russes, beginning in 1909. Fuller and Duncan had foretold the possibilities within dance but, for many, it was only the Ballets Russes that fulfilled these promises.

Ballet in Russia had begun during the reign of Empress Anna Ivanovna (1730–40), when she had allowed a school to be established in 1738. Ballet remained attached to the Imperial Court and was carefully controlled by a director personally appointed by the Tsar. While such control may have limited certain topics for dance action it also gave guaranteed security for the artist and the development of the schooling to produce these artists. Under the ballet master Marius Petipa (1818–1910) such masterpieces as *Don Quixote* (1869), *La Bayadère* (1877), *Sleeping Beauty* (1890), and *Raymonda* (1899) were created. They were formal ballets in three or four acts with detailed mime scenes, many divertissements, a large corps de ballet, and all centered around the prima ballerina. Though similar to the French ballets of the period in outward appearances, there were strong differences in approach, since the Russian school still allowed the male his place on the dance stage while the superiority of the choreographic talents of Petipa, combined often with the musical talents of Peter Tchaikovsky (1840–93) and Alexander Glazunov (1865–1936), produced dance spectacles of the highest order. By the turn of the century, however, such formula presentations were no longer as impressive and Petipa was forcibly retired in 1903. This did not halt the Petipa style, though, and ballets continued to be produced in the mold of the former master, so dance in Russia seemed to be heading for the same rigidity that had confined the French Romantic ballet. Change can take place, though, within the system, rather than as a Duncanesque revolt from without, and one dancer, Mikhail Fokine (1880–1942), while finding faults with the Petipa structure, decided that the balletic schooling was still necessary for the creation of the performing artist. Briefly, Fokine suggested that ballet should be an integrated unit of music, dance, and decor, while traditional mime language should be replaced by a more natural and motivated gesticulation that could be conveyed through the entire body; pointe work should be used as an extenstion of character, rather than as an acrobatic display of bravura technique.[18]

Fokine's proposals were not received with great favor by the Imperial Ballet authorities when he submitted his theories with a ballet scenario for *Daphnis et Chloé* in 1904, but a group of artists which included Alexandre Benois (1870–1960) and Léon Bakst (1866–1924) found his ideas of great interest. Subsequently, Fokine was introduced through these gentlemen to Serge Diaghilev (1872–1929), who had helped produce the magazine *The World of Art* between 1899 and 1904 and had presented in Paris an exhibition of Russian art in 1906, a concert of Russian music in 1907, and the opera *Boris Godunov* in 1908. Diaghilev's French producer Gabriel Astruc (1860–1938) had then suggested the possibility of some of the ballet dancers of the Imperial Theatres being presented

Figure 1.   Jean Cocteau with Serge Diaghilev, ca. 1924
            (Courtesy of the Stravinsky-Diaghilev Foundation)

along with the opera in the next season. When Diaghilev met Fokine, he knew he had a choreographer with exciting vision who could create ballets that would be a true synthesis of all the arts as he, Diaghilev, saw them. Diaghilev also knew he could tap the potential of such dancers as Anna Pavlova (1881–1931), Tamara Karsavina (1885–1978), Adolph Bolm (1884–1951), and Vaslav Nijinsky (1888–1950), since the season could be arranged to coincide with their summer holiday from the Imperial Theatres. Diaghilev had especially become fascinated with the prodigious technique of Nijinsky, who would eventually become his lover, but it was not for personal reasons alone that Diaghilev agreed to exhibit the Russian ballet. Rather, it was to show Paris great dancing such as it had not seen since the early Romantic period and to present balletic compositions different from the Petipa formula.[19]

Paris was ripe for Diaghilev's great experiment. The city was the center for experimentation in music, painting, and literature, and had already witnessed the very personal, albeit stimulating, forms of dance that Fuller and Duncan displayed. Already interested in Russian culture due to the art and music concerts Diaghilev had previously presented, both salon society and the avant-garde in Montparnasse were anticipating the next Russian season. The Ballets Russes would profoundly affect many artists and writers, not least of whom was Jean Cocteau.

2

Jean Cocteau and Serge Diaghilev: The Influence of the Ballets Russes and the Creation of *Le Dieu bleu*

In effect, I was bowed into the theatre with the Ballets Russes *of Serge de Diaghilev which turned everything [in Paris] upside down and brought to this cosmopolitan world such spectacles of luxury and violence that I never had imagined existed.*

—Jean Cocteau, *Le Théâtre et la Mode*

The Ballets Russes particularly affected Cocteau, not only by stimulating him towards involvement with the dance, but also by showing him how this stimulation could be used and assimilated with his own ideas.

Today, when so many changes occur so rapidly and society is accustomed to cultural stimuli that are quickly assimilated and just as quickly rejected, it is difficult to imagine the influential and lasting impact the Ballets Russes had on Western culture. Even contemporary scholars tend to neglect or misunderstand the importance of the Ballets Russes. Not only was Cocteau astonished by "the spectacles of luxury and violence," but so were many other writers, poets, designers, directors, composers, painters and sculptors who used the ideas of the invading Russians for their own kinetic or plastic purposes.

Diaghilev, however, was almost unable to offer a *Saison Russe* in 1909 when the powerful influence of the Russian *prima ballerina assoluta* Mathilde Kschessinska (1872–1971) halted the support of Imperial funds. Her withdrawal from the Parisian enterprise was due to her own annoyance at the choice of roles Diaghilev had given her, and Diaghilev had to turn to private patrons to raise enough funds to pay for the sets and costumes. Gabriel Astruc, in Paris, supplied the funds to refurbish the Théâtre du Châtelet in the grandest possible manner in order that the premiere would be the event of the season. The season included the following: *Le Pavillon d'Armide*, a tribute to the French Baroque designed by Alexander Benois; the "Polovtsian Dances" from the opera *Prince Igor*, which presented such virtuoso and athletic male dancing that women in the audience fainted; *Le Festin*, a hodgepodge divertissement from the Petipa repertoire, but disguised in exotic Bakst costuming; *Les Sylphides*, Fokine's tribute to the Romantic age set to the music of Chopin; and finally *Cléopâtre*, an exotic cornucopia of music, dance, and sensual pleasures clothed in some of Bakst's most luxurious finery. Paris had seen nothing like it, and neither had the young and impressionable Cocteau.

Yet for all his social connections Cocteau was not at the *répétition générale*, which was by invitation only, nor at the opening night, though many authors assume he was at both events.[1] His very first visit to this evening of ballet was with his mother and sister, not his socially important friends.[2] At a turning point in his career but unsure which direction to take, the Ballets Russes became the fireworks lighting the way for Cocteau:

> The Russian ballet of Serge de Diaghilev played its part in this critical phase [of my career]. He was splashing Paris with color. The first time I attended one of his performances (they were giving *Pavillon d'Armide*) I was in a stall rented by my family. The whole thing unfolded far behind the footlights, in that burning bush in which the theatre blazes for those who do not regularly go backstage.[3]

At this performance of *Le Pavillon*, Cocteau states that he saw Pavlova and Nijinsky dance, and as Cocteau watched he experienced a shock which no poetry had ever been able to give him. It was

> a sharp pang of yearning to get a closer view of things unmeasurable and unattainable such as no poem of Heine's, no prose of Poe's, no fever-dream had ever given me, and since, I have invariably had the same sensation, at once subconscious and acute, which I attribute to the silent and nebulous precision of all they do.[4]

Cocteau was here responding to both the technical precision of the trained dancer and sensual pleasure of the beautiful body in motion—so well revealed by Bakst's exotic costuming. Cocteau realized that the performer onstage did not always resemble the person offstage (something he would soon find out about Nijinsky), but that did not dissuade him from seeking admittance into Diaghilev's "inner circle."

The key to his acceptance was Misia Edwards (1872–1950), née Godebska. She was musically precocious and her opinion was respected by many of France's leading musicians. She had married Thadée Natanson, cofounder of *La Revue blanche*, eventually divorcing him for Alfred Edwards, the wealthy publisher of *Le Matin* from whom she separated in 1910 to live with José-Maria Sert (1976–1945), the Spanish painter she would eventually marry. She was a busybody, insufferably snobbish, and enjoyed using her influence in society. She also had an extraordinary gift of musical perceptiveness which was respected by even the

Figure 2.   Cocteau's Drawing of Anna Pavlova, Made in 1955
(*Private Collection*)

surly Igor Stravinsky (1882–1971), the young Russian composer whom Diaghilev was just then bringing to world attention. Cocteau called Misia the "Queen of the Russian Ballet" because of her influence over Diaghilev, and he captured this domineering nature of hers in the character of the Princess in his novel *Thomas l'Imposteur*. Her influence over Diaghilev was due to her support during his earlier enterprises—she had bought up the empty seats the season Diaghilev had presented *Boris Godunov* in order that he would not be disappointed—and her judgment on new musical talent, which Diaghilev always sought. The Russian impresario admitted that she was one of the few women with whom he could get along.[5]

At a soirée of Misia's, Cocteau was finally able to meet Diaghilev, and the French poet claimed "from that moment I was a member of the company," referring to the Ballets Russes.[6] This claim, however, was far from the truth. "Heaven knows," Misia herself remarked, "that Jean [Cocteau] was irresistible at the age of twenty—but it needed something more to claim the right to collaborate with Diaghilev."[7] Cocteau, however, seems to have been irresistible enough to be given a *carte de circulation*, the magical and precious slip of paper that allowed the bearer to go backstage at any time and to see any performance he wished. Misia also seems to have allowed Cocteau to frequent her private box, as Cocteau claims that he only saw the ballet from the wings or "behind Madame Sert, topped with her Persian aigrette, Diaghilev [there also] following his dancers with a pair of tiny mother-of-pearl opera glasses."[8]

While Cocteau was using Misia to get closer to Diaghilev, Misia was also using Cocteau because of his connections with bohemian artistic circles and his knowledge about the young musicians in Paris. Needed as a catalyst, he was not wanted for his own talents and Misia admitted this quite frankly in her memoirs:

> I had the opportunity of putting him [Diaghilev] into contact with all the young French musicians whom I had known through Jean Cocteau, and many of whom owe to Diaghilev and Cocteau, if not their celebrity, at any rate the satisfaction of having acquired it at an earlier age than they would otherwise have done.[9]

However, during this time, Misia made sure that Cocteau was frustrated in his attempts to do anything directly for the company.

Cocteau channeled his frustrations into a literary journal that he started in 1909 entitled *Schéhérazade*, inspired by Rimsky-Korsakov's famous composition and the fascination for the East which the Ballets Russes had engendered, though Fokine's ballet of that name would not appear until 1910. The front cover of the journal was designed by Paul Iribe (1892–1937), a young artist whose drawings were reminiscent of Beardsley, and the contributors to the magazine included many people who would later work with Cocteau on his ballets. Among them were the composer Reynaldo Hahn (1875–1947), a student of the well-known opera composer Jules Massenet and a friend of Marcel Proust, and Marie Laurencin (1885–1956), a young painter whose work would later catch the eye of Diaghilev. The journal, lasting until its issue of 15 March 1911, was popular with the *beau monde* but not with the avant-garde, who were beginning to see anything connected with Diaghilev as too decadent for their tastes.[10] Cocteau's reputation with the avant-garde was also weakened because he spent considerable time with the Ballet Russes. In fact, he became something like a mascot to the company, a position the ballerina Tamara Karsavina speaks about in her memoirs, *Theatre Street:*

> A permanent figure of the theatre was Jean Cocteau, the *enfant terrible* of rehearsals. Like a mischievous fox terrier, he bounded about the stage, and often had to be called away: "Cocteau, come away, don't make them laugh." Nothing could stop his exuberant wit; funny remarks spluttered from under his voluble tongue—Roman candles, vertiginous Catherine wheels of humour. That summer I sat to [sic] Jacques Blanche for my portrait. A quieter refuge from the feverish pulsation of Parisian life could not have been found than in his large studio at Passy . . . [when] the sudden appearance of Cocteau in the studio would bring a boisterous note. As if he vowed never to locate himself anywhere, his voice now spoke from behind canvases, now called from the garden, unexpectedly addressed us from the top of a gallery. Standing there he forestalled our remarks and, pronouncing himself a preacher, a flow of extemporaneous speech immobilized him for a little while.[11]

Later this *enfant terrible* would become, in Benois's words, "the arbiter of French taste," but now he was only tolerated, and was even made the butt of jokes.[12] Prince Peter Lieven (1887–1943), a Russian aristocrat who was a keen contemporary observer of the Ballets Russes, tells of one evening when Diaghilev and Cocteau were sharing a cab home when Cocteau was rather drunk and very sleepy. As Diaghilev descended from the cab at the Mirabeau Hotel, he gave the driver whispered instructions to continue as far as the Hotel des Reservoirs in Versailles. Cocteau awoke, much later, to find himself in the country in the early hours of the morning, miles from his home. Diaghilev would never have played such jokes on Benois or Bakst, or even his principal dancers, but Cocteau, the company "mascot," was not yet a person Diaghilev really respected.[13]

Cocteau studied Diaghilev carefully, and there is no reason to doubt he tried to imitate the impresario's style in these early years. The poet's word-picture of this talented Russian is a vivid and revealing portrait:

> Serge de Diaghilev appeared to wear the smallest hat in the world. If you put this hat on, it came right down to your ears. For his head was so large that any head covering was too small for him.
> His dancers nicknamed him *Chinchilla* because of one lock kept white in his dyed and very black hair. He stuffed himself into a coat with a collar of opossum, and sometimes fastened it with the help of a safety pin. His face was that of a mastiff, his smile that of a young crocodile, one tooth sticking over his lip. Sucking at his teeth was with him a sign of pleasure, of fear, of anger. He chewed his lips, topped by a little mustache, in the back of some stage-box from

which he kept an eye on his artists in whom he let nothing pass. And his watery eye was cast down with the curve of a Portuguese oyster.[14]

Though not without its humor, this description shows the admiration and respect Cocteau had for Diaghilev.

While he would try to emulate Diaghilev, it was Nijinsky who tantalized the young poet and for whom Cocteau would write his first ballet:

> Nijinsky was below average height. Body and soul, he was pure professional deformity. His face, of Mongol type, was joined to his body by a very long and very thick neck. The muscles of his thighs and those of his calves stretched the fabric of his trousers and gave him the appearance of having legs bent backwards. His fingers were short, as if cut off at the knuckles. In short, one would never have believed that this little monkey with sparse hair, wearing a skirted overcoat and a hat balanced on the top of his head, was the idol of the public.[15]

What impressed Cocteau was the man on stage. The foregoing description sets the picture for the transformation of a plain and somewhat gawky human being to an artist of the highest magnitude, one of Cocteau's "monstre sacré," a holy monster. Nijinsky was made to be seen at a distance and under the magic of stage lights. "On the stage his over-developed muscles became slim, his figure lengthened (his heels never touched the ground), his hands became the fluttering leaves of his gestures, and as for his face, it was radiant."[16]

Cocteau was especially fascinated with Nijinsky's performance in *Le Spectre de la rose*, a ballet first performed in 1911 which showcased the dancer's incredible technical virtuosity. It was a simple pas de deux between a young girl who has just returned from a ball and the spirit of the rose which visits her in her dream. Intensely interested in the artist on and off the stage, Cocteau emphasized the dual personality of a performer:

> Instead of watching the performance from out front, I stood in the wings, where there was an even better performance. After lightly kissing the girl, the Spectre of the Rose leaps out her window . . . and lands among the stagehands, who squirt water into his face and scrub him with towels, like a boxer between rounds. What grace coupled with what brutality! I still hear the thunder of that applause, still see the young man smeared with greasepaint, sweating, panting, one hand pressed to his heart and the other clutching a stage brace. He collapsed on a chair, and in a few seconds, slapped, drenched, pummeled, he walked back onstage, bowing, smiling.[17]

Later Cocteau would extend this description to include a technical explanation of the famous leap:

> He [Nijinsky] had noticed that half the final leap of *Le Spectre de la rose* could not be seen from the auditorium. He invented a double leap, a way of tying himself in a knot in the air while offstage and then falling headlong into the wings.[18]

It was this combination of grace and brutality, of the "pauvre athlète" who could transform himself into a god, that always fascinated Cocteau, a duality with which Cocteau would subsequently imbue characters in his films, books, plays, and ballets.[19]

Cocteau make several ink sketches of Nijinsky in *Le Spectre de la rose* in which he caught the dancer panting backstage and being fanned with a towel by his servant, Dimitri, while a concerned group including Diaghilev, Bakst, Misia and José Sert, and Serge Grigoriev (1883–1968), the *régisseur* for the ballet, looked on.[20] Cocteau also drew a humorous sketch of Nijinsky as the Rose in *Le Spectre* including Diaghilev dressed as the young girl.[21] Diaghilev may not have been amused by this joke, though Cocteau's sense of ridicule was not directed exclusively at the impresario.

Grotesque sketches of Bakst, Benois, Stravinsky, Karsavina, and other members of the Ballets Russes poured forth from Cocteau's prolific pen.[22] In some way these sketches are more trustworthy than the poet's later memoirs since the sketches were done at the time of performance. The immediacy of their impact and the quick deftness of line remain a hallmark of the Cocteau style. In the *Le Spectre* drawings, the heavy muscles and mongolian features of the panting and exhausted Nijinsky are captured in a few concise strokes of the pen. For Cocteau this image of Nijinsky—youthful, mysterious, sensual—was to remain the only one. He never wrote or spoke about Nijinsky's subsequent madness and eventual decline. The dancer's broken puppet of *Petrushka* brought forth tears from Cocteau; Nijinsky's golden slave in *Schéhérazade* was like a "fish leaping up and down on the bottom boards of a boat."[23] But on the dancer's madness, not a word. Cocteau seems to have blocked out the personal tragedy and concentrated on the transformation of person to performer, "la déformation professionelle."

His adulation for Nijinsky continued when Cocteau collaborated with Iribe on a limited edition book about the dancer that contained a six line poem by Cocteau with a full-page drawing by Iribe to accompany each line of verse. Although the illustrations emphasized the sensual and erotic characteristics of Nijinsky's portrayals, this was not unusual at this time. Being the first really important male dancer Paris had seen since August Vestris (1760–1842) had leapt across the stages of *ancien régime* Europe, it was not surprising that many artists were fascinated with Nijinsky's combination of incredible technique and sensual charisma. For homosexuals like Cocteau, male dancing represented acceptable voyeurism in a society that had to remain discreet in those post-Wildean days. Cocteau's poem was filled with double meanings and symbolic references, despite its briefness:

> Apollo holds in his hand the string from which he dangles.
> Black slave to the Sultana, he flies as he breaks from his bonds,
> And the decor reminds one of the tail of a peacock.

> He throws, like a Hermes eager to perform his mysterious errands,
> Those flowers which we do not see, then pursues them
> And carries off all hearts on his invisible wings![24]

Is it too much to see the sycophantic Cocteau trying to flatter Diaghilev with his illusion to the impresario as "Apollo" holding Nijinsky's strings? Or could this be a reference to *Petrushka*, which was in the planning stages when the poem was written? However it is interpreted, Cocteau obviously meant to compliment both producer and dancer. But this did not mean that he was respected or admired by the objects of his attentions. Sert and Diaghilev would nickname him "Jeanchik" but, as Prince Peter Lieven remarked, "even at the end of this season [1910], Cocteau was still not accepted as part of the inner circle."[25]

It may seem difficult to comprehend why the young Cocteau spent so much time and effort trying to be accepted by Diaghilev and his entourage when he was already lionized and courted by half the Parisian society. Cocteau saw the Ballets Russes as an important new door in his artistic life, a door that he had to open at all costs:

> My mind went by instinct straight to the mark, but did not know how to use it. . . . I elbowed my way through a mass of quarrels, disputes, trials for heresy. . . . I searched for myself. I thought I recognized myself, I lost sight of myself, I ran after myself, I caught up with myself, out of breath.[26]

At this juncture Cocteau thought that he wanted more than anything else to write a ballet for Diaghilev centering on his idol, Nijinsky. At the end of the 1910 season Diaghilev finally gave Cocteau that chance.

Before returning to Russia in the autumn of 1910, Diaghilev commissioned a ballet to be entitled *Le Dieu bleu* with Cocteau and Frédéric de Madrazo (1890–1922) writing the libretto. Madrazo was a society artist who was closely connected with the Proust entourage and whose portraits were much in demand in salon circles. The composer Diaghilev selected was Reynaldo Hahn, who was connected with Cocteau's magazine, *Schéhérazade*. Bakst was to design the sets and costumes while Fokine would be choreographer. The person responsible for the original inspiration for the ballet is difficult to ascertain. Since the ballet would prove to be an artistic failure, all connected with *Le Dieu bleu* were not inclined to discuss it. Diaghilev mentions it in his notebook, the famous "blackbook" of his ideas and plans, but there is no dating for reference. The blackbook does include a sketch by Diaghilev of his concept of what the seated Blue God should look like.[27] The first dated reference to the ballet is an interesting postcard sent by Diaghilev and Nijinsky to Gabriel Astruc. "Dear Friend," they addressed Astruc, "In the name of all you hold dear not a word to *anyone at all* about the ballet we are planning, and especially about the possibility of including it in the Coronation celebrations."[28] The latter was a reference to the festivities planned in London for the crowning of King George V. The card was signed Hahn, Diaghilev, Bakst, Cocteau, and Nijinsky.

Before the creative work could be started, though, more mundane matters had to be addressed. A study of the Astruc papers in the Dance Collection of the New York Public Library at Lincoln Center, reveals some interesting developments regarding financial considerations, and sheds some further light on the relationship of the collaborators. The first draft of the contract, dated 9/12/1910, shows a typewritten script mentioning Hahn, Bakst, Fokine, and Diaghilev, with Cocteau's name pencilled in. There is no mention of Madrazo until the final draft.[29] In fact, except for his credit on the libretto, one hears very little of Madrazo's contribution to this ballet. Even in the correspondence of Marcel Proust with Reynaldo Hahn there is no mention of Madrazo's explicit involvement, though much about Cocteau.[30] Originally, the contract specified six performances in Paris, Brussels, or Monte Carlo, and six performances in other cities, but these twelve performances are crossed out by Diaghilev and changed to a total of five. In the margin Diaghilev scribbled, "What Folly! To guarantee a minimum of twelve performances per *year*!!" The number was then changed to twelve performances for the duration of the contract, which was to last three years.[31]

In the final, printed contract, Cocteau is listed as "un Homme de lettres" with Madrazo who is given no occupational title. The contract gives Diaghilev exclusive rights to the ballet until 1915. Hahn had to produce the piano score by 8 February, 1911; the orchestra parts had to be ready by June of the same year. The contract specifies Hahn's rights and payments, but Cocteau's and Madrazo's are not set out. They were guaranteed an initial payment and fee per performance, as set by the Society of Authors and Composers.[32] Cocteau felt secure about his rights. "It is just fine," he wired back to Astruc on receiving the contract, and immediately set to work on the scenario. Astruc also asked him to write an article for *Comœdia illustré* on the upcoming season and Cocteau readily complied with a vivid word-picture of the Ballets Russes in a lush, poetic style.[33]

To his friends outside the Ballets Russes such writing, more glorified publicity than literary essay, embarrassed them. They enjoyed the Ballets Russes but did not worship it, and Cocteau's adulation worried some. André Gide (1869–1951), who had just started a correspondence with the young poet, reprimanded Cocteau for the time he was wasting on the troupe, time that could be spent creating more important things. Cocteau, who longed to make Gide one of his close friends, tried to play down his role with the Ballets Russes. "I am only interested in their Vestris and you can keep the rest."[34] Cocteau was obviously playing a double game since he was becoming more and more preoccupied with the Ballets Russes while denying any interest to his literary circle.

Marcel Proust, another friend of Cocteau's, and less puritanical than Gide, looked with wry amusement at his young friend's escapades. The author of *A*

la recherce du temps perdu found the ballet ravishing but could be more percep-
tively critical than Cocteau during this period. Proust recorded Cocteau at one
after-ballet supper which Diaghilev held at Chez Larue, when Proust was chilly
and wished to have his coat for his shoulders:

> To cover my shoulders with satin-lined mink,
> Without spilling one drop from his huge eyes' black ink
> Like a sylph to the ceiling, or on snow a thin ski,
> Jean leaped on a table and dropped by Nijinsky.[35]

Proust was worried that "society" would wreck Cocteau before he reached his
artistic maturity but later saw him develop "little sketches, with his own costumes
and decor, which have brought about in contemporary art a revolution at least
equal to that achieved by the Ballets Russes and are, perhaps, the most extraordinary masterworks of our time." This comment by Proust on his character Octave from *A la recherce du temps perdu* could easily refer to the real life model
for Octave, Jean Cocteau.[36]

Astruc also wanted an appealing poster to advertise the 1911 Ballets Russes
season, which was to open in April. He wrote to Leon Bakst who declined to
design it, but Bakst wrote back with another suggestion:

> My dear friend,
>
>   I thought about the poster you need and I have a good idea. You must get Cocteau to do
> it. He draws very well and will do a stunning Nijinsky, for he has often sketched him. I think
> Diaghilev will agree. What do you think?
>
>   Leon Bakst[37]

Astruc asked Diaghilev, who did *not* agree. "Let us use the Russian poster," he
curtly wired back.[38] The Russian poster refers to the Serov design of Anna Pavlova
which was used for the 1909 season in Paris and Astruc realized that it would
not be good policy to display a drawing of a ballerina who was no longer appearing with the company. Astruc asked Cocteau to try out some sketches which
he hoped might please Diaghilev, once he had seen they were already finished.
Cocteau first tried to adapt a drawing of Nijinsky in *Les Orientales* and then
redid the face on another scrap of paper which he pasted over the first drawing.
The figure shows Nijinsky with outstretched arms and standing on one leg in
plié, while the other leg is drawn up in front in a Siamese-styled *passé*. The second sketch shows Nijinsky in his *Le Spectre de la rose* costume with the legs
extended as they were in the first drawing, but another leg added, extended
backwards, and the arms thrown over the head. This evolved into the final copy,
the now famous poster of Nijinsky in *Le Spectre* with the dancer in arabesque
but, curiously enough, with only the top half of the legs showing. All the other
drawings show Nijinsky full length.[39] Cocteau captured the style of the ballet

Figure 3.   Cocteau's Poster Drawing of Vaslav Nijinsky in
Le Spectre de la rose, 1911
(Courtesy of the Stravinsky-Diaghilev Foundation)

Figure 4. Cocteau's Poster Drawing of Tamara Karsavina in
Le Spectre de la rose, 1911
The profile of the ballerina is closer to a self-portrait of
Cocteau than a representation of Karsavina.
(Courtesy of the Stravinsky-Diaghilev Foundation)

perfectly from only seeing the Bakst costume designs—the piece had not even been choreographed as yet. Cocteau also drew a companion poster of Karsavina in the same ballet, but Diaghilev did not use these posters until the 1913 season, though he allowed them to be reproduced in the program for 1911.[40]

Once Cocteau, with Madrazo, had finished the scenario, it was handed over to Hahn who began to work with great enthusiasm. He, like his mentor Massenet, was fascinated with the East and looked forward to creating an exotic stage piece. He allowed the thematic color of the ballet to be his inspiration:

> the color blue dominates in the tumulous conflicts of these times and places [fantasies in the tradition of *The Arabian Nights*], and we see it all by the blue of the turquoise flame, the fascinating and fierce azure of the skies of Asia Minor.[41]

Hahn's music, however, was not enthusiastically received by the Russian musicians and artists in St. Petersburg in February 1911. Both Benois and Prince Peter Lieven noted the similarity between Hahn and his teacher and thought the piano score "insipid" and "the East seen through the eyes of Massenet."[42] Stravinsky felt "this parlour music" would never stand on its own and hoped the choreography and the Bakst designs would make up for the weakness of the score. Hahn seems to have been unaware of these reservations when he wrote to Proust about the encouraging Russian reaction to his music.[43] If, as Stravinsky said, hope rested with the designer and choreographer, then much care would have to be taken in these two areas. Unhappily, Fokine was already overworked trying to prepare *Le Spectre de la rose*, *Narcisse*, *Sadko*, *Petrushka*, and now *Le Dieu bleu*. Diaghilev decided the production had to be delayed, but he did not use Fokine as the argument. Instead, he mentioned Bakst's designs. Bakst had arrived in Paris in March 1911 to start work on the costumes and sets for both *Le Spectre* and *Le Dieu bleu*. He was also working on the *Le Martyre de Saint-Sébastien* for Ida Rubenstein (1885–1960), a wealthy Russian with exceptional beauty whom Diaghilev had used in various mime roles. She had left the company to form her own troupe and though she had little dancing ability she commissioned ballets centered around herself. She could pay top salaries to the musicians and artists who worked for her, unlike Diaghilev. Diaghilev did not appreciate Bakst's "defection" to Rubenstein, even for one production, and implied to Astruc that Bakst was too busy to finish the work on *Le Dieu bleu*. When Bakst found out about Diaghilev's doubts, he telegraphed him and Astruc in a frenzy of outrage, stating: "SKETCH *DIEU BLEU* FINISHED . . . COSTUMES DESIGNED."[44] Diaghilev, though, insisted the production was too complicated and intricate to be done properly that season; Astruc and Bakst reluctantly agreed.

It was only after the Paris season was over and the company was performing in Berlin in January 1912, that Fokine began rehearsals for *Le Dieu bleu*. According to Grigoriev, Fokine based his choreography on the Royal Siamese dancers, who had appeared in St. Petersburg some years before.[45] Rehearsals continued in St. Petersburg the next month, and the final touches on the ballet were done in Paris in the spring of 1912 before the start of the next season. Meanwhile Diaghilev was privately expressing his doubts about the success of the venture and told Grigoriev he was especially worried about the score, which he considered "dull and ineffective" but which he accepted as a matter of diplomatic policy. This is the closest Diaghilev came to admitting that he used Hahn, Madrazo, and Cocteau because of their connections and influence, not because of their talents, which had not yet been proved. Cocteau himself had lost interest in the ballet some months before and left for a trip to Algiers with a friend; he arrived in Paris only in time for the opening night.[46]

Cocteau wrote the program notes for the ballet, and also a detailed scenario for the published piano score which gives the most detailed description of the ballet as it was performed.

Cocteau begins by talking about himself in the third person: "What befell between the time night took the blue from the water and day put it back into heaven, is what the poet sets out to tell us."[47] The story begins "once upon a time" when a young man who wished to become a priest was tempted "to the ways of the flesh" by the young woman who loved him. "If thou wilt free thyself from the fetters of morality, fortify thy heart, think of Bouddha fighting against the seven arrows of desire, ponder on the jet of water which falleth back into the fountain after it hath tried in vain to mount the pure air of paradise." This, according to Cocteau, was the priests' encouragement for the young novitiate, though one may question how well the dancers' mime could mirror this rather purple prose.

Tempted by his love, the young man almost gives way to the young girl's entreaties, but the priests stop the maiden before she can reach him. They take the novitiate away to help him resist any further temptations and leave the girl within the confines of the cave, which is supported by heavy pillars, crumbling statues, and exotic growing fauna. "The grille doors close behind the columns. The night descends, and she is left with the giant tortoises, the sacred reptiles, and the monkeys." Like the Tsarevitch in *L'Oiseau de feu* the young maiden cannot resist investigating her prison, and in so doing opens a door that releases monsters of terrifying shapes and size. These monsters are "swollen with honey, lambs, and nightingales, who slide out to meet her on their swollen bellies." This is a typical Cocteau touch here and foreshadows his next novel, *Potamak*, which centers around a monster who was fed on shoes, old poems and dead roses.[48] Cocteau's image of the girl in her plight is poignant: "Knowest thou the weakness of the garden's stateliest rose, rooted to the earth by her stem, when assailed by an array of rampant slugs?" The maiden appeals to the goddess of the Lotus for help and succor. "Suddenly there is silence, and in that silence the water ripples and the goddess slowly rises from the water, seated beneath a dais of stamens." The forefinger of her right hand is turned towards the surface of the basin, and almost touching her outstretched hand is another hand, also rising from the water. This is followed by an arm and a head that reveals "the bright form of the young blue god . . . who is the blue of a blazing day." The Lotus goddess commands the blue god to quiet the monsters and, "like a schoolboy at a circus," the young god scampers about and begins a dance that forces all the monsters to circle around him with ever increasing frenzy, a "ronde frené-tique." At the end of the dance, when the violent monsters are dead from ex-haustion, the blue god calmly sits among them in a sedate pose, "de félicité boud-dhique." This scene is an obvious parallel with the scene in *L'Oiseau de feu* where the magical title character dances a round dance that calms the monsters and lulls the evil Kastchei.

When the blue god is finished, the sky changes to morning and the priests enter, expecting to find the remains of the girl offered to the monsters. But to their astonishment the girl is still alive and in the company of gods. They fall on their faces in terror at the miracle before them. The Lotus goddess commands that the lovers be reunited. "No one can tell the true desire of immortals," Cocteau concludes, "as the blue god soars to heaven on a magic golden staircase which unwinds itself beneath his feet." The union of the lovers is blessed by the blue god from heaven and the curtain descends.[49]

There is no question that *Le Dieu bleu* was largely derivative. The ballet had monsters like those found in *L'Oiseau de feu*, exotic dances reminiscent of *Sché-hérazade*, and dancing temple maidens like those found in *Cléopâtre*. The develop-ment of the love interest is similar to *Cléopâtre*, since in both ballets the pivotal theme revolves around two lovers torn apart by a higher force: in *Cléopâtre*, by the queen herself, and in *Le Dieu bleu* the temple priests. In both ballets the young man wants to offer himself for something, either queen or religion, and in both ballets his beloved (ironically both the young girls in the respective ballets were originated by Karsavina) tries to stop him. The difference was the happy ending for *Le Dieu bleu*.

There is also a problem of focus in the ballet. There is no single antagonist, only a group of rather malevolent priests. *L'Oiseau de feu* had the evil magician Kastchei, *Schéhérazade* had the jealous sultan, and *Le Pavillon d'Armide* had the diabolical Marquis, but *Le Dieu bleu* had no single dramatic enemy to rivet the audience's attention. This problem of focus also affects the title character, the blue god himself, a part tailored for Nijinsky. The combination of Lotus goddess and blue god as *deus ex machina* lessens the impact of Nijinsky and one must question why the authors brought in two divinities to help the stricken girl when one god would have worked as well. *Le Dieu bleu* had originally been designed to make amends to Nijinsky for losing the title role in *L'Oiseau de feu*, since Fokine wanted that part played by a female dancer. When *Le Dieu bleu* was written, in 1910, Nijinsky's roles had all been dramatically minor in the plots, and *Le Dieu bleu* followed the pattern. However, by the time the ballet finally appeared

Figure 5.   Tamara Karsavina in *Le Dieu bleu*, 1912
(*Courtesy of the Stravinsky-Diaghilev Foundation*)

in 1912, Nijinsky had already performed leading roles in *Le Spectre de la rose*, *Petrushka*, *Narcisse*, and even the princely leads in revivals of *Giselle* and *Swan Lake*. *Le Dieu bleu* looked redundant by comparison.

Before the ballet had even opened on 13 May 1912, Cocteau had said in an interview that he had wanted a break from writing his first novel, *La Danse de Sophocles*, and had "tossed off" this ballet scenario.[50] Cocteau tried to dismiss his work on this ballet as nothing of real importance—this was a far cry from his verbal proclamations two years before when he had first started working on the ballet.

The French reviews were mixed. They ranged from Valery Svetlov's dismissal of the work as "a failure in every sense of the word—in subject, in musical composition, in setting and stage management. Its one redeeming feature is Fokine's choreography."[51] In contrast, the powerful newspaper *Le Figaro* found the work most pleasing:

> The *Le Dieu bleu* affords a delicious excuse for dancing. To state that its story lacks depth is at once praise for its chief quality. Its authors—I refer to those who compose the synopsis—have had no other end in view. And they have succeeded in producing a poem which owes its success to the inventions of development of the plot, to the manner in which they have afforded opportunities to their collaborators—composer, painters, choreographer, or artists. They visualized, as poets should, the atmosphere and incidents most suited to bringing out the talent of a Bakst, Fokine, Karsavina, or Nijinsky, and whoever has fathomed the distinctive characters of al these artists wil not fail to find the production of the *Dieu bleu* completely appropriate to its subject.[52]

Contemporary criticism, however, must be treated very carefully. This same critic, who found *Le Dieu bleu* so pleasant at the beginning of the Ballets Russes season, was soon ranting against Nijinsky's choreographic debut, *L'Après-midi d'un faune*, a few weeks later—historically a much more important work than Cocteau's debut piece.

Most reviewers spent their columns lavishing praise on the extravagant Bakst sets and costumes of *Le Dieu bleu*, and even the dancers admitted it was the designer's show. Lydia Sokolova (1896–1974), a young English girl who had joined the company (and had her name changed from Hilda Munnings in the process), danced in the first and a few subsequent performances of *Le Dieu bleu* and described the elaborateness of the ballet in some detail in her memoirs:

> *Le Dieu bleu* may not have been much of a ballet, but it was surely one of the most impressive spectacles ever designed by Leon Bakst. The set was a great orange cliff and nearly every person on the stage was made up in varying shades of grey, brown or green. [Lydia] Nelidova was lily white and Nijinsky as the god was plasticine blue all over. Bakst's original design shows Nijinsky in the role as he was originally revealed to the audience at the top of a flight of wide steps at the back of the stage, seated on a throne with legs crossed, holding a flower.[53] The whole company was massed around the stage, making various Eastern gestures. There were

Figure 6.   Vaslav Nijinsky in *Le Dieu bleu*, 1912
            (Courtesy of the Stravinsky-Diaghilev Foundation)

a number of supers, including five little boys, who wore much more elaborate and glamourous costumes than the dancers. Some of their headdresses were of white lace or net on gigantic wire frames about three feet high. The predominating colour of the costumes was white and most of the women wore bell-shaped skirts lined with a very heavy material. Karsavina had a rather thankless part with one solo, which she danced beautifully, maneuvering her hands and feet in the exotic positions Fokine had invented for her.[54]

Fokine did create two outstanding dances, according to Sokolova, that used the Bakst costumes to great effect and which always received the most applause when the ballet was performed:

> One [dance] was performed by our three tall beauties, each carrying a stuffed peacock. They held these magnificent birds by their stiffened claws, allowing the long tail to fall over their shoulders or float in the air, and grouping themselves in lovely poses. The colour of the peacocks' tails was wonderful against the naked midriffs and white veils. Although these girls were very tall, the peacocks' tails were so long that when the birds were perched on their shoulders they would still trail on the ground.[55]

The other was the dance of the dervishes:

> Their costumes were made entirely of white ropes, about a thumb's thickness. Besides the ropes which formed the skirts, there were more attached to their caps, which hung down to about knee length. The ropes were dead white, and the men's bodies were dark greyish-brown. As the dancers spun faster and faster at the end of the dance, they presented an extraordinary picture of wizzing white discs. It is amazing to think that Cocteau was responsible for this scenario as far back as 1911.[56]

Cocteau may have been responsible for most of the scenario, but he was not happy about his first venture with the Ballets Russes. Years later when he was asked to comment about the ballet all he would say was "it was very bad," without supplying his reasons.[57]

In 1913 London was finally able to see *Le Dieu bleu*, and it looked even more dated then. Additionally, the ballet was probably not well served by the choice of accompanying pieces on the opening night program of 27 February 1913: *Cléopâtre* and *Petrushka*. The former showed where the *Le Dieu bleu* ideas had come from and the later showed how far the Ballets Russes had traveled away from such oriental exotica. The Hahn score could not escape merciless comparison with the Stravinsky composition. Most of the reviews echoed the *Daily Mail* which thought

> both the music and the action of the ballet less wonderful and less strange than other pieces. Both [the music and libretto] are by Frenchmen, not Russians, and in both, graceful as they are, one can trace survivals of old conventions rare in the purely Russian pieces.[58]

As in Paris it was the Bakst sets and costumes which drew most of the attention and a ballet cannot last long which is so dependent on its decor. *Le Dieu bleu* just fulfilled its contract by playing three performances in Paris and three in London. It was announced for the Nijinsky-Ballets Russes tour of America in 1916 and even scheduled in the San Francisco program, but it was never performed.[59] It left its mementos, mostly statues and drawings of Nijinsky as the blue god, but it was never revived by Diaghilev after the 1912–13 seasons.[60]

Cocteau did not seem to be despondent over the outcome of this ballet—he always had projects in many areas—but he was more subdued now in his dealings with the ballet world and especially more cautious about his projects and his collaborators. *Le Dieu bleu* could be forgiven as the first try of a young man unsure of the requirements of a ballet scenario, but he could not afford to make that mistake again. Perhaps the generally unfavorable reviews for Hahn's score made the young poet realize that his next collaboration would have to be with a more controversial composer, *au courant*, as Diaghilev would have phrased it. It was therefore no surprise when Cocteau, for his next venture into ballet, began to court the favors of Igor Stravinsky, who had gained recognition with *L'Oiseau de feu* of 1910 and acclaim with *Petrushka* in 1911. However, it was the composer's next ballet that was to cause the greatest controversy and make a profound impression on Cocteau.

3

"Astonish Me!": The Creation of *Parade*

The first chimes of a period which began in 1912 and will end with my death, were rung for me by Diaghilev, one night in the Place de la Concorde. We were going home, having had supper after the show. Nijinsky was sulking as usual. He was walking ahead of us. Diaghilev was scoffing at my absurdities. When I questioned him about his moderation (I was used to praise), he stopped, adjusted his eyeglass and said: "Astonish me." The idea of surprise, so enchanting in Apollinaire, had never occurred to me.

—Jean Cocteau, *The Difficulty of Being*

This famous command gave Cocteau's life a goal, and his work motivation. He called this period the time when he "fell asleep," and that he hoped he would not wake up until his death. "The Ballets Russes could ruin a young man, but this command was my coming of age." Cocteau knocked "at the stern Muses' door. These Muses never ask you to sit down, but point in silence to a tightrope."[1] Cocteau now turned to Igor Stravinsky to join him on his tightrope.

As with many of Cocteau's claims, there seems to be some debate over when he first met the Russian composer. He was certainly not as close to Stravinsky as he wanted everyone to believe.[2] What had impressed Cocteau was the opening night of Stravinsky's *Le Sacre du printemps* on 29 May 1913. It created a sensation, a scandal, an outrage. For Cocteau, it showed him what path he would have to follow to create his own astonishments. The ballet premiered in a new theatre which Cocteau thought was "too comfortable and too cold for a public used to emotions at close quarters in the warmth of red and gold."[3] The conditions were not the only reason for the reaction to *Le Sacre du printemps*, but they contributed. The music was stylistically and aesthetically alien to the Parisian public. The audacity of Stravinsky was quite gratuitous; he did not set out to create a scandal, it just happened. It is a pity Cocteau did not study his own words here since he was often accused of creating an atmosphere to encourage scandal rather than concentrating on the artistic worth of the piece. The sounds of *Le Sacre du printemps*, combined with the shock of Nijinsky's stolid and forceful choreography, turned the fashionable house into something less than respectable. Cocteau continues:

> [The house] is packed. A practiced eye could discern there all the material for a scandal: a fashionable public, *décolleté*, decked with pearls, aigrettes and ostrich feathers; and, rubbing shoulders with tulle gowns and tail-coats, the jackets and headbands and conspicuous garments of that species of aesthete who acclaims no matter what novelty in season and out of season through detestation of the "dress circle" (the unintelligent applause of the former being more insufferable than the sincere hisses of the latter). Add to these the musicians of the "feverish" school, a handful of "moutons de Panurge," hesitating between public opinion and the admiration one ought to entertain for the Russian Ballet. And, without insisting further, mention ought to be made of the thousand varieties of snobbism, super-snobbism, anti-snobbism, which would require a whole chapter to themselves.
>   The audience behaved as it ought to; it revolted straight away. People laughed, booed, hissed, imitated animal noises, and possibly would have tired themselves out before long, had not the crowd of aesthetes and a handful of musicians, carried away by their excessive zeal, insulted and even roughly handled the public in the loges. The uproar degenerated into a free fight.[4]

There is no reason to doubt Cocteau's word. The next part of his story is, however, more difficult to prove, or even believe. Cocteau says he joined Diaghilev, Nijinsky, and Stravinsky for a carriage ride along the Bois de Boulogne after this opening night. He gives us an intimate view of Diaghilev's emotional reaction to the premiere and includes a conversation he had with Stravinsky. "From this meeting in the cab," the poet informs us, his "real friendship with Stravinsky dates."[5]

The story was categorically denied by Stravinsky, who said that Cocteau would never, in the years before the war, have been privy to such a display of emotion on Diaghilev's part. The composer has also said that he does not remember any ride like this taking place, with or without Cocteau.[6]

Stravinsky left for Switzerland sometime in the winter of 1913. He was tired after the opening of *Le Sacre du printemps*, and his wife was ill and needed care. He was not to have peace however, for Cocteau hatched an idea for a ballet that he wanted Stravinsky to consider. It was entitled *David*:

> An acrobat was to do the "parade" for *David*, a big spectacle which was supposed to take place inside; a clown, who subsequently became a box, a theatrical version of the phonograph at a fair, a modern equivalent of the mask of the ancients, was to sing through a megaphone about the prowess of David and implore the public to enter to see the picture inside.[7]

The germ of *Parade*, even its title, is already contained in this sketch. Cocteau was fascinated with the circus street fairs and felt justified in using them as a theme for a ballet. "What I turned to the circus and music hall to seek was not, as is so often asserted, the charm of clowns and negroes, but a lesson in equilibrium."[8] The unusual element of *David* is the biblical theme, which may have been used as an appeal to the highly religious Stravinsky.[9]

In his book *Cocteau*, Francis Steegmuller has published the manuscript letters of Cocteau to Stravinsky about *David*. They show a rather desperate side of Cocteau's nature. "Our *David* must be a success," Cocteau writes; "think of the music!" Cocteau storms and bombards the harried composer with ideas and threatens a visit to him in Switzerland to discuss "our" plans for *David*. When Cocteau finally arrived, he brought with him Paul Thevenaz, a young artist who danced and taught Dalcroze Eurhythmics. Cocteau wanted him to choreograph the piece—it is interesting to note that Nijinsky had used Dalcroze's method in *Sacre*—and wanted Stravinsky to get to know him, Cocteau's "latest discovery." He also told Stravinsky that the ballet was to be produced at the Théâtre Colombier under Jacques Copeau's direction. Stravinsky said later that he did not believe Cocteau really meant to produce the ballet there at all, but used it as a cover so he could present Diaghilev, who was really the only producer who would be interested in the piece, with an accomplished fact.[10] This would seem highly likely as Copeau showed no interest in producing dance pieces and Diaghilev would be more willing to accept Cocteau's ideas backed up by an already completed Stravinsky score.

Misia Sert was piqued that she was not involved in the plans for *David*, even after Cocteau sent her a number of rather sycophantic letters.[11] Nor was Diaghilev pleased about Cocteau's clandestine meetings with his chief composer. That, combined with Stravinsky's increasing reluctance to become involved in the project, forced Cocteau to drop his plans for the ballet. But by the time *David* was dropped Cocteau had found something else to occupy his time—the Left Bank.

"Why did you put him in touch with the cubists? He is a man of the right, not of the left."[12] Thus Paul Morand quotes a very annoyed Misia Sert on Cocteau's latest interests. Whomever she was speaking to, she was quite right. Late in 1913 Cocteau began to court the favors of the various artists he knew in Montparnasse, much as he had with Stravinsky. Maurice Sachs noted that Cocteau with "an Aladdin's lamp in his hands, took the road to Montparnasse, where he was badly received by the poor bohemians."[13] Of course, Cocteau tells a different story: "When I was young and we all lived in Montparnasse, we had no money and no political, social or national problems of any sort."[14] Cocteau, however, never lived anywhere near Montparnasse, and was comfortably well off for his entire life. Also, at this particular juncture, he did not have any radical political leanings that dominated most of the bohemian artistic circles; his "acceptance" by them could be, at most, a toleration.

Such hindrances did not stop Cocteau from involving himself in the artistic world of the Left Bank; his new enthusiasm had a purpose. On the opening night of *Le Sacre du printemps* Cocteau had noted that

there was absent, with one or two exceptions, the young painters and their masters. An absence due, as I afterward learnt, in the case of the former, to their ignorance of these functions to which Diaghilev, to whom they were as yet unknown, did not invite them; in the case of the latter, to social prejudices.[15]

Cocteau was quite correct: Diaghilev was still unaware of this section of the French art world, so dependent was he on his Russian designers, and the bohemian painters were not about to go to the Ballets Russes, which was dependent upon the salon world they had rejected, Diaghilev's "cher snobs."

Cocteau set about breaking the barriers between these two worlds, and for that alone one must be grateful to him, whatever his pretentions later on. His first discovery was Albert Gleizes (1890–1946), a follower of Picasso who wrote the first important monograph on the movement begun by his master, On Cubism (1912). Cubism, as first seen in Picasso's Les Demoiselles d'Avignon (1907), was dramatically primitive and new, though not as yet fully formed. By 1913 Picasso has formulated his approach and he had engendered many followers in the process. Cocteau founded another art magazine in 1914, Le Mot, and he printed pictures by Gleizes in it, hoping to prove to the other Montparnasse artists his interest in their work. Le Mot also reflected new tendencies towards nationalism, even jingoism. This was a natural reaction to the German agression, since World War I had begun by the time the periodical went into production.

Cocteau became involved in the war in a more practical way than just the magazine. He joined Misia Sert's ambulance brigade, a rather motley group of wealthy patrons and salon artists who traveled to the front in converted Parisian fashion-house vans. When Cocteau was not involved with caring for the soldiers at war, he spent most of his free time at Montparnasse where some of the artists began to show some grudging respect for the society poet. Cocteau convinced Albert Gleizes to collaborate with him on a new ballet and to help in the designs. Once more it is a circus scene, but this time Cocteau took a ready-made scenario, Shakespeare's A Midsummer Night's Dream, and transformed it. It was to be staged at the Cirque Médrano and Cocteau convinced Edgard Varèse (1883–1965) to conduct. Cocteau wrote Gleizes sometime in late 1914, when the artist was residing in New York:

> The Dream can and must be a marvel. Médrano orchestra a potpourri of everything we like directed by Varèse—Clowns and everything. My translation is literal—big excisions (the whole "charm and dalliance" bit—untranslatable and boring)—what remains is a kind of cinema of the sublime.[16]

Cocteau wanted Gleizes to design floor rugs in red, canary yellow, and apple green for each of the three acts. Onto these Cocteau planned to project shadows of trees, doves, and other forest life. Cocteau must have been aware of Max Reinhardt's (1873–1943) different productions of A Midsummer Night's Dream in Germany, since an article in Le Mot lamented "Shakespeare deserts to Germany" and suggested a French production as a gesture to the English allies. Many of

Cocteau's ideas had also been explored by the Russian avant-garde movement, but they had little effect on the ballet world.

Amazingly enough, Cocteau convinced Diaghilev's producer, Gabriel Astruc, to present *A Midsummer Night's Dream*. In his memoirs Astruc remembered that "Cocteau's idea was to have Bottom, Flute, and Starveling played by . . . three clowns. Oberon was to make his entrance to the popular song, 'Tipperary.'"[17] Astruc also decided to make the project a benefit for the war wounded.

Cocteau had the producer and the designer for the project—he now went after a composer, Eric Satie (1866–1925). Satie had always opposed lush orchestral sounds, which was the tendency of French music in his early life, and it was this attitude which prevented him from gaining recognition until he was past middle age. His compositions appeared with humorous names and polytonal or atonal content. Cocteau had just heard Satie's "Three Pieces in the Shape of a Pear" and wanted this tongue-in-cheek composer to allow him to use his music for his tongue-in-cheek production. But first he had to maneuver an introduction. At a dress rehearsal of a Ballets Russes production, *Josephslegende*, in May 1914, Cocteau made sure that the author of the scenario, Hugo von Hofmann-sthal (1874–1929), introduced him to a young artist, Valentine Gross (1887–1968). Married to Jean Hugo, another artist who would collaborate with Cocteau, Gross was a great fan of the Ballets Russes and sketched many of the dancers in rehearsal and performance. She had found work for Satie when he desperately needed money, and the composer appreciated her concern. She was not, however, enthusiastic about Cocteau when she first met him. Over the next few months his charm and wit broke down her reserve. By October, Valentine wrote to Satie that Jean Cocteau would like to meet him and discuss some ideas for a ballet. Satie readily agreed because of Valentine's past patronage, and he came to her house to dine with Cocteau and Astruc on 18 October.[18] This meeting must have produced some inspirations since, on Satie's death, a manuscript score entitled "Five Grimaces for 'A Midsummer Night's Dream'" was found among his papers.[19]

By the time Cocteau and Satie met again at Valentine's on 29 November, however, *A Midsummer Night's Dream* was no longer the project at hand. It was at this meeting that Cocteau broached the subject of a different ballet, *Parade*.[20] Whatever happened to the Shakespeare project is uncertain, and Astruc's memoirs are very vague about the reasons. It may have been a falling out with the management of the circus, wartime conditions, or a diminishing of interest. Whatever happened, Cocteau never spoke or wrote about *A Midsummer Night's Dream* again.

By May of 1916 Cocteau had handed over to Satie a pile of notes on the ballet. He was leaving for the front again and told Satie to be careful as "it is my only copy."[21] Soon after this, Misia Sert must have gotten wind of the project, and there is a flurried correspondence between composer and author as to how to placate her ruffled feathers. It was obvious to both Satie and Cocteau that Diaghilev would be the only one who could produce the ballet; therefore, Misia had to be brought in on the project. While he was stationed in Boulogne, Cocteau received a letter from Satie dated 8 June 1916:

> Cher ami,
>   For heaven's sake stop worrying, don't be nervous. I am at work. Let me do it my own way. I warn you, you won't see a thing until *October*. Not a note before that. I tell you so under oath. Will it be all right if I mention you as the author of the scenario? I need to. Madame Edwards [Sert] is all for the project. I told her that she would have to wait until October. I want to do a good job—very much so. . . .[22]

Satie had been flattering Misia to the hilt. He told her that it was at her house that Cocteau and he were "inspired" to do this work, that it was to be dedicated to her, that she would love it, and so forth. "I am working on some 'stuff' that I propose to show you very soon and which is dedicated to you, while I think of it and while I write."[23] Sert printed this flattering letter in her memoirs. But behind her back Satie called her "Tante Trufaldin" after the treacherous valet found in Italian *commedia* plays, who was always saying one thing to one person and just the opposite to another, and causing many complications in the process.[24]

Sert was not very happy that Cocteau was the author of the scenario, even less so when she realized he was also the instigator of the whole project. To avoid the *David* problems Cocteau wrote her a letter, which Sert also reprinted in her memoirs and which was obviously an answer to one of her more vitriolic communications:

> Ma chère Misia,   n. d.
>   The work that I am "pregnant" with begins to get organized, sends me into paroxyms of despair, and gives me many a consolation. Nothing can describe the "androgynous" discomfort of the poet who fertilizes and gives birth at the same time. Satie is an angel (well disguised), an angel from Arcueil-se-Cachan. My part of the work doesn't make things easy for him—on the contrary. I wish our collaboration could move you as much as it moved me the day when I told him what he ought to write. An unforgettable Anjou evening, of such marvelous richness, such electric response. I can see by the cards that things are going the way I most want them to go. It is *his* drama—and the eternal drama between the audience and the stage—in a form as simple as a penny peepshow. You know my *love* for and *cult* of Igor [Stravinsky]—my distress about the stain on the beautiful snow of Leysin [Switzerland] and the book I am planning to write on his character.
>   I hope he doesn't ever imagine that I am "grafting" any cuttings of David; there were two sides to David, one definite and one confused—a part myself, and a part of "circumstances," if one might say so.
>   I bumped into Igor as I progressed towards Satie without knowing it, and perhaps Satie is the corner of the road that will bring me back to Igor. On the whole, the Stravinsky-Cocteau affair was heavy and full of misunderstanding. Our meeting with Satie represents nothing but light and happiness.[25]

Written in the midst of "guns emitting huge flashes of lightning," as Cocteau concludes, the letter shows a desperate man trying to placate the irritated Misia.

There are amusing contradictions in the letter—Cocteau telling Misia how it was Satie's drama but then saying how he told Satie "what" to write. Cocteau's concern for Stravinsky, however, was probably ill-founded as the busy composer probably was indifferent to *David*'s fate.

Between the first meetings of Cocteau with Satie at Valentine Gross's in the later months of 1914 and the notes that were handed over to the composer by May of 1916, Cocteau courted another artist to become involved in his *Parade*. This was Pablo Picasso.

Cocteau had already been introduced to the Montparnasse set at the beginning of the war. While the group gave him inspiration for the stillborn *Dream*, it also allowed him to discover the methods by which the artists created their world of cubism. Cocteau claims he finally met Picasso late in 1916. However, Douglas Cooper, in *Picasso Theatre*, claims the meeting took place in December 1915. If the meeting had been arranged by Edgard Varèse, as Cocteau states, the December date would make more sense.[26] Cocteau also claims that Varèse took him to Picasso's studio, but it seems more likely that Picasso was brought to see Cocteau, who was ill at the time. Cocteau's tendency to romanticize events never left him.[27] However they may have met, Cocteau was immediately fascinated with this "rag-and-bone man of genius," a man who could transform bits and pieces and oddments of all kinds and "raise them to the dignity of usefulness" in any of his paintings.[28] Cocteau also saw the theatrical possibilities in his work and pinpointed this quality in one of his many essays on the artist.

> Let us understand what we mean by this word realism. Picasso has never claimed to do abstract painting. He searches ferociously for a likeness and finds it in such a way that the object or the face at the origin of his work often loses relief and strength when compared to its representation.[29]

Pierre Cabanne, in his biography of Picasso, claims that Cocteau was "the bridge over seven years of asceticism [for Picasso] to a new show to conquer."[30] For Picasso cubism had been an art of teamwork, not in terms of the actual painting but of the exchange of ideas and the general camaraderie of the artists' quarter. Now the team had dispersed, due to the war, and Picasso was left mostly to himself. Cocteau said he "took advantage of a city which was almost empty, waiting to be captured, and it *was* captured."[31] The first step in his capture of the city was the enticement of Picasso to work for the ballet.

Other factors contributed to a change of venue for Picasso and his willingness to work on a stage design, rather than an easel picture. Picasso must have enjoyed the young poet's company as a distraction from the fatal illness of his mistress, Eva, who died in January of 1916. Soon after that, in late February or early March, Picasso moved to 22 Rue Victor Hugo, which put him closer to Eric Satie, an old friend. In their late night walks, the older composer told the young painter about his work on *Parade*. In May, Cocteau brought Diaghilev to meet Picasso, and Satie joined them for lunch. The plans for *Parade* were discussed and the Russian impresario and Spanish artist impressed each other very much. Soon after this, on 24 August, Satie and Cocteau were able to wire Valentine Gross that "PICASSO IS JOINING US."[32] The team was now complete, except for the choreographer. Diaghilev chose his latest discovery, the young Leonide Massine (1895–1979), who had played the leading role in *Josephslegende*. Massine had been trained as both an actor and dancer in the Imperial Theatres in Moscow. He had auditioned and was accepted by Diaghilev when war broke out. Then the impresario set about grooming him to replace Nijinsky, who had married against Diaghilev's wishes and left the company. Diaghilev invited all three collaborators—Picasso, Satie, and Cocteau—to join him and Massine in Rome, where rehearsals would begin.

With the entry of Picasso into the production, Cocteau's influence began to diminish. Picasso brought a whole new set of ideas into the work and slowly transformed Cocteau's original plans. It is relevant to take a closer look at Cocteau's original scenario, given to Eric Satie, and detail the changes that took place until the final version was performed in May 1917.

"In *Parade*, I attempted to do good work," Cocteau said bitterly, "but whatever comes into contact with the theatre is corrupted."[33] This was Cocteau's later reaction when everyone else had transformed "his" ballet beyond his recognition. In his original notebook for *Parade*, Cocteau set the ballet on a Parisian boulevard on a Sunday afternoon. This concept would not change and he reminded Massine in Rome "not to forget that *Parade* takes place on a street."[34] There were to be three managers, one French, one American, one Negro. Each manager was to present a verbal introduction for each of their respective acts: a Chinese conjurer, an American girl, and an acrobat. Cocteau's draft synopsis shows that he could not decide on the best presentation, and he kept changing various aspects of the managers' monologues—at one point they were to come from behind the scenes, then from the audience, then from megaphones placed on the set, and finally from one voice, but using three vocal ranges. There was a complicated set of almost nonsensical gibberish for the managers to say, in the first draft simultaneously, and this babbling was to build to an angry crescendo. The managers each promise the audience more and more wonderful things if they would only come inside to see the show. "If," or "si" in French, is the crucial word in this text. "*If* you would be rich!" cries one manager while the other exclaims "*If* you wish never to be ill!" and the last promises "*If* you want everything you ever wanted!" All these claims become more and more frantic as the managers become more desperate to induce the public to come in. "Si! Si! Si!" they all cry, which can mean both "if" and "yes" in French. All these claims are Cocteau's exaggerated vision of hucksters at a fair. Reproduced in figure 7 is a rendition of a page of this unpublished manuscript with Cocteau's original spelling and idiomatic phraseology.

For the "petite fille américaine" Cocteau gave Satie a sheet of notes to help

Figure 7. "The Cries of the Three Managers," from *Parade*, 1917
Rendition of a page from Cocteau's unpublished
manuscript of the ballet.

Cris des trois managers *ensemble*

rire nègre	(il crache)	(il siffle d'ausin doigts)
Entrez, Mesdames et messieurs /	" ———	" ———
Si vous êtes origins de vivêse	Si vous voulez vivre vieux!	Si vous voulez être riches! /
		Exigez le K! ici!
Si vous voulez ne plus jamais être malades!	Si vous voulez qu'on vous aime!	
Si vous voulez avoir la toute puissance	Si vous voulez qu'on vous aime!	Exigez le K!
Si vous voulez plaine!	Madame! SI vous voulez une belle poitrine!	Si [unclear words] Exigez le K!
Si exigez le K vous voulez gagner au jeu!	Monsieur! Si vous voulez obtenir une situation prépondonaires!	Si vous faire un beau mariage!
		Exigez le K!
Si y r---- voulez faire un beau mariage!	SI Exigez le K on vous trompe!	
		Si! EXIGEZ LE K!
SI!	SI SI	
SI!	SI!	Si!
SI!		SI
		SI SI SI

Les trois managers s'écrouler de tachgue [*sic*]

Source: *Parade*, n. pag. Lines across various phrases are Cocteau's pencilled crossings. They may refer to those phrases being cut or changed, although there is no definite proof. In interview Massine said he could not remember what the lines indicated. This page is not from the Massine notebook handed to him in Rome. Cocteau may have torn it out when the dialogue was cut. However, it did later come into the possession of Massine.

him with associations for the music in her act. Some of these would appear in her final variation, though not all of them. It is interesting to note the associations Cocteau brought to America, a place he had never seen, except through silent movies:

> The Titanic—"Nearer My God to Thee"—Elevators—the sirens of Boulogne—submarine cables—ship-to-shore cables—Brest—tar—varnish—steamship apparatus—the *New York Herald*—dynamos—airplanes—short-circuits—palatial cinemas—the sheriff's daughter—Walt Whitman—the silence of stampedes—cowboys with leather and goatskin chaps—the telegraph operator from Los Angeles who marries the detective at the end—the 144 express—the Sioux—the cordillera of the Andes—Negroes picking maize—jail—the reverberation—beautiful Madame Astor—the declarations of President Wilson—torpedo boats—mines—the tango—Vidal Lablache mercury globes—projectors—arc lamps—gramophones—typewriters—the Eiffel Tower—the Brooklyn Bridge—huge automobiles of enamel and nickel—Pullman cars which cross the virgin forest—bars—saloons—ice-cream parlors—roadside taverns—Nick Carter—Helene Boodge—the Hudson and its docks—the Carolinas—my room on the seventeenth floor—panhandlers—posters—advertising—Charlie Chaplin—Christopher Columbus—metal landscapes—the list of the victims of the Lusitania—women wearing evening gowns in the morning—the isle of Mauritius—*Paul et Virginie*[35]

The Chinese conjurer included images pertaining to the "silence of thunderous events in silent films and the inaudible transmission of messages by telegraph" while the acrobat was to reflect "the heights and the depths, things submarine and stratospheric."[36] Later these images became a score for two voices which Cocteau gave Satie to set to music. He told Satie in the cover letter that he was free to use any or all of the pages—not even to consult him—and that the notes were just "new ideas for the song which might, with their freshness and warmth, come across, above the noises of your orchestra." Cocteau told Satie the lines referred to the mystery of the interior and came from a poem he was then writing, *Le Cap de Bonne Espérance*. The text is scrawled across the onionskin pages in a curving line up and down the page, almost an imitation of some of Satie's own serpentine-formed letters. The cover letter concludes: "How much I like you and how I like our work, *already completed!*"[37]

As much as Cocteau would have liked to believe otherwise, the work, of course, was far from complete. Satie's answer to Cocteau's manuscript sent 2 May 1916 simply said: "I have received the manuscript. Very exciting. I am sorting things out in my mind."[38] One has the impression that Satie was not as enthusiastic as Cocteau about the manuscript, despite his stated "excitement." By June, Cocteau must have been worrying Satie more since Satie told him "don't be nervous" in the letter quoted earlier. This, of course, was during the period when they were both having troubles with Misia Sert. By 15 September 1916, less than a month after Picasso had committed himself to the project, Satie wrote Cocteau that "Picasso has some curious and new ideas for *Parade*. He's marvelous!"[39] The day before Satie addressed this letter to Cocteau, he revealed his true feelings to Valentine Gross:

Parade is being transformed, for the better, behind Cocteau's back! Picasso has ideas which please me more than those of our Jean! What a misfortune! And I "am" for Picasso! And Cocteau doesn't know it! What's to be done! Picasso tells me to continue working on Jean's text and he, Picasso, will work on another text, his own—which is dazzling, stunning!

I am getting crazy and sad! What's to be done! Knowing the splendid ideas of Picasso, I am disappointed to be *obliged* to go on composing to those ideas of our good Jean, which are less good—oh! yes! less good. What's to be done! What's to be done! —Write and advise me. I am going crazy.[40]

However, within a few days of this letter of remorse and panic it was obvious Picasso and Satie had talked to Cocteau, since Satie wrote Valentine joyfully on 20 September that "it's fixed. Cocteau knows everything. He and Picasso have reached an agreement. How lucky!"[41]

The changes Picasso made were mostly to do with the cutting of the dialogue. According to Cocteau, Picasso showed him the sketches for the managers and "we realized how interesting it would be to introduce, in contrast to the three chromos [the circus performers], unhuman or superhuman characters who would finally assume a false reality on the stage and reduce the real dancers to the stature of puppets."[42] Cocteau probably had less to do with the transformation than he claimed, though he still kept part of the dialogue in since he then decided to have three actors in the audience calling out advertisements through megaphones, as the orchestra settled down. Cocteau felt that his *trompe d'oreille* should mirror Picasso's *trompe d'oeil.*[43]

Before they left for Rome the details of the contracts were confirmed. On the same document, dated 10 January 1917, Cocteau and Satie signed and Picasso signed his contract the next day. It is interesting to note in the Cocteau-Satie contract that:

> because of the importance of the libretto of *Parade*, the authors have agreed between themselves that M. Jean Cocteau alone shall receive the author's royalties on each performance until these reach the three thousand francs of the premium which he cedes entirely to M. Eric Satie; after which royalties shall be divided in the usual way between composer and librettist.[44]

This agreement contrasts two sides of Cocteau's nature. To flatter his ego it now stated, in writing, how important he was to the production; at the same time it revealed his generosity towards Satie in regards to the financial arrangement. Neither Satie nor Cocteau saw much of the three thousand francs since *Parade* was not performed frequently.

On 17 February 1917, Picasso and Cocteau left for Rome. Cocteau was very excited about the trip and even Picasso looked forward to it, though he did not usually like to travel.[45] Satie did not go since the piano score was finished, and he was very nervous about leaving Paris, the city he had lived in for his entire life.[46] Cocteau noted with amusement how shocked Montparnasse was to see Picasso "distort the Aristotelian rules of Cubism and follow me to Rome in order to prepare the ballet *Parade*."[47] In Rome Picasso and Cocteau joined Stravinsky, Bakst, Diaghilev, and Leonide Massine. Picasso and Massine had met briefly the previous October when Diaghilev brought him to Paris for a preliminary discussion of *Parade*, but this was to be the first intensive work session.

Massine was the next important factor in the changing of Cocteau's scenario. Although his technical accomplishments were not on the same level as Nijinsky, he would become one of the greatest *demi-caractère* dancers of the twentieth century. In 1917 he was only twenty-two years old and probably rather nervous about working with such a triumvirate as Cocteau-Satie-Picasso, "three laughing cynics," as Walter Propert would call them.[48]

Cocteau took immediate advantage of his inexperience and presented Massine with another notebook filled with ideas about how the choreography should be developed. Even before he arrived in Rome Cocteau had prepared the groundwork for these ideas through Picasso. Cocteau wanted Picasso to make it clear that he would be helping Massine with the choreography. "Massine will be satisfied," Picasso wrote back; "You can write and tell him so. Everything will be alright."[49] What Cocteau wanted to do was mirror in gesture what Picasso was doing for the objects of the set. "I wanted to transfer these realist ideas into motions, into the dance, and Massine and I worked together on these ideas."[50] Massine seems to have taken many of these suggestions and used them in his choreography. The young dancer-choreographer liked "the lean and witty Cocteau, whose outrageous suggestions amused and sometimes irritated Diaghilev. But he [Diaghilev] was ready to listen to them, for he felt that Cocteau brought to the company a breath of avant-garde Paris."[51]

The notebook he gave Massine shows Cocteau's attention to detail. The outline for the Chinese conjurer—the part Massine would eventually play—is divided into nine sections. In brief phrases Cocteau jotted down his ideas for the structure of the dance:

LE CHINOIS
1° Salut par terre—
    vérification des accessoires
2° l'oeuf
2° l'éventail
4° le feu (geste central)
5° danse de jongleur qui lance
    des couteaux   ⎫
                                    ⎬ par immobile
6° Le tour incompréhensible   ⎭
7° l'oeuf
8° l'éventail (TETE COUPEE)
9° Salut par terre[52]

Massine followed this outline closely when working out the dance. Massine said that Cocteau suggested the miming of swallowing an egg when he was stuck for an idea, and the young dancer seems to have appreciated Cocteau's involvement.[53] However, that did not mean that Massine followed his every wish. Far from it. The managers still had dialogue, according to the notebook given Massine, and though Cocteau later claimed that he saw the dialogue would not work and "substituted for the voices the rhythm of footsteps in silence," Massine's account is probably closer to the truth:[54]

> Cocteau told Diaghilev he wanted to incorporate into the ballet every possible form of popular entertainment. Diaghilev agreed until the moment came when Cocteau suggested that the managers should be given lines which they would deliver through megaphones. This was going too far, even for Diaghilev, who pointed out that the spoken word was entirely out of place in a ballet. Cocteau, however, insisted that in this case the use of megaphones was perfectly valid and in tune with the cubistic concept of the production. Although he lost the argument, he eventually persuaded Satie to introduce into the score a number of realistic sound effects, such as the clicking of a typewriter, the wail of a ship's siren, and the droning of an aeroplane engine. All these, Cocteau explained, were in the spirit of cubism, and helped to portray the feverish inanity of contemporary life.[55]

He had legitimate reasons for these effects. He had written in the notebook "Never forget *Parade* happens in a street," and it was within this concept that Cocteau argued. This concept would account for the placing of these various noises in the score, noises that would have been heard by passersby or, as in the case of the typewriter, a deception of the ear to match Picasso's deception of the eye.

Massine had his own ideas for the ballet, and, like Satie and Picasso, had to convince Cocteau to accept them. He made the one male acrobat into two, a male and a female, to create a *pas de deux*, which Cocteau claimed was a parody of the Italian technique of dancing.[56] The American girl, whose idea-sketch was quoted earlier, seems to have stayed the closest to Cocteau's original plans. In Massine's choreography she imitated the silent film technique in Mary Pickford fashion.[57] All this choreography was worked out "in a Roman cellar . . . which was callled the 'Taglioni Cellar.'"[58] An appropriately named place, though one doubts that the spirit of the great Romantic ballerina after whom the cellar was named would have appreciated the antics within.

Cocteau wrote to Misia Sert about the work in Rome and his relationship with Diaghilev. He had told Stravinsky that "with *Parade* I finally feel in rapport with Diaghilev."[59] This, however, seems to have been only an Indian summer of their relationship. "Serge seems to be very nervous," Cocteau told Misia, "and I think he sees me as a hindrance to the work [at hand]." Cocteau quickly added, "I know you will be content. The Chinese [magician] is done—Massine has indicated he would like to play the acrobat but I have shown him that the Chinaman is the part best suited to his talents and abilities."[60] Cocteau was always on the defensive about "his" *Parade*. Earlier he had told Valentine Gross "that I really do count for something in *Parade*, and that he [Satie] and Picasso are not the only ones involved."[61] In Rome he was obviously becoming more touchy.

He wrote Misia with an arrogance that is surprising, considering his earlier letters to her:

> Tell Serge [Diaghilev] that if my staying here [in Rome] does not displease the Powers-that-be [War Office] too much—the work is well on the go—Massine imbued with my ideas, and whatever Diagh. may think, my absence cannot do any more harm to *Parade*.[62]

The letter goes on to tell Misia about the dancer Chabelska, who was playing the little American girl, and with whom he was carrying on an affair. This "affair" was only a show, of course, an imitation of the real affair Picasso was having with one of the other ballerinas. Cocteau had now transferred a large amount of his adulation to the Spanish artist and tried to imitate him in many things, to a ludicrous extent. In the same letter to Misia, he was now making derogatory remarks about Bakst, who was "passe" in Cocteau's eyes. Picasso was the "dernier cri"; Bakst was no longer part of his artistic credo.[63]

Cocteau had noted earlier in his notebook which artist he would have chosen to design each of the performers:

> For the Chinaman look to Braque
> For the girl, Leger
> For the acrobat, Picasso

These were hypothetical choices—*le mot just* as happens since Picasso was designing all three characters. Of all his work with *Parade* and his personal feelings about the changes, Cocteau still felt very proud about bringing Picasso into the theatre. "What concerns me is Picasso as theatre decorator. I drew him to that. Those about him did not believe he would follow me. . . . To paint a *décor*, above all for the Russian ballet, was a crime."[64] He wrote nostalgically about Picasso's studio in Rome where he painted the Chinaman, managers, and the American girl. He also noted that the Italian Futurists, led by Filippo Tommaso Marinetti (1876–1944), helped Picasso in the building of the frames for Picasso's costumes.[65]

Marinetti had first presented his ideas in a manifesto published in the Parisian newspaper *Le Figaro* in February 1909. Copies were sent to Italy where a whole new literary and artistic movement was envisioned—one which rejected traditional forms in favor of the energy and speed of the machine age. The Futurist painters and sculptors were interested in theatrical presentation as well and worked for audience involvement and the physicalization of the performance. Diaghilev became interested in their work and commissioned Giacomo Balla to create a work to Stravinsky's early composition, *Fireworks*. Balla presented an actorless performance in which lights were programmed to change in time to the music. Cocteau was very impressed with the work, though he told Misia they were all avoiding the Futurists.[66] This is an obvious deception on Cocteau's part since the Futurists were helping Picasso in his costume and set construction. Massine himself has stated that the Futurists inspired some of his ideas, as well as popular jazz music, an idiom probably introduced to him by Cocteau.[67]

Two weeks were spent working on *Parade* and then Diaghilev, Massine, Cocteau, and Stravinsky went to Naples before returning to Rome on 20 March. Some painting of the sets then took place, though a major part of the work was later done in Paris in late April and early May.[68] Meanwhile Cocteau and Diaghilev were not seeing eye to eye on many of the ballet's aspects. Cocteau later said that Diaghilev "tried to cheat me out of my role as a choreographer" and even complained to Massine. He told Misia Sert in Paris that "I think up every slightest gesture, and Massine executed it choreographically." Cocteau wrote to his mother: "Massine wants me to show him every slightest detail, and I invent the roles, which he then immediately transforms into choreography."[69] How much of this is true is now difficult to ascertain, but future events would show that Cocteau's involvement with *Parade* was of secondary importance.

On the return to Paris final rehearsals began. Cocteau bothered Satie about more sound effects for the score. The composer and Diaghilev agreed to these additions, though they were later deleted.[70] The managers, now that there was no dialogue, had become moving cubistic structures under Picasso's guidance. These always bothered Cocteau, who felt they destroyed his concept of the work as a *ballet-réaliste*:

> The managers, whose part consisted chiefly in lending to the four characters their delicate, postcard size, constitute a weakness, because they move about under a framework whose form and painting, even when they remained immobile, express movement. Wheareas I apply to the gestures of the four characters [the Chinaman, the American girl, and the two acrobats] the Picassian method of "truer-than-true" (familiar gestures synthesized until they become a dance), the managers, with their subversive aspect, rather fall back into the traditional. They make one think of sandwich-board men, each in a magnificent wooden costume.[71]

As this is one of the most striking features of the ballet, Cocteau may have been overreacting, since he had not thought of the idea originally. On the other hand, he does have a point about the distraction they cause in the presentation of the performers, as well as the limitations the costumes placed on the dancers. Nevertheless, the cubistic managers remained as Picasso had conceived them when the ballet premiered on Friday, 18 May 1917, at the Théâtre du Châtelet. On the same program were *Les Sylphides*, *Le Soleil de nuit*, and *Petrushka*. The night before had been a charity gala at which Paris had seen the premieres of *Les Femmes de bonne humeur* and *Contes russes*.

Opening their programs the audience read that the theme was by Cocteau, the front curtain, sets, and costumes by Pablo Picasso, and the music by Eric Satie. The following plot summary by Cocteau was included in the program:

PARADE

"ballet réaliste"

The decor represents the front of some houses in Paris on a Sunday. A street fair. Three music-hall numbers serve as Parade.

    A Chinese conjuror

    Acrobats

    A young American girl

Three managers are occupied in advertising the show. They communicate with each other in their strange language, noting that the crowd is mistaking the parade for the spectacle within and they crudely try to make the crowd understand.

    No one enters.

After the last number of the parade the exhausted managers collapse, one after the other.

    The Chinaman, the acrobats, and the litle girl come out of the theatre quickly. Making a last supreme effort after the managers have fallen, they try to explain, in turn, that the spectacle is given inside.

N.b. The directors reserve the right of changing the order of the numbers of the parade. Typewriters by Underwood.[72]

There then followed two essays on *Parade*. One was by Guillaume Apollinaire. It presented the manifesto for the new art:

This new union—for up to now stage sets and costumes on the one hand and choreography on the other were only superficially linked—has given rise in *Parade* to a kind of super-realism [sur-réalism]. This I see as the starting point of a succession of manifestations of the "esprit nouveau": now that it has an opportunity to reveal itself, it will not fail to seduce the elite, and it hopes to change arts and manners from top to bottom, to the joy of all.[73]

Apollinaire goes on to talk in some length about Massine, Picasso, and Satie but makes only a brief mention of Cocteau—"Cocteau calls this a *ballet réaliste*"— and never directly mentions him as the ballet's author. This snub must have hurt Cocteau dreadfully, though he remained friends with Apollinaire and wrote the program notes for his play, *Les Mamelles de Tirésias*, which premiered soon after *Parade*.

The *Parade* program concluded with a long essay by Bakst on the various ballets premiered that season—he himself had designed *Les Femmes de bonne humeur*—and while he praised *Parade* he was obviously bewildered by much of it:

Voici la Parade, a cubist ballet, parodoxical perhaps for myopics, at least for me. Picasso has given us a vision of a trestle fair, where the acrobats, the Chinaman, and the managers move in a kaleidoscope, at the same time real and fantastic. A great front curtain, *"passéiste"* in design, conceals this new flower of twentieth-century art from the eyes of the intrigued spectator. [When this curtain comes up] the audience is confronted with two opposing aspects: one, the strolling constructions, masses of cubistic discord of the most sublime; the others are acrobats typical of the circus of today. The choreography has assimilated and rendered both aspects as "réaliste;" the ones [acrobats], faithfully copied from life, the others [the managers], born in the brain of Picasso.[74]

If the spectator had read this far and digested all the material, he was now ready for the rise of the red and gold curtain. What he saw was Picasso's almost naturalistic rendering of a troupe of circus performers waiting to go on; this picture was accompanied by Satie's almost traditional sounding fugue, "le prélude du Rideau Rouge."[75] When this curtain rose, however, a more startling picture met the eye and harsher sounds beset the ear. A topsy-turvy set of cubistic buildings set at all angles and painted in primary colors outlined in black were shown to a series of insistent chords from the orchestra. The first manager, a Frenchman, enters, a walking construction of trees, buildings, pipe and cane. He stomps out his message to the audience and the back curtain parts to the sound of a tambourine. A sign showing "number one" appears and out jumps "le prestidigitateur chinois" (Massine) in an orange and yellow sunburst coat and black and yellow trousers. He circles the stage and bows majestically to the left, right, and center of the audience. He pretends to extract an egg from his pigtail and places it in his mouth; it vanishes but, smiling, he slides onto the floor and pulls it from the toe of his left shoe. He next produces imaginary fire from his mouth and fans it into a pillar of flame. As the pompous march of his entrance music returns, he once more circles the stage in a series of jerky bent *jetés*, enters the booth, falls on his knees and flings back his head. The curtain closes.

In silence the American manager enters. He is like his French cousin in construction but has a skyscraper on his back, cowboy boots on his feet and a megaphone in his hand. In the other he holds a placard that reads:

PA
RA
DE

His fellow manager comes on and they stamp out their disgust at the audience who will not come in. The curtain parts and a card announces "number two." To the lively sound of a two-step "la petite fille américaine" (Chabelska) briskly enters in a series of convulsive bounds. She is dressed in a little sailor coat, white pleated dress, and black shoes (Picasso had not designed this costume but had purchased it at a Parisian sporting goods store). She imitates Charlie Chaplin, then cries, pretends to jump on a moving train, drive a motor car, swim a river; she types and, to the sounds of gunshots, imitates a Western movie. Then, to the sounds of Satie's "Ragtime for a Steamboat," she begins to dance joyfully, until rolling thunder announces a coming storm and she mimes the sinking of a ship. As the music returns to the lively air she skips back into the booth and the curtain closes.

In silence the managers express their fury at the public and are joined by a third, a gawky horse. Originally the horse was surmounted by a dummy Negro but when it fell off at dress rehearsal, Picasso decided to leave it out. The horse does a comic soft-shoe shuffle and alternates kicking his front and back legs.

Figure 8.   Manager, Construction by Picasso for *Parade*, 1917
(*Courtesy of the late Leonide Massine*)

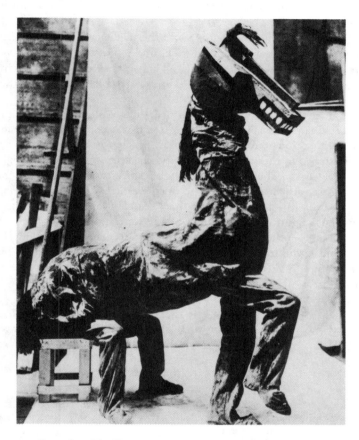

Figure 9.   The Horse, Construction by Picasso for *Parade*, 1917
              (*Courtesy of the late Leonide Massine*)

He is in charge of the third act, the acrobats. As the card shows "number three," the acrobats enter to the sound of a circus waltz. The performers (Nichoals Zverev and Lydia Lopokova) are in tights of blue and white patterned in swirls and stars (Picasso had to paint Lopokova's directly on her before the performance). They slide, twist, and vault on stage as if they were walking on a tightrope. They look up in the air as the sound of an airplane passes overhead, then continue in their pyrotechnics.

The music returns to the ragtime and the managers try one last effort to gain an audience. Their acts perform tricks and repeat their stunts in vain. As they see the audience will not come in, all collapse, except for the Chinaman, who remains inscrutable. The curtain descends as the orchestra repeats the opening fugue.[76]

One can see that the ballet, as performed, differed slightly from the program notes Cocteau supplied. The audience reaction was chronicled in some detail by Cocteau in various publications.[77] In an article for *Vanity Fair* he told the readers "I listened to the storm from behind the scenes, on the first night, and it raged so fiercely that the players actually had difficulty in following the music."[78] This, of course, also happened at the premiere of *Le Sacre du printemps* and Cocteau would relish an imitation of that "scandal." He also told of members of the audience fighting like children, a lady wanting to attack him with her hat pin, and one gentleman saying, "If I knew it was going to be so silly, I would have brought the children."[79] Many historians have accepted Cocteau at his word on these opening night festivities. But some other contemporary observers of this historic occasion saw things differently. Massine, who was dancing in it, said:

> The Paris audience appreciated the novelty of the theme, the wit of Satie's music, and the cubist sets and costumes. They seemed to find the whole ballet entertaining, and yet judging by the reviews, they also caught the serious undertones.[80]

Serge Grigoriev, the *régisseur*, thought that *Parade*

> was witty and entertaining and caused the spectators much amusement. At the same time they took it seriously as a work of art, and realized that in its fashion it represented a synthesis of several modern aesthetic principles.[81]

Paul Morand noted in his diary after the opening night:

> Full house yesterday at the Chatelet, for *Parade*. Canvas scenery by Picasso, circusy, gracile music by Satie, half Rimsky, half dance-hall. The Managers . . . produced a ripple of surprise . . . Cocteau's pivotal idea—freeing dance from its conventions in favor of lifelike gestures—and his modern themes (the gunning of an automobile, photography, etc.), stylized in movement, seemed a little blurred. Lots of applause and a few jeers.[82]

"Entertaining," "much amusement," "lots of applause"—where is the scandal, the cries of horror and outrage that Cocteau insisted occurred? A check of the opening night reviews, while they show a number of negative reactions to Satie's music or Picasso's set, do not mention any outburst by a public scandalized by the action on stage.[83] Does a "ripple of surprise" and "a few jeers" make a scandal? Perhaps in the eyes of Cocteau, who was looking for a scandal. Although a few critics made some xenophobic remarks about what French art should be, one can also find no record of people crying out "Boches!" [Krauts] from the audience, except in Cocteau's writings. It could possibly be explained as a public reaction to a very important battle raging nearby combined with annoyance at Cocteau's calling *Parade* "the greatest battle of the war." But as Cocteau's remark was made years after the premiere any negative reaction was hindsight on the part of later commentators.

In retrospect, this ballet is a landmark of the theatre and was even recognized as such by a number of people at the time. Huntly Carter, reporting the opening night for an English audience (once more no remarks about any outcries of horror) saw, as Apollinaire had stated, the importance of this piece for all the arts:

> The general impression I received from the performance of *Parade* was that of a synthetic movement illuminating passions, emotions, desires, habits, sentiments, etc., of a number of figures, and initiating us into the truth of their vulgar greed and excessive vanity. The main defect I noticed was that Picasso's conception was aesthetic, not dramatic. Though there was a movement with unfolding tendencies, the masks on the figures [referring to the Managers] did [not] change to denote the psychological changes which the figures themselves underwent.[84]

Carter's comment on the managers backs up Cocteau's feeling about the Picasso cubist structures. Carter goes on to say that the French critics made a mistake in calling the ballet "cubist" for "the proper description for *Parade* is 'simultaneity.'" There is "a great possibility of the ideas of *Parade* being developed after the war," Carter concludes, and in this he was quite right. By bringing Satie and Picasso together on one stage Cocteau helped infuse the theatre with elements that had been heretofore neglected. A "scandal" was not necessary to show Paris a new artistic environment.

The ballet was taken to London in May of 1919, and while the critics were fascinated with the combination of talents, it was a mostly lukewarm response. "It is craziness with a touch of genius," said the *Sunday Times*, "a queer, satirical foolery, without beauty, charm, or grace. . . . "[85] W. A. Propert felt that "Satie's satirical humour has before proved too much for British audiences," and Cyril Beaumont thought the ballet "seemed rather obviously planned 'pour épater les bourgeois.'" The ballet was mildly amusing as a joke, he concluded, "but should never have been put forward as a serious choreographic work. It had a lukewarm reception."[86] Grigoriev also noted the London reaction as being quite mild: "They considered the ballet amusing, but no more."[87] Lydia Sokolova, who took over the role of the American girl from Tamara Karsavina in London, disagreed:

> *Parade* has been represented by people who have written about it as a mere stunt. This was not the case at all. The public always seemed to be most enthusiastic, and so was our company. You can always tell when the company approves of a ballet, because you will find a number of them watching it from the wings.[88]

These two opposing views can be reconciled if one remembers that Grigoriev and Beaumont were talking about the opening night reception, while Sokolova spoke of later performances.

That same year the ballet was performed in Madrid for the King of Spain and later in Barcelona. His Majesty expressed his appreciation of the piece, but his subjects were rather bewildered by what their Picasso had done and greeted it with lukewarm applause. Diaghilev did not perform the ballet very often and when asked why said it was one of the best bottles in his cellar and he did not like to shake it up too often.[89] It was revived in 1920 in Paris, with the financial assistance of Cocteau's good friend, Coco Chanel. Due perhaps to Cocteau's influence in obtaining her as backer, Diaghilev allowed him to make some changes in the production, much to the annoyance of Satie. He could not cut the managers but Cocteau did add more noises to the score. Satie wrote Valentine Gross, "Cocteau keeps calling it 'his' ballet. That's fine, but why didn't he write the score, design the sets and costumes, and do the choreography?"[90] André Gide, who had been unable to see the original performance in 1917, went to the revival. He noted in his *Journal*

> Saw *Parade*. Hard to say what is more striking, the pretentiousness or the poverty. Found Cocteau walking up and down in the wings, older, tense, uneasy. He is perfectly aware that the sets and costumes are by Picasso, and that the music is by Satie, but he wonders whether Picasso and Satie aren't by him.[91]

This is rather too vindictive of the older poet, but then both men had a rather uneasy friendship. It does show, however, how much Cocteau enjoyed supervising "his" ballet. He even pretended, in an article in *Comoedia illustré*, that *Parade* was associated with Dadaism. "When we first gave *Parade*, Dadaism was unknown. We had never heard it mentioned. Now the audience will certainly recognize Dada in our inoffensive horse." Cocteau does conclude however that "*Parade* is neither Dadaist, nor Cubist, nor Futurist, nor of any school. PARADE IS PARADE, in other words, a big toy."[92] In typical Cocteau fashion one finds him claiming total originality while dismissing the piece as a mere nothing, "a Punch and Judy show, a wind-up toy."[93]

Parade soon faded into memory and history; many felt it would have been too difficult to revive, not only because of the recreation of sets and costumes, but that it would prove too dated. However, Sokolova said in 1960 that *"Parade* was so delightful that I am sure it would be a favorite if it could be done today."[94] Two years after her statement, Massine revived *Parade* in Brussels for Maurice Béjart, but without the Picasso sets and costumes. It was not satisfactory for all concerned, however, and it was not until 1973 that a full production of *Parade* was finally mounted after more than fifty years of neglect. Robert Joffrey of the Joffrey Ballet brought Massine over to New York to choreograph the piece for his company. Douglas Cooper, an expert on Picasso, supervised the recreation of the sets and costumes.[95]

On 22 March 1973, at the City Center in New York, Picasso's front curtain once again rose on his cubist sets and costumes. Clive Barnes thought the ballet

a triumph. A potent combination of four seminal 20th-century artists. Picasso-Satie-Massine and Cocteau, who was eagerly trying to astonish Diaghilev and the world. The ballet is of dazzling triviality—it is both an exercise of style, and a commentary of the future. Cocteau's theme has the obviousness of suitability . . . but at least Cocteau was the first to recognize the superpublicity type that was to become integral to our century.[96]

Of that, there can be no doubt, since Cocteau created a "scandal" for his ballet's opening that history accepted so readily that it became legend. There was no scandal in 1973 but most critics felt, as did those who saw it in 1917, that it was mainly Picasso's show. Even though Massine created much new choreography (the outlines remained the same), the ballet was dominated by the cubist managers and the prancings of the comic horse. Some critics felt it was nice to see once, as a historical curiosity, but that was all.[97] One critic would have made Cocteau very happy in commenting that the movement looked "wrong for the sculptured costumes [of the Managers]. The result is like watching a sculpture suddenly begin to dance, like a manipulated puppet on wires, or even a building."[98] Arlene Croce, in *The New Yorker*, felt that it was a curious museum piece; for her, Satie's witty score was the liveliest part of the show.[99]

Critics, however, do not always reflect public response. Sokolova noted that every audience enjoyed the ballet, Spain being the one exception. It is difficult to know exactly what the general response was to the original presentation, but Sokolova's account is probably a trustworthy reflection, albeit from the performer's standpoint. The Joffrey Ballet has continually taken the ballet on its cross-country tours of America since 1973 and found audience reaction usually very good. The dancers themselves have said they find the ballet stimulating to perform.[100] The ballet when revived by Festival Ballet in London during 1974 also found *Parade* popular, even on the provincial tours. However, the English critics reacted in the same way as their American counterparts, calling the ballet "a nice museum piece to see once."[101]

Figure 10.   Revival of *Parade* by the Joffrey Ballet, 1973
Ted Nelson as the Manager from New York,
with Donna Cowen as the Little American Girl.
Photograph by Herbert Migdoll.
(Courtesy of the late Leonide Massine)

Perhaps *Parade* has lost much of its impact; it is now remembered mainly for its influence on later works.[102] The premise for the initial presentation of *Parade* was to shock—cubistic designs had not been seen on the ballet stage before, nor was Picasso accepted by the salon clientele that usually patronized the Ballets Russes. When cubism and Picasso became not only acceptable, but sought after and imitated, *Parade* seemed to lose something of its original force. Also, as it continued to be presented the weakness of its choreography became more apparent. When the dance is discovered to be deliberately secondary in what was presumed to be a dance presentation, critics lose respect for the work. Such criticism, however, should not diminish the importance of *Parade* in the history of dance. It jolted ballet into the present by permitting dance to take advantage of the avant-garde and show the public totally unfamiliar areas. For Cocteau, his subject was reality and "only reality, even though well masked, has the power to move one. That is what I tried to do with *Parade*."[103]

4

Independence: The Creation of *Le Boeuf sur le toit* and *Les Mariés de la Tour Eiffel*

There are profound fashions as well as frivolous ones. A musician must submit to these fashions or else create one according to his taste. Every masterpiece having once been in fashion goes out of fashion, and long afterwards finds an everlasting equilibrium. Generally, it is when it is out of fashion that a masterpiece appeals to the public.
— Jean Cocteau, *Cock and Harlequin*

Such pronouncements cover the pages of Cocteau's slim little volume of theoretical axioms, *Le Coq et l'Arlequin*, published in 1918. This manifesto heralded a change in Cocteau's view of artistic enterprises and, in terms of his work in ballet, a breaking away from the concepts that Diaghilev had imposed on Cocteau's past creations. Dedicating his ideas to Georges Auric and expounding a theory of a nationalistic French art, especially in terms of music, Cocteau declared: "Down with the harlequins, who are only scraps of art! Long live the Coq!, which lives on its *own farm*."[1] This meant that artists should look closer to home for inspiration and stop trying to imitate others abroad. Between the lines one could also read Cocteau denouncing his previous Russian influences. The text included much adulatory verbiage on Satie's style of music, a style the exact opposite of German or Russian genres which Cocteau felt heralded a new form of French music. Cocteau also made some surreptitious remarks about Stravinsky, which so infuriated the composer that when the book was reprinted in 1926, Cocteau included a postscript essay to reconcile himself to the Russian. Stravinsky may also have been annoyed because the book impressed Diaghilev; Cocteau had finally gained his admiration without trying for it. When the book appeared in English the critic for *The Times* wrote, "The question remains whether . . . M. Cocteau and his friends are not so far ahead of their epoch that they postulate human organisms that are still nonexistent for their audience."[2]

Nonexistent or not, Cocteau was creating a whole new world with his friends, or, as one author termed it, "inventing the twenties."[3] The friends who helped

Cocteau included authors and artists, but were dominated by musicians. There were six young composers he was especially close to: Louis Durey (1888–1979), Arthur Honegger (1892–1955), Darius Milhaud (1892–1976), Germaine Tailleferre (1892–1983), Georges Auric (1899–1983), and Francis Poulenc (1899–1963). The group always maintained that it was to be considered rather as a band for mutual friendship and attack and defense than as a school, but many observers did not see it that way. With Cocteau writing about their work and presenting their music in concerts they were soon grouped together and Cocteau, in the public's mind, became their mentor. Darius Milhaud remembered how they received the nickname they would forever after be known as "Les Six":

> After a concert at the Salle Huyghens [in late 1918], . . . the critic Henri Collet published in Commedia a chronicle entitled "Five Russians and Six Frenchmen." Quite arbitrarily he had chosen six names [Georges] Auric, [Louis] Durey, [Arthur] Honegger, [Francis] Poulenc, [Germaine] Tailleferre, and my own, merely because we knew one another, were good friends, and had figured on the same programs, quite irrespective of our different temperaments and wholly dissimilar characters.[4]

Collet referred to "Le Groupe des Six" as the French equivalent of the "Russian Five" (Balakirev, Cui, Mussorgsky, Rimsky-Korsakov, and Borodin) and hailed Cocteau as the leader of the group. Cocteau presented the theory of their practice in his book, Le Coq et l'Arlequin, which was looked upon as the "credo" for the six and "always given to generalizations the critics lost no time in hailing Cocteau as the prophet, theoretician, and animator of postwar music."[5] But these words irritated another member of "Les Six," Francis Poulenc, who thought the music critic invented the phrase because he was in "quest of a slogan" and he personally felt the six had little in common. "Our music has always been dissimilar;" he explained; "our tastes and distastes were different. . . . Jean Cocteau, always attracted by every novelty, was not our theorist, as many have claimed, but our friend and our brilliant spokesman."[6] Arthur Honegger felt he was more than that: "Cocteau served as a guide to many young folk. He stood for the general sense of a reaction against prewar aesthetic. Each one of us ["Les Six"] translated that in a different manner."[7] Auric remembered that "Cocteau had almost no musical training. But he was able to go to the piano and play without really knowing the music. . . . He was deeply devoted to both art and artists."[8] Cocteau's simple comment was that Le Coq was a little book he had assembled after listening to all his friends—including "Les Six"—and putting all their comments together. "Le Coq et l'Arlequin was a banquet, a nice book which we all put together. It is not a theoretical work . . . there was no theory for the group ["Les Six"], we were all just friends."[9]

These reservations on the part of the members of "Les Six" came years later. At that time, after the war, their theories were not so rigidly formulated and they gave a number of concerts with Cocteau as director and major domo. These

"Concerts des Six" brought the composers closer together as friends, though not always in terms of musical theory, and stimulated creativity. They frequently met for dinner at Le Petit Bessonneau, went to the fairs in Montmartre, and visited the Cirque Médrano. As Cocteau reviewed their works in a series of articles he was writing for *Paris-Midi* under the general title, "Carte Blanche," he was associated more strongly with the musicians, especially in the public mind, even though it was only Auric and Poulenc who were partisans of Cocteau's ideas.[10] Durey and Honegger did not even like Satie's music, who was considered the godfather for the six.

Cocteau, however, was able to help the musicians become accepted and established. Although Satie was their "godfather" it was Cocteau who had the connections. Auric commented on the "prodigious activity of 'our' poet [Cocteau], whose devotions, affection, and friendship rapidly gained us admittance to the most inaccessible places. At that time he had a passion for the theatre, and he was not long in winning us over!"[11] However, the first person Cocteau won over was not Auric, but Darius Milhaud.

Milhaud had just returned to Paris after having served as Paul Claudel's secretary at the French embassy in Brazil for a number of years where he had even witnessed an impromptu performance of *Parade* by the Ballets Russes company during its South American tour. While in Brazil he found the native folk music fascinating and began to sketch out ideas for a composition:

> Still haunted by my memories of Brazil, I assembled a few popular melodies, tangos, maxixes, sambas, and even a Portuguese fado, and transcribed them with a rondo-like theme recurring between each two of them. I called this fantasia *Le Boeuf sur le toit*, the title of a Brazilian popular song. I thought that the character of this music might make it suitable for the accompaniment to one of Charlie Chaplin's films. At this time the silent films were accompanied by fragments of classical music rendered by large or small orchestras or even a small piano, according to the means available. Cocteau disapproved of my idea, and proposed that he should use it for a show, which he would undertake to put on. Cocteau has a genius for improvisation. Hardly has he conceived the idea of a project when he immediately carries it out. To begin with, we needed some form of financial backing. Jean took the plan of the Comédie des Champs-Elysées [Theatre] to the Comte de Beaumont, who took to reserve in advance, at a high price, the boxes and the first rows of orchestra seats. A few days later, as if at the wave of a magic wand, the whole theatre was sold out, and the Shah of Persia even paid ten thousand francs for a front seat from which he could not see a thing, but was himself in full view of everyone. The expenses of the show being covered, all that remained to be done was to set to work.[12]

Comte Etienne de Beaumont (1883–1956) presented *Le Boeuf sur le toit* as part of his "Soirées de Paris," enterprises that were almost like a private party. Very wealthy and cultured, he lacked the artistic know-how of Diaghilev and depended on others for guidance. With Cocteau he found someone with the right flair and brilliance to create an elegant spectacle.

Cocteau produced a pantomime scenario that was adapted to already existing music. As the music is repetitive though lively, and was written for a silent film—that is, not to stand on its own—it was easily suited to the purposes of a visual presentation, such as a ballet. In fact, Cocteau had the music played twice at the performance, once before the curtain came up so the audience could become used to it, and then as an accompaniment to the pantomime.

The plot was simple. *Le Boeuf sur le toit* is a bar set in America during the Prohibition. Milhaud describes the work:

> The various characters were highly typical: a boxer, a Negro dwarf, a Lady of Fashion, a Red-headed Woman dressed as a man, a Bookmaker, a Gentleman in evening clothes. The Barman, with a face like that of Antinous, offers everyone cocktails. After a few incidents and various dances, a Policeman enters, whereupon the scene is immediately transformed into a milk-bar. The clients play a rustic scene and dance a pastorale as they sip glasses of milk. The Barman switches on a big fan, which decapitates the Policeman. The Red-headed Woman executes a dance with the Policeman's head, ending by standing on her hands like Salome in Rouen Cathedral. One by one the customers drift away; and the Barman presents an enormous bill to the resuscitated Policeman.[13]

Cocteau hired the three Fratellini clowns, whom he had wanted to use in his aborted *A Midsummer Night's Dream*. Paul Fratellini played the Barman, his brother François the Red-haired Lady, and Albert the Lady of Fashion (the Lady in the Low-Cut Gown). All the other players were clowns as well, including a dwarf to play the Negro billiards player. They all wore huge masks over their heads and, in contrast to the fast-paced music, Cocteau had them all move in slow motion. He also wanted them to perform acrobatic stunts which, being clowns, was actually quite natural for them. Thus, it was no problem for Albert as the Lady of Fashion to dance on his hands around the Policeman's head, as Cocteau's scenario instructed.

When asked why he used clowns instead of dancers, Cocteau replied:

> It's always the system of oppositions for the young. At that time I wanted *Boeuf sur le toit* to be the opposite of everything the Ballets Russes represented. This is the spirit of contradiction which is a form of the spirit of creation; or perhaps the spirit of creation is the highest form of the spirit of contradiction.[14]

Though this statement is rather tongue-in-cheek, it was quite true that Cocteau was very anti-Ballets Russes at that moment; *Le Boeuf sur le toit* was his show of independence from Diaghilev's apron strings. Cocteau's mother wrote Valentine Gross, now Mrs. Jean Hugo, that while the Russian Ballet was in town "Jean goes seldom, because of Diaghilev, whom he detests and for good reason."[15] Although the reason is not given, it can be assumed it was due to Diaghilev's treatment of Cocteau's concept of *Parade*.

For this new production Cocteau prepared his usual meticulous publicity.

He wrote a detailed scenario for the program [16] and a long explanatory text, much of it quoted by the *Comoedia illustré* the day before the premiere:

> In 1916, while I was composing the ballet *Parade* with Eric Satie, Picasso, and Leonide Massine, the incomparable choreographer, I had no idea that our meticulous work with music, which embodied the melancholoy of fairs and of steamers on the high seas, would be interpreted by the Parisian public as a simple farce.
>
> It was seeing the word *farce*, used so often incorrectly to describe *Parade*, that I had the idea to do a FARCE—a real medieval farce, with masks, men playing women, pantomime and dance. The timing had to be such that the disorder and improvisation would be effective though by no means accidental. Charlie Chaplin sets an example for us in these modern farces where he achieves real greatness.[17]

Cocteau goes on to say that he did not have any precise idea of how to present this farce until he heard Milhaud and Auric play a double piano version of *Le Boeuf* and then the idea for a dance composition came to him. He saw Milhaud's cinematic concept, but thought the music could be used in a different way: "For centuries our Farce subsisted on characters from the Italian comedy. Now cinematography is, little by little, establishing new kinds of Farce. They deserve to be used in the theatre."[18]

Cocteau subtitled his ballet-farce in idiomatic English "The Nothing-Doing Bar" and the reason, once more, is connected with his Ballets Russes experiences: "*Parade* still contained literature and intention. Here I neglect subject, symbol. Nothing happens, or else what does happen is so coarse and ridiculous that it is as if nothing were happening."[19]

To help visualize this bar where nothing happens, "an American farce done by a Parisian who has never seen America,"[20] Cocteau called in Guy-Pierre Fauconnet to design the sets and costumes. They met at Milhaud's one Sunday and Fauconnet made sketches of characters as Cocteau described what he wanted. They worked very late and Milhaud offered to put the artist up for the night, but Fauconnet insisted on going home. When he did not turn up for their next meeting, Cocteau rushed to Fauconnet's house only to find he had died in the night, while trying to light a fire. He had suffered from an enlarged heart.[21]

Upset, but undaunted, Cocteau asked Raoul Dufy to take over the work, though keeping Fauconnet's designs for the masks and costumes for reasons that he explained in the preface to his farce:

> Nothing in the theatre bothers me more than a lack of transposition: false reality of real objects, real materials, real faces, real tears, only separated from the audience by the footlights. But I also know that the habit is embedded too deeply to change it. The spectator's mind has become lazy and refuses to travel the distance between an object, an emotion, and their representation. He demands them raw.
>
> Here [in *Le Boeuf*] I was bold with carnivalesque liberty and, thanks to Fauconnet and Dufy, I treated myself to rejuvenating the antique mask, to the immobility of an exaggerated face, which gives a mysterious nobility to even the slightest gestures.[22]

Cocteau had already spoken of his idea for Greek masks in the original plans for both *David* and *Parade*. Could he now be demonstrating what he felt was wrong with Picasso's structures? Although there was no dialogue in *Le Boeuf*, the use of the body as a total face was quite different than the use of the body as a walking set-piece, as Cocteau felt Picasso had done with the Managers. As Cocteau explained, "a face is not very clear on stage, unless it supplements the arms and the legs, which then become awkward. If the face is hidden, the actor's body becomes a whole face, expressing at a distance what the real face expresses close-up.[23]

Cocteau also explained why he had his performers move in slow motion and, once more, he drew parallels between *Parade* and *Le Boeuf*. In the former "the dance was adapted too strictly to the music. This creates a kind of redundancy between the eye and the ear, which prevents the audience from either hearing or seeing clearly at the same time. Here [in *Le Boeuf*] I forced myself to move *against the tide*, to put slow gestures with rapid music. . . . "[24] Cocteau also felt that these movements were highly appropriate to the style of an American bar "where night owls move like divers at the bottom of the sea." That was why he used the clowns, because they are the "best mechanical puppets in the world," and highly suited to making such actions look real.[25] Echoing Gordon Craig, Cocteau mused later in his life that a theatrical author could only be satisfied if he could write, perform, and produce his own works and play all the parts. As no such creature had yet been born, one had to accept second best.[26] In the case of *Le Boeuf sur le toit*, Cocteau seems to have been highly satisfied with the visualization of his creation.

Three performances of *Le Boeuf* were scheduled: a closed dress rehearsal for an invited audience on 21 February 1920, and two further performances on the following two days, the last being for the benefit of the war wounded.

Lucien Daudet helped Cocteau organize the performances. A close friend of Cocteau's for years, he had no professional occupation, but he did know everyone in society; so Cocteau, worried about attendance, convinced Daudet to send three hundred "pneumatiques" (special delivery letters), each entitling the bearer to a private box. What happened could be expected. There was an indescribable crush at the doors for seats and it took all of Daudet's diplomacy and tact to take charge and place the audience.[27]

As the ballet was short—less than twenty minutes, less than forty with the music repeated twice—the program also included a number of other pieces. Satie wrote "Trois Pièces montées" especially for the occasion; Auric's fox trot "Adieu, New York," was danced by the Negro dance team of Footit and Jackly; and Cocteau's poems "Cocardes," set to music by Poulenc, were sung by Koubitsky. Vladimir Golschmann conducted the twenty-five piece orchestra. There was also an intermission entertainment entitled "American Coctails" [sic] but when the audience rushed to the foyer expecting drinks, they found that the American "cocktails" Cocteau had planned for them was a jazz band. Despite this typically Coctelian trick the poet did an about-face for this ballet. He purposely went out of his way to avoid a scandal. He went in front of the curtain before the show "and said a few words that put the audience on my side." As he explained:

> A scandal is a very lively thing, but it disturbs the artists, the orchestra, and prevents the few serious members of the audience from grasping the thousand nuances of a work that has taken several months to prepare. I spoke some words to the audience before the curtain came up and was able to make the audience my accomplice. If they hissed, they hissed themselves. I didn't budge.[28]

Even with this paternal warning to the audience from the thirty-year-old poet, the critics looked at the performance as a "declaration of aesthetic faith." The well-known society artist, Jacques-Emile Blanche, called the production "a fight for the music for tomorrow," though with the stellar audience Beaumont had provided, it looked like a very upper-class fight.[29]

Pawlowski in *Le Journal* opened his critique with a rhetorical question addressed to Cocteau:

> M. Jean Cocteau has written charming verses; he has rhythm in his head and not in his feet like so many versifiers: He is a poet. But since he does not always succeed in literally expressing the sensations that assail him, he must call upon all the other arts to speak to us. Will he resort to *writing* of dance, to the *plastic art* of music, to the *art of mimicry* of sounds and to the *sonorities* of colors? He does not know yet because he is still searching. And perhaps from among the snobs he has already found an enthusiastic public before he has even discovered himself?[30]

Despite his reservations about Cocteau's use of his talents, Pawlowski enjoyed the performance very much. "There is great, youthful, and original intention in the *concert-play* composed by M. Jean Cocteau; even musical works of the first order and agreeable circus stylization can be found in it." Explaining that Cocteau was "bruised" and hurt when the public did not accept *Parade* as a tragedy, he noted that the poet cut all symbolism from this farce. Pawlowski thought the large cardboard heads of the performers extremely amusing, "because of the remorseless immobility that they give to the different characters, according to the same method in ancient theatre." The music he described as one of Milhaud's most delightful and interesting compositions in an orchestral ensemble "that is truly remarkable." The critic concluded that nothing equaled the "tragedy of a fixed expression and the powerful, slow movement of the acrobat."[31] Thus, Pawlowski gave Cocteau an ironic compliment by seeing "tragedy" in this ballet, after missing it in *Parade*!

Michel Georges-Michel in *Paris-Midi* thought "the spectacle Jean Cocteau presented yesterday at the Comédie des Champs-Elysées was a considerable success."[32] "Considerable," he added, "in the sense that it surpassed by far the amusing farce ingeniously presented by the poet." Michel felt that it gave the "young and decrepit critics" a chance to find the weak spots that any of the young musicians may have, and to attack them in public.

"How will *Le Boeuf sur le toit* be judged?" the critic asks, and notes that the audience included Picasso, Daudet, and even Diaghilev with the young Massine. Michel himself found the evening highly successful and the music diversified:

> The orchestra simulated a circus parade, but the serious people were not fooled by it; with a capriole the newcomers imposed a new, fresh, distinct art. . . . Here is *Boeuf sur le toit*, a new concept for a play and one hundred times more lively than the painted microphalous characters that we have caught glimpses of until now—yes, caught glimpses of only!—on the stage.[33]

Despite some grumblings from the older critics, Michel concluded that "the entire audience laughed freely, and the old men felt mistakenly that they were clever. They defended themselves badly. 'This is only a farce [one said] and a circus game. It's a success. All and good, young people. But we will attend serious works. . . . "[34] But Michel tells these critics that *Le Boeuf sur le toit* is worthy of attention, for "these children's games are made to give us formidable confidence."[35]

Jean Bastia in *Matinee* gave a poetical, if rather obtuse, survey of the night's activities and insisted that the whole affair was a "Cocteau cubist piece," an approach which must have infuriated the poet. "M. Cocteau delivered an allocation [his opening remarks], moreover, in clear language, and he used clarity in the explication of an obscure thing. That is also very cubist."[36] Bastia felt that by climbing the long stairs of the Comédie the audience reaches "the roof" of the piece, even if there is no "ox" to be found. His account of the audience is amusing, and probably close to the truth, though written in stylish irony:

> There were three types of audience members:
> The Coctellists, fervent, transported, fanatic—the most
>   numerous.
> The Rebellious—a minority.
> The Neutral—a few.
> Some said: —Astonishing! Full of genius!
> The others: Stupid!
> The Neutrals: — . . . .!
> —What imagination! What sensibility!
> —It seems to me that I have caught lethargic encephalitis
>   and that I am awakening in another epoch.
> The Neutrals: — . . . .!
> —It is truly a new school. We should expect great things
>   from it.
> —M. Conductor, is it soon that we will return to France?
> The Neutrals: — . . . .!
> —What a force. . . .
> —What a farce. . . .

What are you sorry for? . . . Aren't you prejudiced in that you
   go to a farce created by him?
—Have you ever heard Eric Satie improvise at the piano?
—Never.
—The Cocteau of the Spinet.[37]

Bastia wrote that Cocteau was not wrong in choosing a theatre that was a few stories off the ground level. "To climb the stairs is one way to rise in the world." With a smirk, he concluded that "no one can miss Cocteau's formal manner, which was more commonplace, more talented and, unfortunately, accessible to all. These 'no ones' are not up to date." Like the poet who installed a dental chair in his office in order to raise himself as high as he wanted, according to the height of the highly elevated poetry he was writing, Cocteau had created this venture in a highly elevated theatre to make the audience think it was high poetry. As the audience were practically all hand picked, according to Bastia, he could not fail. Except, of course, with Bastia.[38]

Louis Laloy told his readers of the *Comoedia illustré*:

For a year now numerous manifestos and panegyrics have given us information on the formation of a new coterie composed of young musicians. No one will be as witty as ourselves [they tell us]. United by a pact of indissoluble admiration, it is not wit but genius that these young men recognize mutually in themselves. They have few friends except a protector, M. Jean Cocteau, and a prophet, M. Eric Satie.[39]

Laloy continued his review very tongue in cheek stating it was somewhat premature to call them geniuses, but "they certainly have a lot of wit." Laloy had a number of reservations about *Le Boeuf*, especially the masks Cocteau had set such store by:

As for the scenic realization [of *Le Boeuf sur le toit*], what it lacks most is fantasy. The idea of masks is good, but why are they similar? Why does the Negro have a Negro's head and the Red-haired Woman a red mop? I was expecting animal jaws, or better still, geometric figures, cubes, ellipsoids or icosahedrons, which would have justified the word "transposition" that M. Jean Cocteau used in his introductory interview. I would say as much for the gestures and steps of the characters, which do not go beyond the ordinary buffoonery of the circus or music hall.[40]

Laloy concluded with a warning, mostly directly at Cocteau: it was a good plan with good intentions, but a plan is not enough, "it must be executed. . . . There is a great distance between an aesthete and an artist," he warns, though he hopes that "Les Six" may someday be able to make him contradict his own maxim."

Paris-Midi claimed not to know whether "Les Six" had founded a new musical era or whether Cocteau had found a new art of performance, but it was, at least, an enjoyable two hours at the Comédie. "M. Jean Cocteau himself said in a preliminary interview that 'We do not claim to be innovating or imposing anything subversive. We want to amuse you while amusing ourselves.' He was entirely successful," the critic concluded.[42] The critic also felt the ballet was performed in "the most fantastic and entertaining manner" and that Cocteau's ideas on movement could be easily transferred to other art forms:

> One of the acts of buffoonery that he [Cocteau] created consists of imposing slow movements on the actors during very fast music. He explained very seriously in his interview that an action agreeing with the music could constitute a repetition and a pleonasm. Already, in the past, in different operas, for example those of Donizetti, the situations of the most tragic gravity were frequently underlined with brisk airs and cheerful flourishes. Perhaps the composer of *Lucia di Lammermoor* created cubism without knowing it.[43]

It is highly doubtful that Donizetti would have appreciated this remark, nor did Cocteau, who did not consider his work in *Le Boeuf* to be particularly cubist. As Massine had never experimented with slow action in *Parade*, *Paris-Midi* was making an incorrect generalization.

The writer in *Le Ménestrel* told his readers: "If you go and see *Le Boeuf sur le toit* you will be amused. What you will see and hear will take no mental effort. There is not a single idea, subject, intention, symbol or hidden meaning in this farce. . . . This is the idea of its author, M. Jean Cocteau."[44] That critic, like Laloy, thought many of Cocteau's intentions and ideas were understandable, perhaps even commendable, but intentions have to be *realized*. "Now, *Le Boeuf sur le toit*, though it seems musically and scenically unified, and tries so desperately at originality, does not hold together as a *réalisation*":

> This [ballet] is an essay in which any love of life or interest in humanity definitely does not manifest itself, and we are less inclined than ever to return to the simplicity [that M. Cocteau speaks of]. Besides, I feel that the reasoning behind this production is too systematic in its neverending theme of the continuous impoverishment of that which is best in man. We do not want to be hostile towards these new tendencies of art which vibrate from the vanities of the young, but who said: "An Artist must open a secret door, fumbling with the catch, but hoping to find what he must behind it, even if he does not understand it." These words are by M. Cocteau and they are from his book *Le Coq et l'Arlequin*.[45]

Although the critic obviously felt that he was putting Cocteau in his place by these remarks, it is also obvious that M. Cocteau had opened a new door. The critic writing for *Le Ménestrel* refused to try to understand what was behind the door, though he did enjoy the "little nothing" Cocteau had prepared for public consumption.

Georges Léon Pondey, writing for the *Musical Standard*, seems to have been the only reviewer to recognize the value of the work and not try to write a review that took snide shots at its author:

Amongst a host of revivals, and much new theatre-art of a stereotyped gender, the new venture of M. Jean Cocteau is very refreshing. Supported by members of the younger musical group . . . this poet has instituted a novel type of entertainment at the Comédie des Champs-Elysées, the first [of its kind].

The music of these performances marks a reaction against the Debussyste "impressionism." The youngest composers are for a sort of "actualism," consisting of humour and decoration extracted from ordinary things, such as a ragtime, music hall performers, popular types, etc.: These they interpret with a *gamin* sense of irony truly Parisian. Cocteau is one of the *réaliste* group which proceeds, by individual methods, from the movement commenced by Guillaume Apollinaire and Francis Carcoe. [Cocteau's] new conception is a sort of materialisation of the "Music Hall" of Marinetti, as outlined in the manifesto of 1913. . . .

The form of the new entertainment is a sort of intelligent development of the revue, without the tedious topical blague generality in that form. The action consists of a number of farcical situations following rapidly upon each other, and of a humorous inconsequentiality. It makes no use of "ideas," as does the social comedy. By the use of masks and artificial cardboard structures which give the actors exaggeratedly large heads and shoulders, after the manner of newspaper caricatures, Cocteau has developed the *maschere* of the Commedia dell'arte heightening the comic effect.[46]

Pondey also felt that this new type of entertainment had immeasurable possibilities for all spheres of modern art and it benefited by making an immediate appeal to the audience, which enjoyed it very much.

Despite this last analysis, most of the reviews approached the whole piece with sarcasm. Milhaud felt that the reviewers treated the production as a joke and *Le Boeuf* "was regarded by the public as symbolizing music hall and the circus system of aesthetics, and for the critics it represented the postwar music."[47] The critic for *Le Ménestrel*, however, seems to have been scared. Cocteau had probably not helped matters by his opening remarks—all the critics made some mention of them—and even less by calling the piece "a mere trifle." But his purpose, as stated earlier, was legitimate, since he did not want too much to be read into *Le Boeuf*. A despondent Milhaud felt that everyone would now look at him as a "clown and strolling musician" and not as a serious composer.[48]

For the general public, *Le Boeuf sur le toit* was an enjoyable success. Jean Hugo noted in his diary the full houses he witnessed every night, and an agent from London convinced Milhaud and Cocteau to take their piece to London for a two-week run at the Coliseum. Cocteau took his first trip to the English capital in early July and wrote the Hugos that "London is a mass of provincial towns. The shops are not chic, . . . I am so *sleepy*. Everything passes in a dream."[49]

Cocteau had a rude awakening, though, when rehearsals began. Milhaud, who joined Cocteau later, remarked that "the charming young man who acted as our manager [in London] only had the vaguest idea of how our show should be organized; instead of acrobatic dancers, he had engaged some weird looking youths who looked as if they had come straight from Whitechapel."[50] The same manager also arranged for rehearsals to be held in the Baroness d'Erlanger's town house, formerly Lord Byron's London residence. Catherine d'Erlanger was a great admirer of Cocteau and the music of "Les Six." How the Baroness reacted to these dubious acrobats performing among her priceless antiques—to represent the bar they had laid her Coromandel screen across two antique chairs—can be imagined, though it seems none of the performers destroyed anything. While Cocteau was rehearsing in the d'Erlanger house, Milhaud was having trouble with the orchestra at the theatre, which did not comprehend his music one iota. When he became too frustrated with the uncomprehending musicians he would call a break and Milhaud remembered the lady horn players felt sorry for him in his predicament and "tried to molify me by showing me photos of their babies."[51]

Le Boeuf was to play two weeks at the Coliseum, sandwiched between a Japanese acrobatic act and either a monologue by the American mimic, Ruth Draper (1884–1950), or a pantomime by the popular Swiss clown, Grock (1880–1959).[52] As even the Ballets Russes had played in the same house under the same vaudeville conditions, Milhaud was relieved. Cocteau was delighted, since he felt *Le Boeuf* was now in its perfect setting. A remark he loved to quote was one he overheard a Cockney workman exclaiming to his wife after seeing *Le Boeuf:* "It ain't that it makes you laugh; but it's different, see, so it makes you laugh!"[53]

Premiering on 12 July 1920, this Parisian import, presented under its subtitle, *The Nothing-Doing Bar,* rather than the French *Le Boeuf sur le toit,* did not exactly enthrall the critics. *The Stage* thought it was "a strange little piece, not without cleverness and interest, but too indefinite in its scope and idea to satisfy English audiences. . . . Though the cleverness of the masks and the movements may provide a certain amount of interest, the whole effect is rather wasted."[54]

The Times was less kind, calling it a "farce without a giggle, much less a laugh, a harlequinade with the tempo worked *adagio* instead of *presto.* A taste for humour of the kind M. Cocteau offers might be cultivated, but a Coliseum audience could make nothing of it." The writer concluded that if the action were speeded up it might look better and remarked that the skit by Grock, the clown, which followed *Le Boeuf,* "was something we could all understand and was more refreshing."[55]

Sackbut found the performance self-indulgent and directed its comments in a very personal way, implying that the whole affair was hatched under the effects of opium. This proved to be a rather ironical comment, considering that Cocteau was not then hooked on opium, but would be a few years later.

The main impression left by the performance [of *Le Boeuf*] was that the work itself was inspired by something considerably more potent than gin—probably *Cannabis Indica*; the nightmare atmosphere of emotional vacuum, the huge dwarfing masks and the slow lethargic movements of the actors all point to it. Regarded as a minutely accurate externalisation of a hasheesh vision the little piece is psychologically interesting; but the worst of it is that whereas a great man like de Quincey can take opium and produce a *Dream-Fugue* and a *Suspiria,* drugs (or drink) only emphasize and exaggerate the littleness and silliness of little, silly men. In any case, whether congenital stupidity was or was not assisted by the Indian herb in the devising of it, this production certainly constitutes the most complete exhibition of imbecility we have ever witnessed on (or, for that matter, off) the stage; and the Coliseum audience seemed to think so too.[56]

The reviewer even classified the ballet as a "dada review" which must have infuriated the dadaists as much as it annoyed Cocteau, who would not relish being classified with his declared enemies.

The *Musical Standard* came to the rescue of Cocteau, this time through the words of Leigh Henry. He thought Cocteau very talented in the representation of this "uproarous skit" of an American Prohibition bar. Pointing out the importance of real clowns playing the parts, Henry emphasized that Cocteau had "deliberately designed the movements to contradict the rhythmic movement of the music, thereby attaining a peculiarly grotesque quality, and a curiously irresistible comic effect."

> Spiritually, this significance of *The Nothing-Doing Bar* is important, in that it marks a departure from the sentimental cliché of the "halls," even as the music forms an example of the new musical tendency to get out into the fresh air, even if it be that of the streets. And though one may hear that the subject-matter may be designated as trivial by the solemn-minded, they are yet as important as the daisies immortalised in the Wordsworthian type of poem.[57]

These London performances of *Le Boeuf* were the last presentation of the ballet under Cocteau's supervision. Over the next decade, however, there were two more productions, though Cocteau was not directly involved. One was by George Balanchine—then known as Balanchivadze—as part of his evenings of "Young Ballet" in Petrograd in 1923; the other production was staged by Elizavets Anderson-Ivantzoff at the American Laboratory Theatre in New York in 1930 and was performed in conjunction with Cocteau's play, *Antigone*, written in 1927. Brooks Atkinson thought Cocteau had set his farce in an American bar *in Paris* and thought his fable "never caught the comic facility of the costumes. When the intelligentzia [referring to Cocteau] attempts the robustiousness of hearty horseplay, culture seems like the curse of civilization. Art was in a moderate mood last night."[58] Robert Littell of *The World*, by contrast, found the ballet very interesting. He thought Cocteau's scenario was very good, but the American interpreters of his piece showed too much effort in the execution and did not understand its style:

> The costumes, the giant cocktail shakers, the policeman with the removable head, the delicately drunken barkeep, the fantastic Negro prize fighter, were dream-colored and dream-sized, though very consciously and elaborately so. The desired effect was achieved, perhaps, but signs of the necessary effort thronged the stage. This pantomime, even if carefully conceived, should be tossed off, with the accent of a gay impromptu. It is a charade, but last night it was a charade on whose brow you cold see drops of sweat.[59]

There is an interesting postscript to Cocteau's creation of *Le Boeuf sur le toit*. In 1922, after the Gaya bar moved to a new residence on the rue Boissy d'Anglais, the owner asked Cocteau and Milhaud if he could rename it after their ballet. They agreed and it opened on 10 January 1922 and soon became a mecca for all the artists and friends of Cocteau. Milhaud complained later that many people thought they had named the ballet after the bar, when it was the reverse. Be that as it may, *Le Boeuf sur le toit* bar became a symbol of Paris in the twenties and the ballet, the "spectacle-farce" of Cocteau's devising, became the precursor to another and even more ambitious dance project.[60]

Once more Darius Milhaud became the catalyst in the production of Cocteau's next ballet, though this time an indirect, rather than a direct, cause. Milhaud had written a ballet score entitled *L'Homme et son désir* and was hopeful that Diaghilev might be interested in producing it. "Diaghilev," Milhaud tells us, "was strongly influenced by the theories advanced by Cocteau in *Le Coq et l'Arlequin* and was distinctly attracted by the amusing direct art personified by Poulenc and Auric."[61]

As much as Diaghilev may have been attracted to the music of these two members of "Les Six," he was not attracted to Milhaud's style of composition. To make matters worse, neither was Misia Sert. Although Milhaud did play a piano reduction of the score in Misia's salon for her, Diaghilev, and Massine, his efforts were met with icy silence. Milhaud knew his ballet was doomed in the Diaghilev camp. As the composer noted rather ironically, "My symbolic and dramatic ballet no longer corresponded to the needs of the day."[62] However, there had now arrived in Paris a competitor to Diaghilev's enterprise and Milhaud tried his luck with this company.

Called the Ballets Suédois, it was under the direction of Rolf de Maré (1898–1964), a wealthy Swedish landowner and farmer who, while a sincere agriculturist, was also interested in the arts. His vast income from his profitable estates gave him the money to support his schemes without stinting on details, as Diaghilev was often forced to do. Maré had founded Ballets Suédois to present programs of native Swedish folk dances, which he felt were an important yet neglected part of Swedish culture. However, his chief conductor, Desiré Inghelbrecht (1880–1965), convinced him to present other, more classically oriented, items on his programs as well.

While Maré's chief conductor was French, his chief dancer and choreographer, Jean Börlin (1893–1930), was from the home country. Maré had hired him on the recommendation of Mikhail Fokine, who had spent some time as choreographer and ballet master at the Royal Swedish Opera House after leaving Diaghilev's company. Börlin, however, was far from having the impeccable classical background that many of the Ballets Russes dancers had, but he made up for his lack of technique by hard work, perseverance and determination. When Fokine was casting *Cléopâtre* in Sweden, he remembered how Börlin "crossed the stage with great bounds, landed with all his force and glided over the boards among the group of bacchantes. What character! What ecstasy! The fanatical sacrifice of a bruised body in order to produce the maximum of choreographic effect. It was a revelation to me."[63]

Börlin collaborated with Maré in bringing not only Swedish dance to the West, but a company that prided itself on innovation. Maré disbanded it four years later when he felt that any further productions would only be a repetition of their previous successes. Maré centered his company in Paris, because he was convinced that the success of his venture meant success outside of Sweden, and Paris was still the artistic capital of the Western world. The company toured extensively, but it was Paris where the premieres were held. French artists also dominated the creation of the themes, music and decor, though the ballets were danced by a mixture of Swedish and Danish dancers.

Maré set high standards and worked quickly to achieve his goals. Immediately after the opening night of his ballet company on 25 October 1920, he began to commission music from rising young French composers, but with important stipulations. He did not want any "ready-made" music. The pieces had to be specifically written for the Ballet Suédois. Milhaud was thus rather surprised when Maré accepted his *L'Homme et son désir*, but perhaps the Swedish impresario wanted to prove that he could produce something that Diaghilev had rejected. In any case, through his contact with the composers of "Les Six," Maré could not help but eventually meet Cocteau since he was interested in using prominent writers for the scenarios of his ballets.

Milhaud had used a well-known French poet, Paul Claudel (1868-1955), as his scenarist for *L'Homme*, and Maré saw the possibility of extending an invitation to Cocteau as well. He asked Cocteau to write a ballet scenario with a score by Auric. Auric, however, was unable to undertake the ballet score at the moment because of other commitments. As the other members of "Les Six" were also engaged in various pursuits that would not allow them to allocate much time for Cocteau's ballet he decided to ask each of them to contribute one section and he would put them all together. All agreed, except for Durey, who had been separating himself from the group for some time. Privately Cocteau expressed his annoyance at this "betrayal" but publicly he claimed that Durey had been unable to accept because he was ill.[64]

The working title of the ballet was *La Noce massacrée* (The Wedding Massacre), and it was not until the ballet was well into rehearsal that Cocteau changed the name to *Les Mariés de la Tour Eiffel* (The Wedding Party on the Eiffel Tower).[65] Cocteau expressed his feelings early on that what he was trying to do in *Parade* and *Le Boeuf sur le toit* could reach its culmination in *Les Mariés*. "To shape oneself is not easy. To reshape oneself still less so. Until *Les Mariés de la Tour Eiffel*, the first work in which I owed nothing to anybody, and which is unlike any other, in which I discovered my cypher, I forced the lock and twisted the key in every direction."[66]

Les Mariés did include a number of innovative, if not unusual, features. The setting is the Eiffel Tower on a spring day in 1900. The backdrop is a bird's eye view of the Champs-Elysées. Upstage right is a camera with a black funnel that extends in the wings so that the camera front is a door from which people can jump out of the camera. Downstage, right and left, are two phonographs—actors disguised as such—who speak through the large megaphone contraptions which were part of gramophone players at this period. The author gave directions in the script that the actors playing the phonographs "should speak very loudly and quickly, pronouncing each syllable distinctly."[67] In some of the early performances Cocteau himself played one of the phonographs. The actors disguised as phonographs spoke all the dialogue for the play, even for the other characters, and the dance action happened simultaneously while the text was spoken by the two disguised actors on each side of the stage. Cocteau felt these phonographic commentors "were the renovation of the Greek chorus."[68]

After a sprightly overture by Auric, the phonograph machines discuss the ostrich which is crossing the stage, followed by a hunter. In his pursuit the hunter has accidentally shot a radiogram, which falls from the sky onto the stage. The manager of the Eiffel Tower storms in and complains about the noise. A photographer then rushes on because he is looking for the ostrich which has escaped from his camera. He explains to the manager that usually a little birdie jumps out of his camera when he shouts "watch the birdie!" but the last time an ostrich popped out. Meanwhile, the manager has opened the radiogram and found it is addressed to him: A wedding party is coming for breakfast on the Eiffel Tower, and he rushes about getting everything ready for their appearance.

To a bright wedding march by Darius Milhaud the party enters: the sweet bride, the rich father-in-law, the handsome bridegroom, the stuck-up mother-in-law, the pompous general, the burly ushers, and the bridesmaids, sweet as roses. The general makes a speech, gesticulating and miming his words to the sounds of Poulenc's musical depiction of this discourse. After the speech the general tells of a mirage he once saw in Africa when running tigers appeared as small as wasps on a pie he was eating with the Duc d'Aumale. Suddenly a girl on a bicycle appears on stage. She is on her way to Chatou and stops to ask the general for directions. After she leaves, the general explains to the assembly that they were merely viewing a mirage and not to be concerned. The photographer is ready to take the wedding picture and as the guests prepare themselves, the phonograph machines comment on the position of the Eiffel Tower, not in terms of geographical placement, but her position in society. Once she was the Queen of Paris, now she is just a telegraph girl. "Well," Phono I comments, "a person's got to do something for a living!"[69]

When this exchange is finished the photographer takes the picture of the company, but as he shouts "Watch the birdie!" a Trouville bathing beauty pops out, "pretty as a postcard." To sparkling music by Poulenc she dances a polka

Figure 11.   Jean Cocteau Posed inside One of His Phonographs from
Les Mariés de la Tour Eiffel, 1921
Photograph by Isabey.
(Private Collection)

Figure 12.   The Wedding Couple from *Les Mariés de la Tour Eiffel*, 1921
Costumes by Jean Hugo.
Photograph by Isabey.
(Private Collection)

as the wedding party gazes in rapt admiration. Finally, by convincing her it is a bathhouse, the photographer lures the bathing beauty back into the camera. The photographer exclaims: "Since these mysteries are beyond me, let's pretend that I'd arranged them all along."[70] He accepts the applause of the assembled company, though he realizes he cannot arrange to have the pretty girl repeat her number, though the assembly pleads for an encore. He is never sure what will come out of the camera next. Once more the photographer snaps his shutter and this time a little child jumps out. He calls the groom "papa" and the bride "mama" and all recognize him as the child of the future. They discuss whether he will become a captain, an architect, a poet, President of the Republic, or perhaps a pretty little corpse for the next war. The child searches in the basket he is carrying and takes out some *balles* (in French *balle* can be translated as both sportsball or bullet) and bombards the wedding party; he is massacring them. The photographer takes out a whip and tries to chase the child back into the camera. All the while the child keeps shouting, "All I want is to live my own life."[71]

There is so much noise that the radiograms are scared. They flutter down onto the stage one by one and when assembled, they perform a waltz to music by Tailleferre. The child insists that he must have his picture taken with the general; this time the click of the camera brings forth a lion. Everyone runs and hides except for the general who assures them all it is only another mirage. Mirage or no, the lion chases the general under the banquet table and emerges a few minutes later with the general's boot in his mouth. Immediately the general's funeral is prepared, to a dirge by Arthur Honegger. Orations are given in honor of the departed, but are suddenly interrupted by the "Garde Républicaine" playing a quadraille by Tailleferre.

All the company dance to the charming melody, and the ostrich comes on to join them. To hide the poor bird from the hunter, who is in close pursuit, the company places a hat over the ostrich's head, since an ostrich is always invisible when his head is hidden.

Why does the company suddenly freeze in midaction, Phono I asks. The reason, says Phono II, is the appearance of the art dealer and his client. The former has come to show the latter this masterpiece, "The Wedding Party on the Eiffel Tower." Phono I voices the dealer's lines and Phono II speaks for the client.

Phono I: It is one of God's very latest compositions.

Phono II: Is it signed?

Phono I: God never signs—but I ask you: is it *painted*! What texture! Observe the style, the nobility, the *joie de vivre*! It might almost be a funeral.

Phono II: I see a wedding party.

Phono I: There you are wrong. It is more than a wedding. It is *all* weddings. It is more than all weddings. It is a cathedral.

Phono II: What do you want for it?
Phono I: It is not for sale, except to the Louvre or you. See here: you can have it at cost price.[72]

Here Cocteau parodies the pretentions and commercialism of the art world, which he carried one step further in the play when the client tells the photographer to take a picture of the wedding party with a "Sold" sign hanging on it; it is to be printed in all the American magazines as proof of his purchase for "10,000,000,000" (of undesignated currency). The photographer prepares to oblige this whim of the patron when his camera speaks to him. It wants to give up the general who is inside. The general comes out—minus a boot—and joins the composition. The new owner of the picture is sure to be pleased with this addition, the phonographs inform us, since unexpected details are always a delight when found in great masterpieces.

This time as the photographer clicks, the little bird finally appears, and one by one, the wedding party enter the camera to the sounds of Milhaud's wedding march. The manager comes on and announces that it is closing time, and the hunter rushes off to catch the last train which he seems to have missed. As he goes, the camera starts to move to the left, its bellows stretching after it, like railway coaches. Through window openings the wedding guests can be seen, waving handkerchiefs and, underneath, their feet are seen in motion as the curtain falls.[73]

How does one classify this piece? Cocteau had called *Parade* a "ballet réaliste" and *Le Boeuf sur le toit* a "farce" or a "spectacle concert." Cocteau answered the question himself in a preview article on *Les Mariés*. "Is it a ballet? No. Is it a play? No. Tragedy? No. Rather a sort of secret marriage between the antique tragedy and the modern review. Between the ancient chorus and the music hall turn."[74] It was certainly a wedding of many stage elements: dance, music, speech and spectacle. A major delight of the work is the marvelous witty dialogue, which is filled with double entendres and a brilliant play on words and sounds, impossible to convey properly in any English translation of the text. For example, Cocteau uses the word "cliché" in both its meanings: the click of the camera or something that is passé, mundane. "Objectif" can mean both a photograph negative and the underside or hidden reality of something, and Cocteau uses it as both verb and noun when the photographer is explaining his technique to the wedding party. In most English translations of the play the child is said to be throwing bullets at the company, but the original French word is "balle," which can mean not only a bullet, but a ping pong ball, thus making the child's actions both a massacre and a sport. Cocteau not only plays with words but also with established conventions. For Cocteau the Eiffel Tower is nothing more than a telegraph station and the radiograms that fall from its pinnacle turn out to be a lovely set of Tiller-like girls performing a two-step. Mirages appear from nowhere and turn out to be reality, like the lion. A child symbolically kills his parents as a theatrical gesture of the traditional rebellion of the young against the old.

Add to this mixture the delightful dance sequences, such as the polka of the Trouville bathing beauty or the quadrille of the guests and the music of "Les Six"—minus one. The music has a delightful bounce and gaiety and blends remarkably well together, if one can judge from a recording made many years later.[75] Milhaud said in his memoirs that he thought only one or two sequences were any good, but his comments dating from 1933 were more complimentary.[76] Alexandre Tansman thought that even if the different sections of the music for *Les Mariés* were not evenly good, "it still represented an important evolution in the development of 'avant-garde' music. It took great courage to present this *Oeuvre de ce caractère* in 1921."[77] Cocteau's courage was rewarded by later recognition but even at the time he was able to take delight in the bewilderment of the music critics over the ballet. He wrote about one trick that especially caused embarrassment:

> Arthur Honegger amused himself by making fun of what our musicographers gravely call: MUSIC. It is unnecessary to add that they all fell into the trap. Hardly had the first notes of the *Funeral March* sounded when all those long ears pricked up in grave attention. Not one noticed that the march was beautiful as a sarcasm, written with taste, an extraordinary feeling for appositeness; not one of the critics, all of whom praised the piece, recognized the waltz in *Faust* [by Gounod] which served as its base![78]

All of "Les Six" enjoyed such deceptions and would continue to add them to their respective compositions in future years. Critics became more circumspect and careful after this initial joke in *Les Mariés* though not always more receptive.

Since *Les Mariés de la Tour Eiffel* was the only theatrical piece "Les Six" did together, the ballet is of historic importance. As a deliberate commissional potpourri that could have been a disaster, it is a tribute to Cocteau's artistic knowhow that the piece came off so splendidly. It is reminiscent of commissions made by Italian princes of the Renaissance who had various composers write different sections to form a complete *intermezzo*.

In terms of decor and costumes, Cocteau was at first indecisive as to who would do what and when. Jean Hugo, now married to Valentine Gross and an established designer and artist, gives a full picture of the situation in his journal:

> In the winter of 1921, on my return to Paris, I ran into Cocteau on the Rue d'Anjou; he was occupied in creating *La Noce massacrée*, which was later entitled *Les Mariés de la Tour Eiffel*. . . . He had decided to design the decor himself. In a miniature theatre made from four wooden boards he painted the Eiffel Tower in a number of colors, in the style of Delaunay. . . . He asked me to help him with the work one afternoon and I ended up staying four hours.
>
> To design the costumes he thought of asking Irène Lagut, a painter of delicate harlequins and circus horses. He brought her to Sunday dinner with us and told her all about the piece. She laughed like a child: "I can already see electric lamps for the eyes of the lion."[79]

Some days later Hugo was told by Cocteau that he had changed his mind and wanted Hugo to design the costumes! Cocteau explained to the bewildered artist that he had seen Hugo's engraving of a cyclist for "Les Joues en Feu" and thought he would be better suited for the work on *Les Mariés*. Irène Lagut (1886–1950) was, as Hugo said, a painter of child-like simplicity and her style was well suited to Cocteau's concept. She was naturally vexed when Cocteau decided to replace her with Hugo as costume designer. She was supported by Georges Auric, a close friend, who now refused to contribute his piece of music for the ballet. Either because he was dissatisfied with his own set renderings or, more likely, in order to placate the ire of Auric and Lagut, Cocteau offered Lagut the chance to design the decor. She agreed and Auric promised to deliver his overture and three *ritournelles* for the ballet as soon as possible.

For the costumes Hugo began research with the *Dictionnaire Larousse*, looking up cyclists, lions, bridegrooms and so forth. He designed the lion to resemble the marble models that guarded the Louvre and he put the cyclists in culottes and the bridegroom in a gray morning suit. He had difficulty with a concept for the director of the Eiffel Tower but when he saw a pompous porter one day at a hotel—one with slicked mustaches and a self-satisfied air—he decided to model the director after him. Cocteau, however, had a better idea: "No, the director is . . . Guepratte!" Guepratte was a French admiral famous for his pompous manner and short staccato walking style, due to his small feet. He also had a penchant for smoking large cigars and wearing all his medals for every occasion. Hugo designed his director of the Eiffel Tower with this sea lord as his model.[80]

Cocteau's concept and Hugo's designs dictated that the costuming would totally encase the dancers, including large masks over their heads to emphasize the comic nature of each character. Valentine helped her husband put the final touches to these head coverings, almost cartoon-like with their wide eyes, primary colors and cotton-wool hair. Cocteau was delighted with the realization. He had wanted his characters to resemble those large Greek masks from the ancient plays except his had tiny bodies attached below. "Echelle épiques [on an epic scale]" he called them.[81]

These sculpted heads were difficult for the dancers to work in and Jean Börlin had to choreograph by counts, since they would not be able to hear the speakers or the music very well or even see from the masks. There had to be most extensive rehearsals for this ballet, because of this technical adjustment, but Maré said that each of his dancers performed extremely well and danced with rigorous precision.[82] Cocteau was at all rehearsals and dictated much of the action to Börlin, since so much was mime rather than dance. As with Massine on *Parade*, Cocteau would make suggestions and verbalize ideas that would be visualized by the choreographer. With *Les Mariés*, however, Cocteau's involvement was much more intense than with *Parade*. The poet had learned much more from directing and choreographing *Le Boeuf sur le toit* himself.

Figure 13.   The Child with One of the Bridesmaids from
Les Mariés de la Tour Eiffel, 1921
Costumes by Jean Hugo.
Photograph by Isabey.
(Private Collection)

Meanwhile Irène Lagut was designing a set in pastel colors which gave that bird's eye view of Paris, "a dizzy glimpse of the streets below and the birds above."[83] Hugo admired the painted birds and tricolor flags of the backdrop, as well as the perspective of the Seine with the jade trees running along each side of the bank.[84] The girders of the tower encompassed the entire set to give the audience the feeling of suspension on the observation platform.

Everything would not have been complete without a preview article from Cocteau, which had now become a tradition with the poet. He wrote this one for *La Danse* and humbly claimed, as he did with *Le Boeuf*, that nothing happens in this ballet. "Nothing is described." He said that Hugo had made his characters more real by the use of the masks—a claim Cocteau had already made for *Le Boeuf*—and the poet told his readers: "Thanks to Irène Lagut, our Eiffel Tower brings to mind those Parisian postcards at the sight of which I have even seen little Arabs sigh in Africa."[85] Cocteau then explained his basic thesis for the ballet:

> I have been asked if the text [of *Les Mariés*] were satirical. Wherever there is reality, there is satire, and I cannot endure work which, however far from subjective realism it be carried, has not its deep roots in the reality about us. I have tried to avoid tinkering with style, to avoid originality; I have tried to write freely.[86]

Cocteau also wrote an article of appreciation of the Ballets Suédois. It is interesting to compare this piece with his earlier article for the Ballets Russes; the sycophantic style of the former has now been replaced by a more mature approach:

The Ballets Suédois and the Young

> Little by little we are seeing born in France a new sort of theatre which cannot properly be called ballet and which has no place at the Opéra, the Opéra comique, or even the popular theatres of the Boulevard.
>
> This new genre, more consonant with the modern spirit, which is roughly sketched on the music hall, remains an unexplored land, rich in possibilities. The enterprise of M. Rolf de Maré, the indefatigable work of M. Jean Borlin, has helped greatly in opening the door of this new world to explorers. By the grace of the Ballets Suédois the young—the new generation—will continue to create with new forms in which the fairy, the dance, the acrobatic, the pantomime, the drama, the satire, music, and the spoken word will combine to produce a novel genre; unaided they will stage pieces which the official artists will take for studio farces, pieces which for all that will be no less than plastic expressions of poetry.
>
> By giving us this program, MM. de Maré and Borlin have rendered a great service to France. They are delivering this child of art. They are slowly correcting the old routine art so that its disappearance will not even be noticed or create a scandal, and we will be astonished by the mirror that the Swedes have held up for us.[87]

There are certain thematic similarities in this manifesto which appear in Cocteau's preview articles and writings about his previous works. The idea of a "new door" runs through many of the articles as well as the mentioning of the wealth of material that could be found in the music-hall but which was too often neglected by the artist. He continually emphasized the use and combination of various art forms and the fact that even the most mundane can be made interesting. Cocteau thought the revolution started by Maré and Börlin would be accepted without the tumult which had met *Parade*: the old blending imperceptibly with the new. Cocteau received a shock on opening night for the presentation of *Les Mariés* created quite a disturbance although less for what it actually presented than for the person who created it.

On 18 June 1921 *Les Mariés de la Tour Eiffel* opened to a gala audience at the Théâtre des Champs-Elysées. Dadaists, however, had infiltrated the audience and every time the phonographs spoke any dialogue, they would stand up shouting "Viva Dada!" The numerous pronouncements Cocteau had made about the Dada movement—especially his claim that *Parade* was the first Dada piece—infuriated the followers of that style. Although Cocteau had tried to pretend he was "great friends with Dada followers" though not one himself, this demonstration at the opening of his ballet made him realize that he was "the *bête noire* for Dadaists."[88] There were, however, other reasons for the raucous opening night.

Dadaism was a reaction against the horror of World War I. Tristan Tzara (1896–1963) was the movement's principal spokesman and in manifestos he presented the Dada view of life: a rejection of the past and an embracing of discord and chaos to replace unity, balance and harmony. The Dadaists produced deliberately illogical works and relished direct confrontations with the public. To disrupt a Cocteau opening night was just the sort of "spontaneous" reaction they enjoyed, but there was more to this particular demonstration. The Dadaists were also lashing out against the managers of the Théâtre des Champs-Elysées because they had kicked them out of the building the day before. In the hall above the theatre the Dadaists had been holding a "salon dada" for the past few weeks. On 18 June the theatre below the hall—where *Les Mariés* would open the next night—was hired out to Marinetti and other Italians for a Futurist "Concert bruitiste," which made use of atonality, improvisation, and "nonmusical" sounds. Tzara and the dada followers situated in the hall above heard the noise and came down to break up the proceedings. A fight developed and the management took action by locking the Dadaists out of the building the next day when they were supposed to have a matinee performance. Cocteau and *Les Mariés* bore the brunt of the Dadaists' frustrations displayed on the ballet's opening night.

The reviewers had to concentrate on describing the decor and the action and few mentioned the text, since it was rather difficult for them to hear it over the shouts.[89] The performance did receive cheers, however, and so much so that after the last performance on 25 June, Jean Hugo could write in his diary: "Success." Maré was so pleased with the ballet's reception that he took the collaborators and company to lunch on the platform of the Eiffel Tower and Frenchman toasted Swede with aquavit.[90]

Some reviews turned into a personal attack on Cocteau, rather than the production itself. One was by Henri Baraud, never a fan of "Les Six," who wrote in the *Mercure de France:*

> They debase a profession into which they introduce themselves like parvenus into a club, by greasing palms and feeding parasites. There is more talent, conscientiousness, and originality in the least important revue by Rip and Gignoux than in all the past and future work of M. Jean Cocbin [the critic's slang name for Cocteau]. *Les Mariés* is nothing less than avant-garde mystification . . . and a monstrous, desperate kind of buffoonery.[91]

A review such as this hurt Cocteau terribly and in a long letter dedicated to Jean Börlin and written after the opening night reviews, he expressed his feelings about the critical analysis of *Les Mariés* and the misunderstanding. Cocteau expresses some very important views about theatre in the letter and much of it would later be incorporated into the preface for the published version of the ballet play.[92] In *Order Considered as Anarchy* Cocteau wrote:

> In *Les Mariés de la Tour Eiffel,* I provided poetry with a powerful transmitter, adapted to theatrical presentation. In this piece I claim to have shown for the first time—in spite of an absolute and universal failure, ever on the part of my admirers, to grasp what I was aiming at—a true poetry in terms of the theatre; for poetry merely transferred to the theatre is a mistake; it is like a piece of fine lace seen from a distance. My rope-lace was incomprehensible. People saw through it, and applauded a farce, a satire, but nothing which I had intended. For I suppress all imagery and subtleties of language. Nothing remains but poetry—that is to say, to modern ears, nothing at all. Anglo Saxons think *Les Mariés* is nonsense.[93]

The last comment was in answer to the English reviews of the ballet, which thought the piece rather bewildering. Cocteau always emphasized that *Les Mariés* was a "poésie poétique," by which he meant not just the words he produced but the words in conjunction with the costumes of Jean Hugo, the sets of Irène Lagut, the choreography of Jean Börlin and the music of "Les Six." Only the combination alone should the piece be seen, and through this combination Cocteau was trying "to substitute a *poésie de théâtre* [theatre poetry] for the usual *poésie au théâtre* [poetry in the theatre]."[94] In a 1951 interview Cocteau expanded his ideas about the "rope-lace" poetry he had talked about in *Order Considered as Anarchy:*

> Poetry *in* the theatre is very delicate, almost invisible. I would like poetry to be like a coarse rope as the Eiffel Tower itself is a coarse rope of poetry, but made of metal. She was the premiere farce of 1889. When she was first built, she raised a *scandale,* then she became accepted, and finally commonplace.[95]

The former queen becomes a telegraph operator, to make herself useful. Cocteau was always amused when his early works, such as *Parade* or *Les Mariés,* became acceptable to the critics and frequently to the same critics who had originally condemned the work. But Cocteau was scared of becoming like the Eiffel Tower—

an accepted commonplace—so he always searched for the "very latest thing," *le dernier cri*. "What disgusts me is the process of prolonging works, splitting them into halves and quarters and eights, serving them up with sauces, and chewing them over and over to the point of exhaustion."[96] Cocteau never repeated the trick of *Les Mariés* again; he did not want to be classified, accused of imitating his past success or being *expected* to repeat his past work.

Les Mariés, despite any critical reservations, was a popular success. Maré noted "the applause increased as the action progressed till it was a veritable tumult at the end. This, much to the embarrassment of Cocteau's detractors. It was the same every night."[97] The ballet continued to be popular every season, having twice as many performances in the last season, four years after its premiere.[98] An American who saw the ballet wrote an article for *Vanity Fair* and pinpointed a number of elements of the ballet that contributed to its popular success:

> Cocteau is in love with all the droll and homely aspects of the Parisian world—the music halls, the revues, and the *bals musettes*, the Eiffel Tower with its photographer and its postcards of beautiful bathers, the popular fairs with their side-shows and their jingling merry-go-round tunes. Cocteau protests repeatedly that he wants to make something *real*; and it is true that, for all his nonsense, he does make something real. When he turns a bourgeois wedding into a side-splitting harlequinade, we none the less get the feeling of a vivid reaction to life, of a bodying forth of objects which the artist has seen and felt. It is precisely this seriousness about his art which . . . differentiates Cocteau. . . . The Frenchman theorizes about his art; he formulates an aesthetic doctrine; he relegates his own contribution to the body of art of the world.[99]

The author, Edmund Wilson, Jr., goes on to say he does not know which to admire most: "the classic-mindedness of a public which requires to have such [*sic*] simple, if fantastic, spectacles explained to it, or the artistic seriousness of a writer who takes a charming harlequinade as a pretext for laying down aesthetic principles in the manner of Aristotle."[100]

Wilson thought that American audiences would appreciate Cocteau's brand of nonsense better than the French and expressed hope that *Les Mariés* could be brought to the United States or that Cocteau would produce a ballet especially for America. Happily, when the Ballets Suédois did bring *Les Mariés de la Tour Eiffel* to America in 1923, the critics found the whole production a delightful spectacle. *The New York Times* thought the audience listened to the "very modern music" and avant-garde productions with great attention and applauded each ballet. *Les Mariés* was "a ballet pleasing and yet grotesque in its modern day representation of *gargouilles* as seen on the façade of Notre-Dame; they were designed by the grandson of Victor Hugo, Jean Hugo. The masks made all the figures of the ballet most remarkable."[101]

With the demise of Ballets Suédois in 1925 *Les Mariés de la Tour Eiffel* was never seen again. In fact, for years it was thought that the music for the ballet had been completely lost. However, in 1956 the manuscript score, along with most of the costumes, were found in a museum in Stockholm where Maré had deposited them. Subsequently, Darius Milhaud was able to conduct a recording of the music from the ballet, thus preserving a part of Cocteau's fantastic creation.[102]

As for being fantastic and important, *Les Mariés* left no doubts among Cocteau's admirers. For Cocteau, the frustration of *Parade* had led to his experimentations with *Le Boeuf sur le toit* and the realization of his expectations in *Les Mariés de la Tour Eiffel*. "A question I often ask myself," Cocteau stated in *Professional Secrets*, "is why spectacles like *Parade*, *Le Boeuf*, and *Les Mariés* are so revolting to the professional, and give rise to such sustained animosity, when there is no question of them competing with anything else."[103] Perhaps the theatrical professionals who were accustomed to dealing in specific categories—a dancer, an actor, a singer, a musician—found the mingling of genres, and the new demands such presentations put on the performers, to be a threat to the established precincts of their respective arts. Others, however, welcomed such demands as a means of expanding their talents. With the production of the three works mentioned above, Cocteau had shown audiences that accepted theatrical conventions did not always have to be followed in the presentation of dance compositions.

5

"La Danse de son Temps": The Creation of *Le Train bleu*

Do not fear a certain pomp which will create style.
—Jean Cocteau, *Le Train bleu*

Cocteau had now formulated his ideas for dance presentations and was able to return and work for the Ballets Russes on his own particular terms. With the productions of *Les Mariés de la Tour Eiffel* and *Le Boeuf sur le toit*, Cocteau had established himself as both a theatrical artist and producer who could be as innovative as Serge Diaghilev, albeit independent of the Ballets Russes. Cocteau also began to copy Diaghilev by "sponsoring" artists whose talents were being overlooked by all of Paris. In 1919 Cocteau met fifteen-year-old Raymond Radiguet. A disheveled, morose young boy with a desultory talent for writing, Cocteau took him under his wing and with Svengali-like devotion transformed him into one of the literary sensations of the early twenties. Publicizing and promoting the young boy's books with an energy that even outdid the enthusiasm Cocteau always gave to his own works, he soon felt of Radiguet as more than a "ward of genius" but "as my own son."[1] However, by early 1923 the young boy became very ill and died on 11 December 1923. The official cause was typhoid fever but the excesses of opium and drink accelerated the progress of the disease.

Cocteau was totally crushed and utterly despondent over his young protégé's death. He was so depressed that he felt he could not work, think, or even breathe; "his death tied my hands," he was to say some years later.[2] His friends, who missed the gay and witty poet, thought he was carrying the whole thing too far and nicknamed him "La Veuve sur le toit" [the Widow on the roof]. All of Cocteau's correspondence at the time is filled with self-pity and little about his work; he implies that nothing can get done since he has lost all joy in life. The loss of his erstwhile lover had made Cocteau feel deprived, alone, and senescent, but such a condition could not be tolerated for long. It had also made him more aware of death, though he tried to avoid such preoccupations through humor or through drugs.[3] At this point, however, Cocteau escaped thoughts of death by throwing himself into a series of theatrical works that premiered one after the other in the first months of 1924. Obviously, Cocteau was busy at work while publicly protesting that he could do nothing.

The first person to help give Cocteau impetus in his creative endeavors was Diaghilev. Diaghilev sent a personal invitation to him to come to Monte Carlo to watch the rehearsals of the Ballets Russes and to discuss plans for some new ballets. Cocteau arrived soon after the New Year and stayed to see the premieres of two ballets, *Les Fâcheux* and *Les Biches*. The former had music by Auric and the latter was written by Poulenc. Cocteau felt a personal interest in the works, since he was "father" to all the members of "Les Six." Cocteau also had a hand in both scenarios for the ballets, though this is rarely mentioned in discussions of Cocteau's works.[4] He had to give up work on the ballets for a number of reasons. First, of course, was the health of Radiguet, which occupied Cocteau during the latter months of 1923 when both ballets were in the production stage. Second was the completion and promotion of Radiguet's last book, *Le Bal du Comte d'Orgel*, which took priority over anything else at the time. Most probably Cocteau also lost interest in both ballets from a literary point of view. *Les Fâcheux* was based on Molière, and Cocteau had difficulty in identifying with that playwright. While *Les Biches* was more his style—a brittle picture of high class society in the early twenties—Cocteau found himself competing for Diaghilev's attention with the impresario's new secretary, Boris Kochno (b. 1904). As Cocteau had to stay with Radiguet, and Kochno was more readily available for consultation, Cocteau's continued work on both ballets seems to have been dropped by mutual agreement, *before* Radiguet's death.[5] It would have been impossible for Diaghilev to have asked Cocteau to write both scenarios after Radiguet's death since both ballets premiered less than a month after the young writer's demise. Cocteau's initial involvement with both ballets also shows that the rift between Diaghilev and Cocteau must have been healed much earlier and that Radiguet's death was not the deciding factor.

Les Biches premiered on 6 January 1924, and *Les Fâcheux* on 19 January. Cocteau was in Monte Carlo for both premieres and mentions how impressed he was with the dancing of Anton Dolin (1904–1983) who even performed *en pointe* in the latter ballet.[6] Cocteau received no credit for his preliminary drafts for both ballets and this does not seem to have bothered him at all since he wrote a number of complimentary articles and the introductory essays for both printed scores.[7] In both the article and essay, Cocteau is highly complimentary of the designers, choreographers, and dancers. He makes no mention that he had an early hand in these works, but neither does he mention the final writers for the ballets. All contemporary programs for both these ballets give no credit for the scenario of *Les Biches*, while *Les Fâcheux* is credited to Boris Kochno, after the play by Molière.[8]

That January in Monte Carlo saw a new phase in Cocteau's life that would have a profound and often disturbing influence on his later working career. "I was so sick, so sombre, that my friend Laloy who had written a marvelous book on opium, counselled me to take some to remedy the situation."[9] This was Cocteau's first introduction to opium, its charms and its hazards, and he would spend the rest of his life indulging in its uses and then rush off for intense cures, alternating between two worlds. Louis Laloy, the French author of *Le Livre de la Fumée (The Smoke Book)*, and the critic who was rather sarcastic in his review of *Le Boeuf sur le toit*, was both an addict and a defender of the drug. Cocteau was ripe for Laloy's enticement. Satie, who was also in Monte Carlo at the time, returned to Paris disgusted with the indulgences he saw there.[10]

How much the drug affected Cocteau's work would be difficult to gauge, but it is important to be aware of this habit since he would continue taking opium for most of his life. Obviously, Cocteau was strong enough to continue his work and when he enjoyed his work he would take the drug less; the problem was finding work that interested him.

While in Monte Carlo Cocteau began work on his first ballet for Diaghilev since 1917, *Le Train bleu*, but he was also concurrently working on another theatre project quite separate from the Ballets Russes organization. Considering Diaghilev's jealousy towards anyone who "defected" from his troupe it is surprising that he allowed Cocteau to work on these two projects at the same time. Then again he may have felt indulgent toward Cocteau under the circumstances of Radiguet's death. Whatever the reason, Cocteau was working on *Roméo et Juliette*, a "pretext" based on Shakespeare.

Cocteau's commission for *Roméo et Juliette* was, in a roundabout way, due to Diaghilev. Leonide Massine, Diaghilev's main choreographer and protégé after Nijinsky, left the company to venture out on his own and away from his patron's demanding presence. However, like Nijinsky when he married, Massine found it difficult to obtain work so long as he was on Diaghilev's blacklist. Massine had befriended Comte Etienne de Beaumont, the wealthy dilettante who designed as well as sponsored various theatrical functions such as Cocteau's *Le Boeuf sur le toit*. Beaumont hatched the idea of presenting "Soirées de Paris" to benefit the frustrated Massine, both choreographically and financially, as well as displaying his own taste as a patron. To disguise the charity aspect of the event Beaumont asked Cocteau to devise a work *not* featuring Massine; then the Comte even asked Tzara to give a dramatic reading of *Mouchoir de nuage* as well. Originally, Cocteau decided to write an "Impromptu de Montmartre" on the lines of Molière's *Impromptu de Versailles* but perhaps due to the limited time allowed or his loss of interest in the subject (the fate of *Les Fâcheux*), Cocteau decided to present his own adaptation of the Shakespeare play, an adaptation he had already written in 1916.[11] Strictly speaking, *Roméo et Juliette* is a play, since it has a spoken text. However, it can be looked at as part of Cocteau's *danse oeuvre* for two reasons.

First, Cocteau explained his own concept of *Boeuf sur le toit, Les Mariés de la Tour Eiffel,* and *Roméo et Juliette* as a series of "spectacles meant to save the Parisian theatre at whatever cost."[12] All three productions depended on a choreographed stage picture, though two of the three have dialogue. Secondly, Cocteau insisted that the play was not to be directed but choreographed. In the program for the soirée Cocteau gives himself credit not for his direction but for his "choréographique de mise en scène." He also added a significant note to the printed text that explained this concept: "I have tried to indicate in this text some of the action that cannot be conveyed through the dialogue alone. It is a pity there does not exist some way of conserving and capturing on paper the details of the choreography which I can here only indicate in a very vague way."[13] Thus, the historian has a difficult time, as Cocteau noted, in judging the production only from a reading of the text. In fact, one can even misinterpret what Cocteau wanted to do with Shakespeare if it is looked at strictly as a play. Jean Hugo, who designed the costumes and set for the production, stated that Cocteau called the piece "un essai de Chirurgie ésthetique" (an essay in aesthetic surgery) and while such a term can be looked at as another of Cocteau's fanciful theatrical subtitles for his stage works, the term does help define Cocteau's conceptual vision of the Verona tragedy.[14]

The text is taut, brief, and terse. Most of the comic scenes are cut and all speeches whittled down to their absolute essence. The balcony scene hardly lasts more than half a page; scenes change swiftly to pace the action faster. It is no longer Shakespeare but an outline of Shakespeare: the Bard was only an excuse for Cocteau to display his wit and invention as stage director. The prologue was spoken by an actress-dancer who flew on wires during the entire scene. Hugo, who called her "Miss Aerogyne," said that the trick of flying was concealed by the bright red lights on the performer and the black drapes of the design.[15] Cocteau claimed collaboration: "Jean Hugo [and] I had invented an entirely black set, in which only the colors of certain *arabesques,* costumes, and props were visible. Red lights framing the stage kept the audience from seeing anything else."[16] Hugo, himself, said that the design was a reflection of Shakespeare's time when "The stage was hung with black and I perceive / the auditors prepared for tragedy," and Shakespeare himself had said, in *The Rape of Lucrece:* "Black stages for tragedies and murders fell."[17] With this concept in mind, Hugo devised a set of heavy black drapes and stylized Elizabethan costumes in black and white. Even the stagehands were all in black and became part of the production, making sets and props disappear mysteriously when the action required. When Mercutio's sword fell, one black-clad hand wisked it off and when the passage of time had to be shown two stagehands rolled a long black tape across the set. These "valets de scène" were choreographed by Cocteau as part of the action, and a number of trained dancers were cast in these mobile parts.[18]

Cocteau's stage directions in the printed script are choreographic in tone and content: Benvolio and Romeo were to move to a dance rhythm, a regulated walk "always moving to a hidden tempo."[19] Cocteau had rehearsed both characters to a particular dance piece and removed the music before the performance. He would perform the same trick on his dancers some twenty years later when he would stage *Le Jeune homme et la mort*; this time, however, the music was not replaced by a different piece but with silence, so the actors had to move to an inner "dance." Cocteau also said that Romeo should move in contrast to the other characters like a somnambulist while Tybalt, Benvolio, Mercutio, and the other "young dandies" of Verona moved with a "certain aggressive march."[20] When Romeo and Juliet meet at the ball, their love making is mimed in dance by two dancers, and the whole death scene between the two star-crossed lovers is also mimed in a balletic fashion.

Neal Oxenhandler, in his analysis of the text, has called the piece "a *poésie du théâtre* in its most material form, that is, the parade, the spectacle, the imitation of minor beauty."[21] What Cocteau substituted for the poetry of the text was a poetry of devices, "trucs," and the whole was dependent on these mechanical parts. For that reason, and contrary to Oxenhandler, the "pretext" must not be judged by its text alone, since Cocteau considered the written word only as an excuse for his choreographic picture: a picture in black and white costumes against black drapes with red lights and stylized gestures accompanying dance movements, with a circus trick or two thrown in for good measure. Cocteau felt that the kinetics of the stage demanded a structured form; dance movement for him was the best way of accomplishing harmonization in presentation. This was a quality one would also find in Cocteau's films: the choreographed movements of the performers rather than the directed steps.

In his dedication of the "pretext" to the Comte and Comtesse de Beaumont, Cocteau posed a question and then answered it: "Would a real theatre director have given me carte blanche? I doubt it."[22] Certainly, the Comte had given Cocteau the freedom to create what he wanted; in this particular case Cocteau not only wrote and directed *Roméo et Juliette* but played Mercutio as well. Acting was a totally new experience for him and one he found stimulating, as well as terrifying. It also gave him a new confidence in all three capacities, and, after "Les Soirées de Paris" were finished, Cocteau returned to Monte Carlo to continue work on *Le Train bleu* with a new sense of determination and purpose.

There are many conflicting stories on the creation of *Le Train bleu*. Serge Lifar (b. 1905), then a new dancer with the company, attests that during this period he was spending much of his free time with Cocteau, a situation which upset and annoyed Diaghilev very much. To appease Diaghilev, Cocteau devised a ballet for the other "favorite," Anton Dolin, and thus, according to Lifar, *Le Train bleu* was born. Lifar is the only contemporary source to give this version and further doubts are cast on its authenticity by other contemporary accounts, as well as Cocteau's own writings.[23] Francis Steegmuller in his biography of

Cocteau repeats the Lifar version, but his only source is Serge Lifar.[24] Lifar dismissed the ballet as "slight, silly, and without novelty" and emphasized the fact that it was never revived. He believes that the ballet was never well received and that Diaghilev lost interest in it. Anton Dolin, the young English dancer on whom the ballet was created, pointed out that he left the company soon after the ballet was premiered and that Diaghilev wanted Lifar to learn the part that Dolin played. Lifar, however, was unable to pick up the rather difficult acrobatic stunts that had been so tailored for Dolin's technique; the ballet, therefore, had to be dropped at the end of the season. This story is confirmed by Serge Grigoriev, Lydia Sokolova, and Boris Kochno, who had just joined the company as Diaghilev's secretary.[25] All three of these contemporary witnesses also mention the rivalry between Dolin and Lifar. This was probably only natural since they would both be competing for the same male parts in the Ballets Russes productions, and one can understand that Lifar would be upset when he was unable to perform Dolin's part in *Le Train bleu*. Lifar's competitive spirit may also have affected his attitude towards this particular ballet when he came to write his memoirs of the Ballets Russes in later years.

The germ idea of the ballet seems to have come to Cocteau in the early weeks of January 1924, when he was in Monte Carlo watching the company rehearse. He saw Dolin practicing a number of acrobatic steps on stage, something which the young English dancer excelled at, as his dancing *en pointe* for *Les Fâcheux* had already shown. Cocteau then told Diaghilev that he was interested in composing a work centered on this "beau garçon." As Dolin tells the story:

> During the January season in Monte Carlo I had been practicing for my own amusement and showing off a natural quality that belonged to my dancing, one which, for want of a better term, I will call acrobatics. I had a knack of being able to fall without ever really hurting myself, for I had an athletic strength and vitality, quite apart from what grace I possessed as a dancer.
>
> The rehearsal room was divided into two halves by a curtain down the middle and whenever there was a break I used to go to whichever side of the room was unoccupied and practice these tricks. At times, I would be joined by one or two other members of the company and I used to get the men to swing me round by one leg and arm as I had seen Divina's partner [a cabaret dancer] do. Later these particular steps were actually put into *Le Train bleu*.
>
> Jean Cocteau often came to rehearsals. He was in Monte Carlo on a holiday and as Auric and Poulenc were his friends, it was only natural that he should be interested in witnessing the first production of these new ballets for which they had composed the music.
>
> I can still see him leaning against the practice *barre* watching me; and it was then undoubtedly that the idea of *Le Train bleu*, the ballet showing life on a *plage* as he saw it, was born.[26]

Although Dolin states that Cocteau was on holiday, it has already been pointed out that Cocteau was there by Diaghilev's invitation. The young dancer would have been unaware that Cocteau was definitely looking for new ideas and Dolin's acrobatics gave the French poet the right impetus to create a new stage work.

Cocteau suggested, and Diaghilev agreed, to commission the score from Darius Milhaud, though the impresario had never found Milhaud's music much

Figure 14.   Anton Dolin as Beau Gosse in *Le Train bleu*, 1924
(Courtesy of the late Sir Anton Dolin)

to his taste. Like Cocteau, Milhaud had been asked to write something for Beaumont and as both scores had to be finished practically at the same time Milhaud worked on them simultaneously. "My twins" the composer called them.[27] Beaumont's's work, *Salade*, was composed between 5 and 20 February, and *Le Train bleu* between 15 February and 5 March. Cocteau subtitled the piece an *opérette dansée* and Milhaud was instructed to write a score with no direct, recognizable melodies, yet still inspired by the popular songs of the period, such as those heard in French music halls. It was to be an "operetta without words." By asking Milhaud "to treat this subject of Cocteau's, gay, frivolous, and frothy in the manner of Offenbach, Diaghilev was perfectly aware that I [Milhaud] would not be able to produce my usual kind of music, which he did not like."[28] Milhaud's diary for the period shows he approached work on the piece with relish and humor:

> 16 February. This ballet for Diaghilev is quite a folly. Music in the manner of Offenbach, Maurice Yvain and a Verdi-like finale with all the true harmonies *plates d'un bout à l'autre: Pas une syncope*. It is Paris, vulgar, dirty, and sentimental, with many polkas, galops, waltzes, etc. . . . I am a little frightened [of all the work] but I am very amused by the whole adventure.[29]

The music Milhaud produced is not profound, just as it was intended. Milhaud created the perfect accompaniment for Cocteau's scenario of beach antics by stringing together a series of popular sounding tunes which just escaped recognition, since they were all Milhaud originals. Milhaud took the style and rhythm of vernacular music, without directly plagiarizing his sources. Anton Dolin made his entrance to a bounding piece in three-quarter time with brusque syncopation effects and Sokolova had a solo to a quick little number that sounded like a children's playground song. The finale, the squabble between the tennis champion and golfer, was entitled "Fugue de l'engueulade" (the French word for the American slang expression, "bawling-out"), which developed into a frenzy of orchestral effects.

The choreographer, Bronislava Nijinska (1891–1972), was also influenced by Cocteau's conception for the ballet. Nijinska, the sister of Nijinsky, had also danced with the company but had not really been noted for her choreographic abilities until her work on Diaghilev's London production of *Sleeping Beauty* in 1921. She then choreographed a number of Stravinsky ballets, including *Le Renard* (1922) and *Les Noces* (1923). For *Le Train bleu*, Cocteau took Nijinska to see ballroom dancing and talked to her about music hall and cafe concert performances, which he so often attended.[30] Cocteau based his whole concept on popular forms of entertainment, "Offenbach seen through the eyes of a circus," as he had told Milhaud.[31] The music hall was not an art, but in transforming it in his own way Cocteau hoped to take the "mundane" onto a higher plane.

A main theme that continually runs through most of Cocteau's ballets is the presentation of the vulgar, the everyday, the commonplace, but seen through the eyes of an artist. Cocteau was also stimulated by Dolin's acrobatic technique, and, perhaps more importantly, his youth and energy. From what we know of Cocteau's life through his own comments, he was continually trying to surround himself with the young—to stay young himself. Through the ballet he could create for youth and youth alone, since classical dance demanded young artists. The Ballets Russes with its continuing influx of fresh, young blood stimulated Cocteau in the pursuits of these concepts of eternal youth. It may be for this reason that Cocteau would continue to create for the dance because through the dance he could escape age. He said: "As far as I am concerned, dancing is the language in which I would prefer to express myself, and my favorite theatrical formula."[32]

Cocteau's involvement with *Le Train bleu,* almost to the point of interference, was greater than Cocteau had ever dared before with Diaghilev. Even the tone of his letters to Diaghilev on the ballet have a ring of authority missing from his previous correspondence on *Parade* or *Le Dieu bleu:*

> Darius [Milhaud] is in good form. He has recopied the fourteen minutes, and is working ahead. Ask Nijinska how she's feeling about me. I am not going to make a move unless I am sure she will listen to me, for ridiculous diplomatic games are useless. I do not insist that my name appear on the program as director (although my researches in relation to details of staging have a logical place in the work), but, in exchange, I do insist on being listened to.[33]

As may be gathered from the above letter, Cocteau's relationship with the choreographer, Bronislava Nijinska, was not always harmonious. Cocteau had not been very pleased with her choreography for Stravinsky's *Les Noces,* but, at least in print, he was quite impressed with her work on *Les Fâcheux* and *Les Biches.* However, the world of *Les Biches* was not her world, and the sophisticated humor of *Le Train bleu* was even more alien to her quiet, enclosed nature. The worldly milieu *sur la plage* was not a happy assignment for Nijinska and to make matters worse for her, Cocteau decided that he would involve himself directly in this ballet; he would "insist on being listened to."

Cocteau insisted that Nijinska incorporate acrobatic sports movements and steps into the ballet. For Cocteau the artificiality of sports fit well into the artificiality of the dance. He himself termed dance "la grande gesticulation," an expressive use of motion when speech was inadequate. *Le Train bleu* needed this combination of sports and dance if it was to be successful as a series of picture postcards showing various games played on the beach by a motley assortment of gigolos, swimmers, tennis players and golfers.

But to bring these pictures to life Cocteau had to communicate his ideas to the choreographer. This was no easy matter considering his strained relationship with Nijinska. At first they seem to have tried to cooperate and work as a team. Cocteau would take her to movies or show her pictures, such as the Prince of Wales playing golf, which she was supposed to try to emulate. Nijinska did incorporate an almost movie-like slow motion section in the ballet when a plane, which is not seen by the audience, flies over the heads of the bathers below. This slow motion effect which Nijinska "stole" from the silent films created quite a sensation when first seen since it was such an unusual piece of stage business for a ballet. From the scenario it is definite that this was Cocteau's idea, visualized for him by Nijinska.[34]

Still, Nijinska and Cocteau did not get along well as this ballet progressed. Cocteau stated that all he wanted was a scene "frivolous and gay" played on the beach by *tout-le-monde*. It was to be playacting of a series of sports—golf, tennis, and acrobatics—but done very tongue in cheek. As the rehearsals progressed Cocteau had to be away in Paris for work on *Roméo et Juliette* and during that period Nijinska visibly relaxed and began to make changes in Cocteau's detailed outline. The *pas de deux* between the tennis players changed from a comic flirtation to a love-duet and various extra story elements were added to clarify Cocteau's purposely amorphous scenario.[35]

When Cocteau returned to Monte Carlo, it was only in time for the final dress rehearsals. Kochno states that Diaghilev was so upset by what he saw on stage that he ran to the last row of the balcony. From here the sources conflict. Kochno states that Cocteau substituted pantomime scenes for a number of dances Nijinska had produced. Dolin explains that Cocteau was upset that there was not enough dancing, especially of the acrobatic kind. There is substantial support for the later account. A study of the manuscript score reveals many of the stage sequences marked in over the music, then crossed over as new sequences were added. Although it is difficult to be precise, the writing seems to indicate the addition of dance steps and sequences and the trimming of the purely mime passages. This is confirmed by the contemporary accounts of Sokolova and Grigoriev, as well as the later memoirs of Milhaud, all of whom claim that the amount of dancing was increased over the last days of rehearsal and that Cocteau was on stage rapidly making changes during these tense *répétitions*.[36]

Diaghilev probably let Cocteau have his own way and this allowance widened the breach between Diaghilev and Nijinska. During rehearsals Nijinska had shown increased signs of stress from having to work on so many ballets in succession, and she had never worked well under pressure. Nijinska also hated being ordered about and one can imagine how much worse this must have been when it came to her taking orders from Cocteau, since he knew little Russian and she understood little French.[37]

The revision rehearsals went on practically until the curtain was going up for the first performance. Kochno felt the ballet he had seen that afternoon was nearly unrecognizable by the evening premiere, and Dolin remembered he was afraid he would forget sections because so many changes had been made so rapidly in such a short time. From the iconographic evidence it does seem that much of the choreography was not in the style previously associated with Nijinska. The angular movements of *Les Noces* and *Les Biches* were there, but neither of those ballets emphasized the acrobatic. In *Le Train bleu* there was one part where Dolin did a double pirouette into a cartwheel and then ended in Woizikowsky's arm in a fish dive. Perhaps it is an ironic comment on the classical *pas de poisson* for the feet are pointed, the arms elegantly held, although one cannot prove this. Other pictorial evidence shows headstands, bathers performing swimming motions, the humorous intertwining of arms for the tennis champion and her partner. Lydia Sokolova in her memoirs describes the difficult maneuver of the "Blue Train Waltz" when Woizikowsky "had to throw me up spinning in the air, then catch me as I came down, and I cannot imagine how we never came to grief, because my woolen costume was impossible to grip."[38] How much of these action concepts were Nijinska's and how much Cocteau's is impossible to determine, but considering the amount of evidence on Cocteau's interference at the final rehearsals and how much of the ballet was changed so quickly it may not be wrong to credit the ballet with choreography by Nijinska and the direction by Cocteau.

The physical aspects of the production were rather disappointing. Diaghilev had commissioned the set from the Rumanian sculptor Henri Laurens (1879–1935), who designed a backdrop in blue and white with a scalloped sea as well as diving fish painted on to the wings stage left and right. Diaghilev, not happy with the set, used the now famous Picasso drawing of two nude women running on a beach as the front curtain during the overture. Diaghilev also had Auric write a special fanfare for the curtain that segued into the Milhaud overture. The costumes by Gabrielle "Coco" Chanel (1883–1972) were very chic and historically important, since it was the first time the one-piece bathing suit, the female bathing cap, and costume jewelry for bathers were seen on stage. The designs may have affected fashion in the twenties, but they did not have the theatrical impact of a costume by Bakst or Picasso. Recent evidence also indicates that Chanel invested money in *Le Train bleu*, as she had also put up the money for the revival of *Parade*, due to her friendship with Cocteau. She had also convinced the powerful and influential Princess Edmond de Polignac (1864–1943) to invest in *Le Train bleu*.[39] This may be another reason for Diaghilev's acquiescence to Cocteau's demands on this production, since his friends had helped finance its realization.

The reviews of the ballet compliment the sets and costumes, but it seems fairly clear that the decor did not create the visual impact *Parade* had done. *The Queen* said that "it is impossible to imagine more skillful dancing than this, where the effects are unheightened by artifice and the defects unsmothered by glamour of costume."[40] Certainly, the total decor was not as important in this ballet as it had been in Cocteau's previous works.

The ballet opened at the Théâtre des Champs-Elysées in Paris on 20 June 1924. The principal roles were as follows:

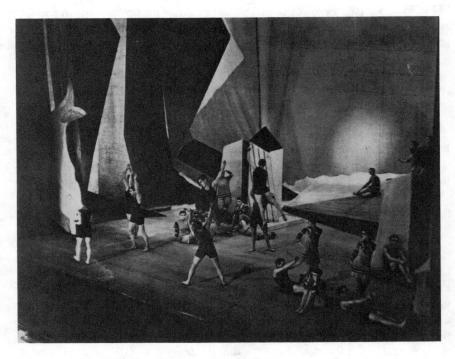

Figure 15.   The "Chicks" and "Gigolos" Cavorting on the Beach in
             Le Train bleu, 1924
             Set designed by Henri Laurens.
             Costumes by Gabrielle "Coco" Chanel.
             (*Courtesy of the late Sir Anton Dolin*)

La Championne de Tennis	Mme. Bronislava Nijinska
Perlouse	Mme. Lydia Sokolova
Beau Gosse	M. Anton Dolin
Le Joueur de Golf	M. Leon Woizikowsky
Poules et Gigolos	[Assorted "chicks" and their "escorts," among them being the newcomer, Ninette de Valois][41]

The cast remained the same for the London performances except that Tamara Gevergeva (Geva) took over Mme. Nijinska's role when she left the company. The Paris performances were conducted by André Messager and the London performances by the composer. In the program Diaghilev inserted the following capsule of the ballet; it is more than probable that Cocteau had a hand in its composition since it reflects his style of writing and his sense of humor:

> The first point about *Le Train bleu* is that there is no blue train in it. This being the age of speed it has already reached its destination and disembarked its passengers. These are to be seen on a beach which does not exist, in front of a casino which exists still less. Overhead passes an aeroplane which you do not see. And the plot represents nothing. . . . Moreover the ballet is not a ballet; it is an *opérette dansée*. The music is composed by Darius Milhaud, but it has nothing to do with Russian ballet. It was invented for Anton Dolin, a classical dancer who does nothing classical. The scenery is painted by a sculptor, and the costumes are by a great arbiter of fashion who has never made a costume.[42]

The ballet was a great success in both Paris and London, though the reviewers were often bewildered by Cocteau's concept. Jean Brun-Berty in *Le Ménestrel* talked about this at some length:

> It is being established today that, from the point of view of choreography, the theatre we know today is turning to the music hall to present something new and different. This is a reversal of previous history. *Le Train bleu* which is now being presented by the Ballets Russes confirms this tendency.
>
> The scenario of M. Jean Cocteau does not recount anything very explicit to the unexpectedly popular-styled score of Darius Milhaud. It is simply a view of any moment on an exclusive beach where the female bathers are known as "chicks" and the male bathers are known as "gigolos."
>
> And yet this hasty sketch—which is entitled an *opérette dansée*, God knows what that means—is, at the same time, great fun and yet very involved. The movements done in slow motion are particularly interesting, successful and amusing. There is an infinite amount of variety to the choreography, seen for example, by the ingenuity of the dancers and danseuses who move so quickly in their becoming bathing costumes.[43]

Brun-Berty complimented all the dancers, noting especially the acclaim that Dolin received from the crowd and which proved that he had been established as "sacré grand danseur." But he also asked if such a piece really added anything to the Diaghilev crown. Though the work was "amusing, alert, and up-to-date," would it, in a few years, be proven "out-of-date?" The author also questioned the worth of glorifying do-nothings and idlers on a beach as a stage representation; at the

Figure 16.   The Four Principals from *Le Train bleu*, 1924
Lydia Sokolova, Anton Dolin, Bronislava Nijinska, and
Leon Woizikowsky.
(*Courtesy of the late Sir Anton Dolin*)

same time he thought that he could be proved wrong and that the ballet might prove to lead the way to a new and exciting style of art.

The *Revue de Paris* concentrated on the incredible acrobatic tricks of the choreography but noted that "Jean Cocteau has contributed a charming scenario."[44] *La Nouvelle revue française* did not talk much about Cocteau, though it did note that his scenario gave "the perfect pretext to show off the dancers' unusual skill, especially the energetic and astonishing Dolin and the lovely and flirtatious Sokolova."[45]

Music critics in Paris were less pleased with this departure for Milhaud. One reviewer asked "Who the devil thought of using café-concert music?" Cocteau replied to the newspapers that it was *his* idea and then gave a typically nonsensical reason, "Give me music which one would hear at the cinema when a certain type of film is showing: for example, Mme. Millerand [wife of the French president] visiting a foundling hospital."[46]

When the ballet reached London, it was an immediate success. *The Bystander* noted that. "It is as difficult to get a seat for *Le Train bleu* as it is to get a seat in the thing itself during the height of the Riviera rush."[47] The *New Statesman* thought Cocteau's concept "not really a skit or parody," although it pretends to use the "characteristic conventions" of the musical comedy style. "It is much more in the nature of an elaborate mannequin parade of bathing and other fashionable French seaside costumes by the house of Chanel, but all done at a much higher degree of self-consciousness and from more than one point of view."[48] The *Illustrated London News* thought Cocteau's "musical comedy" ballet, as they called it, "was wonderfully expressed in terms of dancing . . . one of the very effective ballet novelties to be seen in some time. The charming originality of this adaption of modern sports to the uses of ballet has proved remarkably popular. It is like a bathing beach scene from a musical comedy, but danced instead of sung." The *News* thought Cocteau had supplied a "thread of a plot which affords some material for characterization" but it was the basic fun and frivolity of the piece that made it so successful.[49] *Musical America*, whose London critic reported back to the States, thought that Cocteau had brought out "the deliberate artificiality of the place [Deauville] and the unreality of its people, who are at the same time delightful and gay." The critic also felt:

> It is in its insouciance and its light sophistication that the ballet is charming. It is not a moral sermon. It is simply a caricature and a subtle one. It is written not in regular ballet form, but in a typically operetta style, with solo dances instead of songs. It is a novel idea, that of *Le Train bleu*, and it has been interpreted by Mr. Diaghileff with all his old time understanding and charm.[50]

Phyllis Bedells in *Dancing Times* struck a note that was being leveled at Diaghilev more and more after the war which, while praising the new, nostalgically longed for the old:

> I wonder if everyone *really* likes *Le Train bleu* or if they are showering so much praise on it just because it was the Diaghileff ballet? Have most London audiences the courage of their own convictions, or will they continue to praise all and everything *the* Russian ballet does? Personally, I was interested and amused by the performance and the extraordinary first night audience. I'm afraid I could not greatly admire either, though both left a very strong impression on my mind. The ballet was certainly new, and by all means let us "get out of the rut" if we can, by advancing towards originality and *beauty*, but I am afraid I could not find anything beautiful in *Le Train bleu.* It seemed an awful pity to me that such obviously great artists should spend their efforts on "cartwheels," "handsprings," and slow-motion running attitudes, and even choose the least attractive swimming positions for their posturing—I cannot call it dancing. I am afraid the whole company must be laughing up their sleeves at the great British public! I cannot think that anyone can really admire and prefer such a performance to the ballet produced by Fokine for Mons. Diaghileff at Covent Garden before the war.[51]

The earlier works of the company set a particular style and design which Miss Bedells has applied to *Le Train bleu.* This narrow sense of beauty and limitation of criteria was also noticed by Cyril Beaumont when he discussed the English reviews. All the London papers praised the ballet, he said, but tempered their attitude towards "a certain facile smartness and atmosphere of the very latest thing." They did not stint their praise for Dolin, however, and even Beaumont was impressed with the young dancer's performance as Beau Gosse:

> Dolin danced like a man in ecstasy, like a man who suddenly felt possessed of a divine power of movement which raised him above mere mortals. His dancing was not pure classical ballet but his sportive movements had the grace and beauty which comes only from a thorough training in the technique of classical ballet. . . . All those complicated bounds, leaps, handstands, and backbends were, in essence, stunts if you like, but they were done with such grace and apparent ease, that it was only when you began to examine them, that you realized how dangerous they were. I say quite frankly that at any moment Dolin might have done himself serious injury and ruined his career, but he never faltered, and when the curtain fell he was accorded a well deserved ovation.[52]

Dolin himself said in interview that "nothing seemed to hurt me. How I had control I don't know, but I did not feel any of the cuts and bruises until after the performance was over."[53]

Reviews mean nothing, however, if the public does not come and see a work and voice their own approval. In Paris and London the new ballet was enjoyed by a large percentage of the audience, more popular than the limited appeal of Diaghilev's other "avant-garde" works. Beaumont records the nightly ovations *Le Train bleu* received and Arnold Haskell mentions that it was one of the most popular ballets that season. The papers also commented on its phenomenal reception, such as *The Bystander* quoted above, and how difficult it was to obtain tickets to see it. Of course, it could be argued that *Le Train bleu* was a failure because it was dropped after one season. But *Le Train bleu* was not dropped because it had failed. When Dolin decided to leave the company, he tried to teach the role of Beau Gosse to Lifar,[54] but Lifar was unable to pick up the complicated acrobatics

Figure 17. *Le Train bleu,* 1924
(left to right): Sokolova, Dolin, Cocteau, Woizikowsky, and
Nijinska.
(Courtesy of the late Sir Anton Dolin)

and finally all plans for its continuance had to be dropped. Even Sokolova mentions that without Dolin the ballet could not continue in the current repertoire. Nijinska had now left the company so it would have been difficult to change the choreography, but to change the acrobatics would have diminished its audience appeal. Haskell states that Cocteau could not sit through the last performance of his ballet in London, but left the theatre overcome with emotion realizing that, with the loss of Dolin, his ballet's existence was at an end.

About its future claim to fame Haskell continues: "This ballet influenced dance production for a time in a way that many great works have failed to do and it came at an opportune moment during the Paris Olympic season." But what exactly was this "influence?" Here Haskell leaves the reader in the dark and even many years later he can only add "that it [Le Train bleu] made its mark on the music hall and operetta, besides opening up a new field, that of modern folk art. It is also the precursor of innumerable sporting ballets."[55] However, there had been an earlier ballet that had used a sporting theme, Jeux, choreographed by Nijinsky in 1913, and Nijinska, who was with the company at that time, could not help but be influenced by her brother's ideas.

These hypotheses of Haskell's are difficult to prove or disprove, but it may be true that Le Train bleu did have a wider influence than shown heretofore. It was around this period that the English and French music hall became more topical in its approach and sporting themes began to enter certain theatrical genres. The connection is tenuous, however, and needs further investigation. As to the "innumerable sporting ballets" it is difficult to trace more than one or two in the next decade from the Ballet Russe de Monte Carlo period, Beach by Massine in 1933 probably being the most noticeable.[56]

The influence of Le Train bleu may be less obvious than Haskell would have us believe, albeit just as important. The introduction of novelties into the world of dance had always been a part of every Ballets Russes season and perilous feats had been part and parcel of ballet for quite some time, whether it be the antics of the acrobatic dancers in a Carolingian antimasque in the 17th century or Carlotta Grisi's famous leap as La Péri into the waiting arms of Lucien Petipa in 1843. But Cocteau was not concerned with an oriental dream world or an aristocratic arcadia; he was concerned with the present day but the present seen through rose-colored glasses. He loved taking the vulgar and making it snobbish, "a certain tradition which, in spite of being vulgar, is nevertheless very elite."[57]

W. A. Propert wrote a prophetic analysis of Le Train bleu soon after it was created, complimenting the use of acrobatics and ballet:

> These acrobatic but balletic feats were questioned by the more academic critics, but as no one has as yet been able to define the borderline between dance and acrobacy, the question remains unanswered. In certain ballets of the later years the controversy became more acute, as the choreography of Massine and Balanchine turned more and more towards the angled line and away from the sinuous curves of the Schéhérazade epoch.

To the author it seems that all rhythmic movement is dancing, with whatever part of the body the movement is made; and that whether that movement is stiffened into angles or relaxed into flowing curves, whether the dancer is leaping through the air or even turning somersaults, then providing there is rhythm and continuity and intention, there is also dancing. There may be action which in itself is grotesque or even uncouth, but if, like a deliberate discord in music, it has definite meaning or is a stage in the evolution of a new harmony, such action is legitimate and has by no means forfeited the right to be called dancing. Moreover, the acrobacy of a trained dancer differs subtly, but quite unmistakably, from that of the ordinary athlete.[58]

The difference between an athlete and a dancer is not distinguished by training—if acrobatics are to be used—but in the *way* the skill is used. Athletes are in competition, whether singly or as a team, and they use their training for the purpose of winning in a competitive situation. Dancers are more concerned with the presentation of their skills in a particular theatrical situation. In sports there is a spontaneous use of skill depending on the circumstances of the game; in dance the skill is used within the context of the choreography, which is generally set by opening night.

Even dancers found the new style of acrobatic dancing something of a shock. In an interview with Alexandra Danilova in February 1978, the great prima ballerina who had just joined the company in 1924, thought that

the Ballets Russes style was revolutionary compared to the Imperial Ballet. To tell you the truth when I joined the Ballets Russes and first saw Anton Dolin dancing *Le Train bleu* I was shocked. I saw him do two pirouettes and then an *entrechat six* and a handstand and, I thought, how does he do it? To me it was more acrobatics than dancing; it was gymnastics. But then, after awhile, I was housebroken. . . .[59]

If a dancer would feel this way, is it any wonder that the contemporary critics either thought Cocteau and Diaghilev were laughing at the public or introducing music hall elements into an art form that was, hypothetically, above such things?

The ballet itself was pencilled in for revival when Dolin rejoined the company in 1929. A letter from Dolin to Diaghilev asks the impresario to take him back "to play roles unsuited for Lifar."[60] The death of Diaghilev in that same year prevented any future plans for revival in the Ballets Russes; however the Royal Ballet of Sweden did perform an entirely new version in 1934 with settings by Jon Aud, but it was never seen outside that country.[61] In late 1940 Nijinska planned to revive the ballet for Anton Dolin in America but many problems occurred, including the difficulty of tracing a full orchestra score. Nothing came of the project—set for a Chicago opening—and nothing more was heard about the ballet until 1977 when Dolin staged some of his solos for the brilliant English dancer, Wayne Sleep. These dances were performed at a gala benefit—with the Chanel costumes—and were staged again by Dolin for Kevin Haegen in 1979 for the Nijinsky Gala in Hamburg.[62]

Cocteau would not write another ballet for almost twenty years. During that time his attention would be turned to plays, poetry, essays and finally film. There are probably many reasons why Cocteau did not return to the dance world for so long, but some of his negligence towards the ballet may have been due to the frustrations that occurred with Le Train bleu and the fact that this particular work of art disappeared from view so quickly, not because the ballet was deemed a failure but because it was so dependent on one performer.

6

Postwar Paris: *Le Jeune homme et la mort*

Our machine disrupts itself a little more each day and each morning man wakes with a new impediment. I recognize this. I used to sleep right through the night. Now I wake up. This sickens me. I get up. I start working. It is the only means that makes it possible for me to forget my blemishes and acquire beauty at my table. This "writing-face" being, when all is said and done, my true face. The other a fading shadow.
—Jean Cocteau, *The Difficulty of Being*

Le Train bleu was Cocteau's last involvement in dance for almost twenty years. After this final work for Diaghilev, who would die five years later in 1929, Cocteau abandoned the ballet. Why?

In addition to the problems surrounding *Le Train bleu*, discussed earlier, part of the answer may lie in his production of *Roméo et Juliette*. Cocteau was experimenting with a play which he transformed into a choreographic picture. He found the lure of the theatrical play more inviting than the ephemeral and frustrating world of dance. He later admitted that he had many ideas about how to present dance on stage but lacked the vocabulary that is the lexicon of technique so important for a choreographer. It was comparable to trying to write music without knowing tones and scales. In 1926 Cocteau had his first success as a playwright with the production of *Orphée*. When it was revived in 1927, he himself played the part of Heurtebise, the underworld angel who would haunt many a Cocteau play, film and drawing. Between opium cures and publications of poetry and novels he spent the thirties and forties writing plays, most of which proved to be quite successful. These included *La Machine infernale* in 1934, *Les Chevaliers de la table ronde* in 1937, *Les Parents terribles* in 1938 (which included a curtain-raiser for Edith Piaf entitled *Le Bel indifférent*), *La Machine à écrire* in 1941 and *Antigone* and *Renaud et Armide* in 1943. The last play, a verse drama, was the first of Cocteau's plays to be presented by the Comédie Française.

During these same years Cocteau, who was becoming more and more fascinated with the world of film, began to experiment with cinema and its techniques. The first of these experiments was *Le Sang d'un poète* in 1932. These delvings into what Cocteau would later call the "tenth muse of poetry" would continue throughout the next two decades.

This activity helped wean Cocteau from the world of dance, for as author, stage director and especially as a film director, he was able to exert total control over his work of art. Also he may have felt, as many did, that the death of Diaghilev would plunge dance back into the nether world of operatic dance divertissements and music hall turns.

With the outbreak of World War II such speculations were far from anybody's mind as survival became a primary goal. In September 1940 Cocteau moved to a temporary lodging: rooms in the Hotel de Beaujolais, overlooking the gardens of the Palais-Royal. Living in the same building were the designer Christian Bérard (1902–1949) and Diaghilev's former assistant, Boris Kochno. Spending much time together, the three men chatted often about their great love for dance and what would happen to the art. At the time, perhaps, none of them was aware that these discussions would lead to the production of actual ballets.[1]

Another former member of the Diaghilev troupe, Serge Lifar, was also in the city and working now as principal dancer and choreographer for the Paris Opéra. He helped keep the dancers in work, albeit in front of the Occupation forces and Germanophile Frenchmen. Later, after the war, this activity would lose Lifar his job, since he was accused of collaboration. But at the time everyone was grateful for his efforts to keep them all in work: dancers, musicians, stage hands, designers and costumers. Lifar also arranged recitals for those dancers he felt were most promising. In 1943 Lifar asked Cocteau for permission to use the theme from one of his poems in the collection *Plein Chant*, which had been published in 1923. This was a series of love declarations addressed by the poet to his mysterious angel, elegiac rather than lyrical. Cocteau had always felt "their personal meditation needed music" and he readily granted Lifar permission for the poem's use in a dance recital. When it appeared as a concert piece for the dancers Colette Marchand and Serge Perrault of the Opéra, Cocteau's involvement was minimal, but it did help to revive his interest in the dance world and he began to observe the budding dance artists who were trying to establish their own artistic credo under such trying wartime conditions.[2]

Two of the most interesting and innovative of these young dancers were Roland Petit (b. 1924) and Janine Charrat (b. 1924) of the Paris Opéra. Petit, who was barely twenty at the time, had studied in Paris and had joined the Paris Opéra in 1940 where he was quickly promoted to soloist due to his technique, energy and dramatic stage presence. Charrat, six months younger than Petit, had studied with Lubov Egorova and Alexander Volinine, and made her debut as a dancing child star in the film *La Mort du cygne* in 1937. She joined the Opéra in 1941.[3]

Both Petit and Charrat soon found the atmosphere of the Opéra stultifying for them both as dancers and as choreographers, since the Opéra gave them no outlet for personal creative work. Seriously considering a move from the com-

Figure 18. Colette Marchand and Serge Perrault in *Plein Chant*, 1943
Photograph by Serge Lido.
(Courtesy of the Stravinsky-Diaghilev Foundation)

pany, they decided to test their wings first in a series of concert pieces. Impressed with *Plein Chant*, they decided to ask Cocteau to aid them in their first endeavor. Janine Charrat remembered their first meeting with the poet as both nerve-racking and stimulating.

> I remember . . . when Roland Petit and I decided to give our first recital! I will always remember the first time we went to his [Cocteau's] house on the Rue Montpensier [by this time Cocteau had moved from the Hotel de Beaujolais]. We were very "bold" and asked him for the use of his play *Orphée* [for a dance piece].[4]

The forward young dancers not only asked Cocteau for permission to use his treatment of the ancient myth but also wanted *maquettes*, that is, models or sketches from him for the set and costumes. Afraid that he would refuse such an audacious request, they were surprised by his reaction:

> At once Cocteau flared up. . . . He told us that in our youthful enquiry we had found the most original solution for a dance recital . . . because it is a theme at once universal and incorporated what every artist sought: originality. The idea [of a danced *Orphée*] was at once *original, novel* and so *primordial!*[5]

At once Cocteau overwhelmed the young dancers with ideas for the ballet, and they "listened to the great master with fervor and admiration!" as Charrat recalled. When it came to the costuming of Euridice, Cocteau came up with an original solution which Charrat considered very striking at that time: "a white *maillot* with a hood of the same color, a small slip of black tulle, and . . . that is all!" For the period it was a revolution in Franch balletic costume design "since one was so used to the ornate costumes that required so much work for both dancer and designer." Cocteau also helped them on the décor, which was simple and stark by reason of a limited budget. The set consisted of a large panel of the head of Orpheus done on a black background with the hair flaming out from around the brooding face, almost like a sunburst. On his right shoulder a toga was lightly sketched in black, flowing lines. For Petit as Orpheus, rather than have him hold a harp in his hand and be encumbered as he danced with Charrat, Cocteau devised a headdress of cardboard which was the harp itself and which was strapped to Petit's head. There was no color in the realization of the designs; everything was black and white in a grey underworld of shadow and gloom.[6] Although Cocteau was busy with many other projects at that moment, Charrat said he never stinted in his help or work during the final rehearsals. "If I ever had a problem," Charrat continued, "I knew only Cocteau would come up with the right solution that would always succeed . . . and he always found a solution so unique!" Cocteau also drew portraits of the two artists for their program and poster and when, during the rehearsals, he was unable to help in alterations in his designs, he asked Jean Marais to supervise the costume changes and fittings.[7]

Thus, Cocteau had been seduced back into the dance world, and he began to take a renewed interest in creating within that idiom again, but the right circumstances would have to present themselves for any future work.

These circumstances came about when Petit and Charrat left the Opéra soon after the liberation and collaborated with Irene Lidova (b. 1907), the French ballet critic, and the impresario Claude Giraud, in a series of recitals styled *Vendredi de la danse*. These concerts were intended to afford an opportunity for young French artists of promise to show their talents both as dancers and choreographers. The first of these soirées was given at the Théâtre Sarah Bernhardt on 1 December 1944. Petit's style of choreography excited and interested many; two of the most important were Boris Kochno and Christian Bérard, who, as mentioned before, were living in the same building as Cocteau during the early months of the war. These two, along with the composer Henri Sauguet (b. 1902), collaborated with Petit on a ballet entitled *Les Forains*, which premiered on 2 March 1945, and was acclaimed as Petit's first important work.

The ballet was about a group of traveling street performers and Kochno's scenario owed something to Cocteau's outline for *Parade*, but the manner and style of presentation of these circus performers was very different in Petit's hands, since his style was more energetic and acrobatic than Massine's.[8] On the same program Petit presented *Les Deux pigeons* to music by Jean Hubeau,[9] followed by *Guernica* with music by Paul Bonnaut, which evoked the celebrated painting of the same name by Picasso, who gave his blessing to the enterprise, and finally the *Mephisto Waltz*. For the last ballet Petit found himself running out of money and did not know what to do to costume the piece. Lidova, like Charrat before her, turned to Cocteau for help.

> It was always Jean Cocteau who saved us, and always at the last moment when we could think of no way out. . . . [For *Mephisto Waltz*] Cocteau jumped on the stage during the last rehearsals, asked for five meters of red tulle. He then took the white *maillot* he had designed for Janine Charrat for *Orphée* and cut, tore, shaped, and adjusted the chiffon around the tights to create a whole new costume. Out of a piece of black paper he fashioned a mask and gave Nina [Vyroubova] a pair of red gloves: all of this was done within half an hour.[10]

This first concert program was so successful that a second was planned at the same theatre. This time Petit's father, who was a proprietor of a bistro in Paris near Les Halles, gave the financial backing for the evening's work. This recital included *Les Rendezvous*, a ballet about Paris street life in a Baudelaire-like setting, and *Le Poète*, a divertissement. When the program was presented at the same theatre on 15 June 1945, Petit had already established himself as a rising young choreographer, but a choreographer without a home and a company.

It was Roger Eudes, then director of the Théâtre des Champs-Elysées, who came to his rescue. Realizing that Petit needed a place to keep a company and have a steady income in order to build a repertoire of ballets and establish a

Figure 19.   Cocteau Rehearsing with Nathalie Philippart and
Jean Babilée for *Le Jeune homme et la mort*, 1946
Photograph by Serge Lido.
(Courtesy of the Stravinsky-Diaghilev Foundation)

reputation, he gave Petit his theatre for a short season, the month of October 1945. Petit formed his dance associates into a company called "Les Ballets des Champs-Elysées" with Eudes as manager, Kochno as artistic director, and himself as principal dancer and choreographer. Janine Charrat, Nina Vyroubova (b. 1924), and other dancers from the Paris Opéra joined his troupe, and Petit's father entered the company as an associate producer with Eudes. The company soon established itself as innovative, exciting, and stimulating. Seasons were extended and the company began to tour in the provinces and then abroad where they were favorably received and praised for their freshness and vitality. Although Cocteau became involved only as an observer from the sidelines, he cheered enthusiastically and encouraged the newborn company.

For their first season Cocteau wrote the program notes which give an excellent picture of his thoughts on the dance in postwar France:

> All that was left to us of the unforgettable Phoenix, Serge Diaghilev, were his ashes. But we know the myth, this Phoenix died to spring up again from its ashes. Boris Kochno, who assisted Diaghilev in his work, is now organizing a veritable festival of youth and dancing. Once again we see him grouping the painters, the choreographers, the dancers. Around Roland Petit, the dispersed quicksilver reassembles itself and forms a block, which vibrates and sparkles. The Phoenix meditated upon its substance, reorganized its great soul and its multicolored plumage, in the secret of the fire.[11]

Most interesting about these notes are Cocteau's references to Petit as "gathering the dancers together like quicksilver" with the dance "rising out of the ashes" like a Phoenix. These words echo, almost phrase for phrase, Cocteau's description of Fokine rehearsing his dancers for that first Ballets Russes season many years before—his first program notes written for that company.[12] Obviously, Cocteau looked for Petit to revive the dance world as Fokine had done; it is also obvious from the notes that Cocteau realized the new company could not imitate the Ballets Russes style but had to look ahead. The new ballet still had to have the fire and sparkle of the old, but reorganized into a new and totally different image. The Phoenix that rose out of the ashes could not be like the old Ballets Russes for this new bird had lived through World War II and the new dance would be a reflection of this changed environment. This theoretical approach of Cocteau's must be reckoned with when considering his next contribution to the ballet and his first for the new Petit company, *Le Jeune homme et la mort*. At the time of its premiers *Le Jeune homme* was acclaimed as both a masterpiece and a monstrosity. While it may have dated as a viable theatrical piece, it was extremely important as an influence on ballets in that decade and typified the general aesthetic philosophy that pervaded Paris after the war. At the time it showed the world that Cocteau, even after twenty years, could still shock, stun and stimulate with a dance composition.

The concept for the piece was first discussed sometime in May 1946 when Cocteau was having luncheon with Christian Bérard and Boris Kochno. Kochno confided to Cocteau that he was looking for a new ballet that would personify the present-day period, much as Fokine's *Le Spectre de la rose* had evoked the dreams of the Romantic style. It took Cocteau only a few moments to think and then express his interest in creating such a ballet. According to Cocteau's own diary, the suggestion gave him the pretext for working on an idea he had had for some time: "the mystery of accidental synchronization."[13] He had already worked with this idea in film, "in which any music of quality integrates the gestures and emotions of the characters. It remained to prove that a dance, set to rhythms suiting the choreographer, could do without them and gain strength in a new musical climate." In other words it was to be a counterpoint of dance and music wherein neither would necessarily compliment the other and any harmony would be accidental; "it is from a delicate arrangement of unbalance that balance draws it charm," Cocteau commented. To test his theory Cocteau decided that the dancers should rehearse the piece to jazz rhythms as an aid for counting and tempo, but that at the last minute a classical composition totally alien to the work such as Mozart, Schubert, or Bach, should replace the rehearsal music. The performers therefore would only hear the classical music at the final rehearsal.[14]

Within days of the luncheon Cocteau was putting his plan into action. As with *Le Spectre* Cocteau decided that his composition would be a dance dialogue for two and choose two new members of the company for the parts: Jean Babilée (b. 1923) and Nathalie Philippart. Babilée fascinated Cocteau as Nijinsky, Dolin and others had before him. Babilée, who was only twenty-one, had a brash and temperamental quality both on and off the stage that hinted at a brooding and almost demonic nature. His tendency towards moodiness was exactly what Cocteau needed to fashion the part of the young artist tense with sexual frustration. Babilée also had a fantastic technique, especially when it came to *batterie* combinations and jumps, while his attitude towards this natural gift was almost slovenly. He rarely seemed to warm up and paid no attention to proper *port-de-bras* or *épaulement* and seemed to be more interested in his motorcycle than his dancing. This offhand attitude towards dance combined with an energy and inner fire made him the perfect vehicle for Cocteau's young man: a dancing Darglos who combined brilliance with disdain. Philippart, who would become Babilée's wife, had a brittle technique and a cool, sophisticated, aloof quality. She needed little coaching to become the girl who would personify both love and death.[15]

Early on Cocteau decided that his involvement in the ballet would be as supervisor and producer, rather than as director. He decided "to take a hand only in so far as to describe in detail to the scenic designer, to the costumer, to the choreographer and to the performers" what he expected of them. For the decor Cocteau chose George Wakhevitch, "because he designs film sets and I wanted this high relief from which the cinematograph draws its dreams." For the costume realization he chose Karinska and Bérard "because they know stage optics better than anyone else." For the choreography he selected Roland Petit "because he would listen to me and translate my ideas into the dance language which I speak fairly well, but of which I lack the syntax."[16] This last remark is of crucial importance as it points out both Cocteau's love of dance and his frustrations over not being able to take a direct hand in the choreographic operations. But his attitudes at this point were colored by his recent work in films, and he approached the ballet almost as one would a film: dictating his ideas and concepts to the various technicians and artists who could make the equipment work but who needed his ideas. Thus the program credits for the ballet read: "*Le Jeune homme et la mort*, Dance, decor and costumes explained [*raconté*] by Jean Cocteau to Roland Petit, choreographer, Wakhevitch, designer, Karinska, costumes."[17] Georges Wakhevitch (b. 1907) was a Russian designer who had just settled in France and this was his first important theatrical assignment, while Barbara Karinska (1886–1984), also Russian, was more a maker of costumes than a designer. Both, therefore, were quite willing to take dictated ideas.

Cocteau's synopsis for the program was disarmingly simple:

> A young man waits for the girl who does not love him. She arrives. He pleads with her. She insults him and runs away. He hangs himself. The room disappears. Death comes in female form. She takes off her mask of death and puts it on the young man. She is the girl. She leads him away over the roof tops.[18]

The ballet was rehearsed in fifteen days and the dancers worked out their movements to the plot outline by Cocteau with a percussion jazz band accompanying their movements. Cocteau decided soon after rehearsals began to use Bach's Passacaglia, reorchestrated by Respighi, since organ accompaniment was unavailable and impracticable for the theatre. The Bach piece, though chosen early, was not heard by the dancers until their final *répétition générale*.[19]

Cocteau wanted the setting to evoke the world of Baudelaire, so Wakhevitch was instructed to use dark colors and neutral tones. The set is a studio, a Parisian garret "of a most unhappy painter." In the form of a triangle, the set is composed of two walls plus a third wall formed by the proscenium arch and footlights. The set encloses the center of the stage, and at the apex of the room there is a post, slightly off-center, which rises from the floor to the ceiling. This post forms a gallows supporting a beam which crosses the stage. From this post hangs a rope with a slip knot. Nearby on the crossbeam hangs the iron frame of a lamp, wrapped in old newspapers. The right wall is in rough cast and scarred with dates, scribbled phrases, and forgotten engagements. Also on the wall are drawings, these being done by Cocteau himself, his one graphic contribution to the ballet. Against the wall is an iron bedstead with a red blanket and dirty sheets trailing across the floor. Against the left wall, a dirty washstand and crumpled towels. In the left foreground a door. Near the footlights are a table and some straw-bottomed chairs, and other chairs and objects are strewn around the chamber; one chair is just under the rope. The whole room is lit by very harsh lighting which is let in by a glazed skylight revealing the Parisian night sky. Thus the room is composed of "pools of light" rather than general lighting so that the characters can move in and out of the shadows as the drama progresses.[20]

For the performance the orchestra struck the first chords of the Bach composition, and then the curtain rose. The young painter is seen lying on his back on the bed with his right foot raised against the wall. His head and one of his arms are hanging over the red blanket. Like the personification of one of Cocteau's own drawings for his novel, *Les Enfants terribles*, the posed man conveys the feeling of expectancy and tenseness. He is smoking and wears nothing but a pair of overalls, a "boiler suit" which is stained with paint and dirt and, as Cocteau explained, "calls to mind Harlequin's motley." The trousers are rolled up close to the knee and old slippers are on his feet. Cocteau continues his description of his ballet: "From time to time he impatiently looks at his wrist watch" which begins the first phase of the drama. This phase shows the viewer the young man's "anguish, nervous tension, dejection." Pacing the room or stopping to listen for a sound or to the ticking of his watch is mime action which, "carried to excess, incites the dance. One of the motifs being that magnificent, circular and airy movement of a man consulting his wrist watch."[21]

Suddenly the door bursts open and a young girl appears with long dark tresses flowing to her shoulders onto a simple pale yellow dress which has very short, puffy sleeves almost child-like in design. On her hands she wears long black gloves. "Right from the door, which she closes behind her, she pricks out her ill humor *sur les pointes*." This *pointe* work is used by Cocteau and Petit to emphasize the dominant and aggressive nature of the woman: a nature with a streak of sadism. The young man brightens up immediately when he sees his love, but she spurns him and strides across the room. The second phase of the drama, according to Cocteau, begins with the girl's entrance and continues through this strange courting and spurning. She leans disdainfully on the table; he presses himself to her but she pushes him away. He tries to clasp her legs but "she brutally kicks him in the face."[22] He goes to a chair and wearily sits on it as she goes to the table and slowly lights a cigarette. Rising from the chair while extending his leg *à la seconde*, the young man moves towards her as if hypnotized by the smoke, and his movements are now almost mechanical, echoing the girl's quality of gesture. The smoke drifting in his face, he knocks the cigarette from her hand and stamps it out on the floor. She sits disdainfully, disregarding his anger and remains "absolutely oblivious to him, as if she were at a cocktail party and he was one of many people who were naturally looking at her."[23] The man takes a chair and stands on it over her, but she moves away. He chases after her with bold *jetés*, *tours* and frenzied leaps. When he finally reaches her, he lies on the floor and tries to hold on to her, but she slaps him away, knocking him backwards on to his head with his feet pointed into the air. "Three times she stamps her heel on this poor kneeling fellow who falls, spins, collapses, straightens up again with the extreme slowness of heavy smoke, short of Anger's exploding thunderbolts."[24]

Figure 20.   The Opening Scene of *Le Jeune homme et la mort*, 1946
Jean Babilée in the principal role.
Photograph by Serge Lido.
(*Courtesy of the Stravinsky-Diaghilev Foundation*)

This dance is on the extreme left of the room, and the young man now indicates the rope with an outstretched arm. "And now the young lady cajoles him, leads him to a seat, sets him astride it, climbs on to the chair under the beam, adjusts the slip knot, then comes back and turns his head toward the gallows."[25] During this sequence the girl has become softer in her approach and the young man more dreamy "at this unwonted tenderness."[26] Finally, however, she flees from the room with a leer as he chases after her and tries to grasp her hair.

The third phase of the ballet begins with the young man left alone. He flattens himself against the door the girl has just slammed in his face and then proceeds to dance out his fury in a series of tour-de-force steps. He whirls chairs in the air and breaks them, drags the table towards the makeshift gallows, "clutches his breast in pain and makes cries of pain which we see but do not hear." Finally his pain and loneliness steer him to the hanging noose. He circles the post with a stool—"his frantic, nervous shadow seen reflected against both converging walls."[27] He steps on the stool and puts the noose around his neck and then pushes the stool away with his feet. The stage darkens and two crossed beams of light focus on his hanging body, the legs trembling in a series of spasms which are suddenly stilled.

The fourth and last phase of the dance-drama now begins. The room disappears in the dark, leaving only the triangle of the floor and the furniture, the framework of the gallows and the lamp. "These are now seen against an open night sky, in the midst of a surging sea made up of chimneys, of garrets, of electric signs, of rain-pipes, of roof tops. In the distance the letters of the Citroën light up in turn on the Eiffel Tower."[28] Across the rooftops of Paris comes the figure of death, and like the princess from the underworld in *Orphée*, this Cocteau personification of the afterlife is an elegant woman. She is in a ball dress, perched on high buskins with bracelets and a diamond necklace and a tulle train that floats behind her. She also wears a skeleton mask which is framed by a red hood and a pair of matching long red gloves. Her right hand rises and indicates the void; she advances towards the footlights, turns away and then crosses to the extreme right where she snaps her fingers. Slowly the man frees himself from the noose and slides down the beam onto the floor. Death removes her hood and mask and reveals herself as the young girl. She puts the skeleton mask on the face of the young man who moves around her and stops. Cocteau concludes his scenario: "Then Death holds out her hands. This gesture seems to urge on the young man more dreamy "at this unwonted tenderness."[26] Finally, however, dancers sets out across the rooftops."[29]

Within this scenario Cocteau connected two distinctly discernible yet radically different influences: romanticism and existentialism. The romantic tradition is linked by the dual use of love and death combined as one: eros and thanatos, the love desire and the death wish, a *liebestod*. The young artist, like James in the romantic ballet *La Sylphide*, is frustrated by the pursuit of his desire, and

Figure 21.   The Young Man Hangs Himself in *Le Jeune homme et la mort*, 1946
Jean Babilée in the principal role.
Photograph by Serge Lido.
(Courtesy of the Stravinsky-Diaghilev Foundation)

though he realizes his situation, he continues nonetheless. *Le Jeune homme et la mort*, while rooted in this romanticism, is also structured by the existential atmosphere which pervaded Paris immediately after the war. This philosophic approach to art placed a heavy emphasis on personal despair, dissolutionism, and desperation. While the female in the dance-drama is very close to her counterparts in other romantic ballets, notably the black swan Odile from *Swan Lake*—since she promises *l'amour* to the young man but delivers *la mort*—the young man sets himself up for such treatment by his almost masochistic and subjective relationship to her. He does not fight the fate she has in store for him but seems to succumb willingly to her desire for his destruction. This is a very different temptress from the sweet Giselle or the fragile Sylphide; this temptress is a stark, icy, and glacial beauty who is out to conquer both mind and soul. She taunts the man to violence through her hostility and thus to his death. Unlike the romantic hero, the young man has no alternative paths to avoid his fate. Albrecht could have avoided hurting Giselle if he had wanted to and James did not have to follow the Sylph into the woods, but this young man's will seems to be subjected to a much higher force. The viewer senses his doom from the moment the curtain rises.

Le Jeune homme et la mort had some technical problems before it reached the stage of the Théâtre des Champs-Elysées on the night of 25 June 1946. The company had just returned from a tour of Switzerland and everything had to be reassembled very quickly to make the deadline for the final *répétition générale*. Cocteau said that he had a hard time convincing Philippart to make her last entrance in high buskins, that Babilée's boiler suit was finished just in time, and that the set gave continual problems:

> In short, at seven o'clock in the evening, while the stagehands cleared the stage, we found ourselves faced with the prospect of disaster. The choreography came to a halt with the hanging of the young man. Roland Petit had refused to do anything about the last scene in my absence [while the company was away from Paris and touring Switzerland]. The dancers were half dead with exhaustion. I suggested that we [Petit and Cocteau] should let them sit in the auditorium and mime their parts to them. This we did.[30]

After Petit and Cocteau had shown the dancers what to do, Cocteau returned to his rooms at the Palais Royale to dine. He was back at the theatre for the *répétition générale*, which, as always in the French theatre tradition, was open to a paying audience and which was planned to begin at ten o'clock. The house was sold out and crammed with a tensely expectant audience; Cocteau's reputation "to astonish" had not diminished one iota since the days of Diaghilev. As *Le Jeune homme et la mort* was third on the program, the garret set had to be assembled during the interval and, unhappily, proved to be very difficult for the stagehands. The audience, growing impatient, began to boo and hiss while stamping their feet or clapping. Finally, Kochno ordered the house lights dimmed, and the orchestra struck up:

> From the very first chords of the Bach, we had the feeling that an extraordinary calm was pervading the whole place. The semi-darkness of the wings, full of running feet, of shouted orders, of feverish dressers (for Death had to be dressed in one minute) was less chaotic than one would have dared hope. Suddenly I saw Boris [Kochno] looking distraught. He whispered to me: "There's not enough music!" That was the danger of our experiment. We called to the dancers to quicken their pace. They were no longer with us.[31]

Cocteau may have colored the picture here for story value, but it was a truly unusual experiment and as the dance piece and the music had never been practiced together, one could not be sure of the timing of music and dance. Luckily, the experiment worked and the last chords of the Bach composition were played just as the dancers were leaving the stage. At the second performance a few nights later the orchestra played ahead of the dancers so that the music came in on different movements. Yet, according to Cocteau, the whole stage picture still worked, albeit in a different way. As the room was late in taking flight, Babilée was left hanging from his beam. "This produced a new beauty as a result of which the Entry of Death was even more startling."[32] This new effect, which was due to a stagehand's tardiness, was so admired by Cocteau that he later decided to keep it in the ballet for all subsequent performances.

The ballet caused an immediate sensation and reviewers spent much time discussing the philosophical pros and cons of the piece, the use or misuse of Bach's music, and the introduction of acrobatic technique into the classical ballet. *Dance News* summed up the Paris critical scene in a survey article headlined: "Morbid Ballet by Cocteau Stirs Paris Controversy":

> Talk of the town of the summer dance season was Jean Cocteau's *Le Jeune homme et la mort.* The controversial ballet premiered June 26, by the Ballets des Champs-Elysées. . . . The ballet evoked a great deal of discussion in the press and among the spectators. Most critics accepted the ballet as a beautiful composition, coherent, harmonious and marked by the peculiar qualities of Cocteau's poetry which has the power to transform things and people.
>   Those who accepted the ballet with reservations criticised mainly the showing of suicide on the stage and the perfunctory treatment of Bach's music. There were also those who, like A. Schaikevitch, commented that "actually Cocteau only wanted to provoke a feeling of indignation toward his audacity from those who still possess a reverent attitude toward Johann Sebastian Bach and toward the artistic enthusiasm of Noverre and Viganò."[33]

Janet Flanner (Genet), who reported the Paris scene for *The New Yorker*, thought the ballet was

> one of the high moments of the theatrical season and proved that the most indestructible talent in Paris is still that of Jean Cocteau. . . . The audience felt the same sense of astonishment that

Cocteau aroused with everything he laid his pen, pencil, or imagination to between the two World Wars. The passage of time seems neither to wither nor even to interrupt the hothouse ripeness of his talent.[34]

Pierre Tugal called it the highlight of the Paris dance season of 1946–47, which he thought generally mediocre. *Le Jeune homme et la mort*, however, would have stood out in any season, but because of the slack quality of other works presented before and after it during the year it "deserved a special place in the annals of dance." Tugal felt it was Cocteau's literary background combined with his theatrical capacity which made this ballet work so very well:

> It is imperative that from time to time a poet should succeed in spiriting away our consciousness that we may enjoy art by a species of logical catastrophe, which is what happens in Cocteau's ballet. . . . Thanks to the vision of this preeminently nonconformist poet, our poor Reality is indeed spirited away. Normal situations and characters no longer exist. Cocteau is perhaps more visionary than poet, and certainly more morbid visionary whose hallucinations sound the very depths of the soul. But unlike those of Dostoievsky, another dreamer, Cocteau's visions are not progressive stages towards liberation, even liberation through Christianity, they are paths which Cocteau would have us follow, that he may take delight in leading us to the very gates of hell. The performance given of this [work] by Babilée and Philippart will be unforgettable for all of those who have seen them.[35]

Tugal's remarks on Babilée and Philippart were shared by most critics and as the ballet began to be taken abroad reviewers concentrated on these dynamic performances, rather than the work itself. When the ballet was seen in London the next year, 1947, Cyril Beaumont called *Le Jeune homme et la mort* "a master-piece" although the performance could vary in intenseness "because that is the nature of interpretations of this type which emotionally have to be recreated at each performance." Beaumont also gives the reader one of the best word-pictures of these two performers in two incredibly taxing parts:

> Babilée, and Philippart, the latter at times reminding one of a certain portrait of Rachel, give an inspired performance; their individual contributions are so nicely balanced and so integrated that it is impossible to imagine one artist without the other. . . . Mlle. Philippart, with her secretive air, suggests all the youth and all experience, a *fleur du mal* such as Baudelaire might have imagined. Those vicious stabs with her *pointes*, that half disdainful, half inviting, provocative gaze, which, preceded by a malevolent twist of her lips, sometimes assumes a smiling mask to lure on her would-be lover with specious promise, only to humiliate him once more, haunt one's memory long after the ballet has ended. Babilée is superb as the desperate lover, alternatively rejected, enraged, and finally, through his utter wretchedness, driven to commit suicide by hanging. His movements have a rare beauty, partly from his masterly execution and partly from his subtle sense of line and his admirable timing, which are most inspiring. Notice how, when he turns a somersault, his legs, exactly together, rise with a rhythmic sweep upwards, remain poised for an instant, then, continuing the chord of the circle, descend in a downward course.[36]

No other dancers in the Ballets des Champs Elysées ever took these parts while Babilée and Philippart were with the company; it would have been extremely difficult, as Beaumont's description shows, to capture the right quality that these two artists had.

Other English reviewers were also very favorably impressed with the work. Gladys Lasky called it "a great and beautiful ballet" not only in its inventiveness but in its authentic capturing of emotional stress and prestigious choreography.[39] *Dancing Times* thought *Le Jeune homme* the "perfect answer to all those adherents of modern dance, who decry the achievements of classical ballet, saying it has no contact with real life." The magazine commended Cocteau and Petit for the "brilliant use of a stylized form of classical dance which allowed the dispensing of any *épaulement*, setting every *passé-à-la-seconde* directly *en avant*. This gives a strength and ugliness of line so necessary to such a bitter theme."[38] The reviewer also thought the use of *pointes* especially effective in emphasizing the girl's cruel walk and posturings, while the acrobatics gave to the lovers' fight a sense of realism often missing from classical dance.

Dancing Times verbalized a complaint that some had seen in the Paris production and would be noticed later by other non-French reviewers:

> People will complain such realism has no place in ballet. Perhaps it has not. But this work can hardly be called a ballet, rather it is a dance-drama. The French have been masters of realism in horrific plays—the *Grand Guignol*—for many years and to use such methods so successfully proves that they have still a great deal to contribute to the art of classical dance, if it is to continue to be a living art and not an academic art.[39]

While thus applauding Cocteau's efforts in this line by stretching dance further, the same reviewer also tempered his praise with some questions about Cocteau's methods in transferring realism to the balletic world. It was the final scene that particularly bothered the reviewer of *Dancing Times*:

> The meaning of the second scene is obscure. Is Jean Cocteau asking us to believe that the Young Man loves Death? The libretto seems to suggest this. Will he only find happiness in death? If so we find it strange that the only happiness he gets after donning the death mask is to walk amongst the glittering signs of the Eiffel Tower.
>
> It is in this scene one feels this discrepancy between the theme and its choreography—and the music. Hitherto the dancing has followed the surge and urgency of Bach's great C minor Passacaglia. It forces the tragedy onwards. But Bach's wonderfully exalting final chords mean much more than a twinkling Citroën sign, an overdressed woman and a figure in dungarees. Is this death? Surely not, for such music rises to the greatest heights and these two dancers, having proved themselves great artists, deserved a genuine ending, not a banal picture without meaning.[40]

The reviewer here, as many subsequent American reviewers did, defined realism and applied it too strictly to the ballet. It must be remembered, however, that Cocteau never stated that the ballet was realistic; only the critics applied this term to the work. Cocteau considered *Le Jeune homme* an experiment and a workshop. "I simply grope about and manage the best I can," he later said about the piece. He did see, however, that critics would have trouble with the ballet and could trip up on trying to interpret it,

> accustomed as they are on the one hand to Voltaire's metronome, on the other hand to Rousseau's hazel switch. The precarious balance between these two extremes is perhaps the winning over of the modern trend, but for [the understanding of that] the critics must explore the zone, visit its mines and let in the unknown.[41]

It was the exact juxtaposition of the Bach with the simple exit that gave the ending of *Le Jeune homme* one of its peculiar qualities, and while one might disagree with his intention or the use put to Bach's music, it is hard to try to simply categorize the final sequence as "a banal picture without meaning."[42]

In 1951 Babilée and Philippart were invited to appear as guest artists with American Ballet Theatre in New York. They brought *Le Jeune homme et la mort*, which premiered for American audiences on 9 April 1951, at the Metropolitan Opera House. Doris Hering in *Dance Magazine* called the movement "literal, ferocious, and acrobatic," and thought the two performers "exciting, audacious, and unconventional."[43] Lillian Moore, who had seen the piece before, thought "the vehicle, in its effectiveness, was marred by Petit's peculiar mannerism of repeating each combination of steps or movements exactly three times, neither more nor less."[44] Moore felt this lessened the wonder of the piece and took the edge off the theatrical excitement. Walter Terry thought the ballet "a stunning theatrical piece. Perhaps it is not strictly a ballet in the formal or technical sense but it is a theatre-dance of a potent kind." Terry also noted the pictorial impact of the opening scene with the young man sprawled across the bed, motionless. It was still dance for Terry since "great dance is implied in the highly charged inaction of this figure as a young man. . . . Ballet actions, both pure and adulterated (by impulsive movement), are combined with gesture, acting and a kind of apache-like genre of violent motion."[45] He thought the use of Bach might be considered startling to accompany this brash melodrama "but its noble flowing beauties provide, I believe, a wonderfully satiric counterpoint to the frenzied patterns of this choreography."[46]

John Martin of *The New York Times* did not agree. While he praised the dancers highly, he thought the work itself "not very important" and "of little value" without such stunning performances. He was disturbed by the "misuse" of Bach and thought the ballet should have been accompanied by "vulgar street songs" for "the broad and noble organ music of Bach has no bearing whatever upon the situation or its esthetics."[47] One can well imagine Cocteau replying to such a criticism that that was exactly what he intended: the parallel "mystery of accidental syncronization." Both Terry and Martin noted that the French designs of Wakhevitch were unable to be used for the American production and Oliver Smith had to design a substitute variation. What this meant was that the American audiences did not really see the ballet as Cocteau had intended, since the whole final scene of the rooftops of Paris was replaced by an intangible and less definite skyline.

Le Jeune homme et la mort received a totally different kind of fame by setting an important precedent in a court case ten years after its creation, when it was still being performed with regularity. This event occurred in September 1956 when M. Eudes, the director of the Théâtre des Champs-Elysées, claimed that he should receive author's rights to the ballet since he had commissioned and paid for the work. He also claimed that no performance could be allowed without his permission. The case was taken to the court of Paris, and Cocteau, representing the company and Petit, claimed sole right of artistic ownership. The judgment of the court would have far-reaching consequences since, if it judged in Eudes' favor, other impresarios could claim rights as recipients of royalty checks from the works they produced, as well as designers, composers, choreographers or costumers. The debate was over who owned a ballet and who had the right to present it: "the right of presentation of this work when it is produced in the theatre" [le droit de l'exploitant sur l'oeuvre qu'il monte dans son théâtre]. Cocteau argued his point of view brilliantly and asked the court the rhetorical question that if producers should have royalty rights, why stop there? Why not let machinists who run the sets and stagehands who move the furniture also participate in the sharing?[48]

The tribunal decided in Cocteau's favor and by so doing set an important precedent by recognizing the rights of choreographers as equal to those of librettists. Cocteau, in his capacity as both choreographer and librettist for this ballet, was able to help choreographers gain the rights librettists and scenarists had enjoyed since Scribe founded the "Societé des Auteurs et Compositeurs dramatique." The court stated that producing a work did not give the producer the right to the piece, even as a seamstress would not have the rights to the design the costumer had created, nor the painter the rights to the set design he was painting from another's sketches. The court also decided that choreographers should be included in the rights and privileges of the Societé due to the "very particular characteristics" of dance since choreography was an essential element of the composition and not extraneous. This court case also helped form the "Comité d'Etudes pour la Défense du Droit des Chorégraphes," an important step in the international recognition of choreography as legitimate for copyright protection.[49]

There are three further revivals of *Le Jeune homme et la mort* that are important to consider. The first was for the famous Russian defector Rudolph Nureyev (b. 1938) and the French dancer Zizi Jeanmaire (b. 1924) which Roland Petit supervised in 1968 for French television. This time Cocteau received credit only as the author of the libretto, and the screen credits read "Choreography by Roland Petit based on a scenario by Jean Cocteau." The sets were still credited to

Wakhevitch, but no costume credit was given. This was due to the fact that the boiler suit was now replaced by a simple pair of jeans and the woman was dressed in a simple sleeveless practice dress. The former change certainly helped update the production, but the latter innovation destroyed most of Cocteau's symbolism. What was probably more startling was Petit's decision to cut the final scene, for the television film ends with the figure of Nureyev hanging from the supporting beam. It was certainly no longer the ballet Cocteau had originally conceived.[50]

Petit supervised another revival in 1975 for another Russian ballet star, Mikhail Baryshnikov (b. 1948) and the American dancer Bonnie Mathis (b. 1942) for American Ballet Theatre. This time the ballet's overall design was left more or less as Cocteau originally planned it; though credit once more read "based on a scenario by Jean Cocteau." The costumes and set were credited to the original designs of George Wakhevitch, although Wakhevitch had had nothing to do with the original costume designs. This revival actually followed Karinska's realization, although the woman's sleeves were longer and the young man remained in bluejeans, as Nureyev had worn. Baryshnikov explained that it was Anthony Tudor who suggested he try the ballet. Of course, choreographic changes were made by Petit to fit Baryshnikov's particular talents, but there were also changes in Cocteau's concept. As Baryshnikov wrote:

> I consider *Jeune homme* a successful "popular" ballet. True, it is a period piece, but the questions it raises are timeless; if it is perhaps a cliché, it has the *force* of a cliché. It is about loneliness, and it is a naturalistic as well as surrealistic drama: pure Cocteau. Roland [Petit] used Cocteau's libretto, retaining the most important aspects of the story and strengthening them. I think their collaboration worked perfectly. Roland understood how to use the peculiar theatricality of Cocteau's story and, at the same time, make it clearer for the stage.[51]

However, despite Baryshnikov's enthusiasm and Petit's adaptation of the ballet for the young Russian, the revival did not jell. Perhaps Eric Aschengreen put it most succinctly when he noted "there is something depraved in that ballet, an impotence and fear for life which is not in Baryshnikov's very sane kind of talent to express."[52] Arlene Croce also noticed this when reviewing the ballet: "Baryshnikov, more angel than thug, is physically so vital and radiant, so unstrainingly precise, that he unconsciously undermines the expressive intentions of the ballet."[53]

The expressive qualities that the critics felt were lacking in Baryshnikov's performance in 1975 were definitely present when Patrick Dupond (b. 1959), the young star of the Paris Opéra Ballet, performed the part with Roland Petit's Ballet National de Marseilles during its New York season at the Metropolitan Opera House in July 1983. *Dance Magazine* critic Mindy Aloff thought *Le Jeune homme* was the most forceful work of the season and that Petit's choreography came across the strongest in his *pas de deux*. Petit restored the original costuming for his production—painter's overall hooked over one shoulder—and returned to the original ending. Dupond's interpretation gave the part a power and dynamic intensity that many critics felt was the closest to Babilée's original interpretation. Luigi Bonino, who alternated in the role, was also complimented on his performance. Since 1983 marked the twentieth anniversary of Cocteau's death a number of critics reanalyzed the work and gave it higher marks than they had eight years before.[54]

Throughout its nearly forty-year history, *Le Jeune homme et la mort* has come in for much analysis, speculation and discussion. Deirdre Pridden felt that Cocteau always used dance and adapted it to his theories of the moment; thus the postwar existentialism was fitted into the format Cocteau devised for this particular work.[55] Jerome Lemaitre saw *Le Jeune homme* as representing the young adolescent looking for the ideal but unable ever to obtain it, and the woman who is death as an "avenging angel" who leads him into a world where the ideal can be found. Thus, according to Lemaitre, the *corrida* is reversed as the bull, symbol of death, is the woman, and the toreador is the victim. Only when the young man is led away from his flat, "the bullring of life" into the universe of poetry do the roles reverse and the man is free: the moment he takes the mask of death from the woman. Lemaitre also contends that this liberation of the poet was an obsession with Cocteau and that it represented not only an artistic liberation but a liberation from the matriarchal, preying female, "the woman." Lemaitre explains that Cocteau's homosexual inclinations would naturally lead him to such a view.[56]

While Lemaitre's theory is interesting and has many parallels with other Cocteau works—the fascination with angels, the use of the color red, the symbolism of the bullring—Lemaitre's approach may be reading too much into a simplistic statement. Cocteau himself expressed apprehension soon after the ballet's premiere that too much would be read into the work: "There is neither magic nor master's eye [in *Le Jeune homme*]. Only a great deal of love and a great deal of work." Cocteau also, as he did with all his dance works, refused to classify it as a ballet. It was

> a drama in mime, in which mime broadens its style to that of dance. It is dumb show in which I endeavor to endow gestures with the high relief of the cry and the spoken word. It is speech translated into the language of the body. It consists of monologues and dialogues that use the same vocabulary as painting, sculpture, and music.[57]

However much Cocteau may be praised or chastised for this creation, it is obvious that much depended upon the personalities of the two lead dancers. Was this ballet a masterpiece, as some critics claimed, or was it a masterpiece totally dependent on its original performers, Babilée and Philippart? Is it best to see the dance-drama as a "period piece," representing attitudes of that time which have since become dated or seem to be no longer relevant? Richard Buckle, in an obituary notice for Cocteau in 1963, said that the ballet was the most remarkable creation of the Ballets des Champs-Elysées but, like Cocteau's earlier ballet, *Le Train bleu*, epitomized its period: "It was the time of the cold war, of existentialism, of bombed-out buildings, peeling wallpaper, and cynical pessimism. The young man who hanged himself on a beam for love could not know that if he had waited a year or two he would be one of those to take over and rule a new world."[58] The combination of both factors, the personalities of the two original dancers, as well as the representation of postwar neurosis, may make *Le Jeune homme et la mort* historically important, but not presently viable as a performable ballet, unless the right interpreters are available, as with Patrick Dupond.

In 1946, however, such considerations were far from Cocteau's mind. One thing was sure, and that was the artistic quality and exciting stage presence of Babilée and Philippart. Previous commitments and a very busy schedule prevented Cocteau and the couple from working together for another two years. In January 1948, Petit and Kochno had a disagreement, and Petit left Les Ballets des Champs-Elysées to form another company, Les Ballets de Paris, taking with him Jean-maire, Vyroubova and Marchand. Choreographic responsibility for the former company was now divided, and one of the dancers given a chance to create ballets was Jean Babilée. Although he had done one short concert piece for Lidova's *Soirées de la Danse* in 1944, this ballet would be his actual choreographic debut for a professional company. He began to look around for help and encouragement.

One day Babilée and his wife were visiting Cocteau at Milly where he was absorbed in the preparations for the filming of *Orphée*. The couple talked to Cocteau about some ideas for a ballet and became so desperate that Babilée cried out "Save us!!" [Sauvez-nous][59] Cocteau, though very busy, could never resist such a plea for help, and though he had very little time, he told the Babilées he would help them and do everything in his power to make their choreographic endeavor a success.

The scenario they evolved was based on the Apuleius tale of Eros and Psyche. In the story Psyche is a human whose incredible beauty makes Aphrodite so jealous, since mankind is neglecting her temples and worshipping this human, that she sends her son Eros to avenge her. Eros, however, falls in love with the princess and spirits her away to a secret garden where he makes love to her every night, though she is never allowed to see his face as he disappears by morning. Psyche's jealous sisters visit her and tempt her to break her promise. She does so and finds out her husband is a god, and so he leaves her. After falling into the hands of the still jealous goddess Aphrodite and going through a number of trials, Psyche is finally enabled to return to her husband and Zeus grants her immortality.[60]

Cocteau suggested that they use only the first part of the legend as set down by Apuleius and end the ballet with the seduction of the princess. For the music Cocteau suggested César Franck's suite *Psyché*, which was composed between 1887–88. Cocteau had used part of this score previously for the *Orphée pas de deux* danced by Philippart and Petit at their first recital. Now, however, rather than being used as background accompaniment, Cocteau's scenario followed the story outline of the composer's symphonic poem, although the chorus was cut and only a section of the suite was used.[61] Cocteau gave the ballet the title of *L'Amour et son amour*, and he gave this simple and typically enigmatic explanation for the ballet in the program: "Love has no explanation—do not seek a meaning in love's gestures."[62] Working from the basic outline Cocteau had devised for him, Babilée choreographed while Cocteau, between work sessions on *Orphée*, literally phoned in his designs to the costumer and the scenographer. In his instructions to Karinska, Cocteau said that Babilée's wings as Eros must be made of the same material as "Marlene Dietrich's plumes . . . in the film, *Shanghai Express*" and that the harness connecting the wings should be red, that recurring symbolic color which is found in so many Cocteau works.[63] To Michel Lavaret, the young painter who was executing his set designs, Cocteau explained exactly how to compose the background scenes of earth and heaven and even where each line should be placed. Unlike the "dictated" designs for *Le Jeune homme* in which Cocteau had given the designers a more or less free hand, Karinska and Lavaret were executors of his specific plans since Cocteau decided, for the first time for one of his ballets, to design the sets and costumes himself.

The ballet premiered at the Théâtre des Champs-Elysées on 13 December 1948. Babilée did not portray the literal details of the story but tried to convey through movement the quality of love that gave rise to the myth. The legend could be looked at not only as a myth but as an allegory, since the Greek word "psyche" means the soul. Babilée may also have taken his cue from the librettists for César Franck, Sicard and Fourcaud, whose text and outline for the piece are followed, almost to the letter, by Babilée.

The ballet begins with an entr'acte to part I of the suite, "Le Sommeil de Psyche." "Psyche sleeps. . . . In the dim regions of her dreams, her spirit becomes aware of some perfect bliss not of this world, which she feels will yet be hers."[64] The audience first sees the drop curtain Cocteau designed, dazzling white and showing the profile of a young man whose eyes are directed towards a small opening in the painted frame that contains his image. First violet, then green light plays off the image as the curtain rises. The first scene is earth with a painted backcloth patterned in pale blue, brown, white and mauve, and is so colored and shaped to represent a map of earth. The wings, also in a pastel hue, are outlined in a Greek design.[65]

Psyche enters from the right in a flesh-colored skintight leotard around which is wrapped a dark blue tulle skirt, although streaks of a lighter blue appear here and there in the material. Her hair is long and on her brow is a flat headpiece that is almost like bull's horns. She moves as in a dream, doing *bourées* across the stage. Two men enter, kiss her hand, and worship her beauty. They lift her in various poses but her attention is elsewhere and she continues to dance with soft, voluptuous gestures. As Franck's music changes [Psyché enlevée par les Zéphyrs], "suddenly the air vibrates to strange sounds . . . " and seven zephyrs enter in misty green gowns that float behind them. Around their shoulders fall "narrow strips of cloth coloured green, pink, red and yellow, which undulate as they move."[66] The Zephyrs encircle Psyche, and she dances through them and with them, although she can never escape them. They weave in and out of formations and flutter their hands over her head to the sound of a harp. She falls into their arms and is carried off to Olympus as the drop curtain falls and the light slowly changes to twilight.

Scene two of the ballet is set to part II of Franck's score, "Les Jardin d'Eros." Cocteau's second backdrop shows a sketch of the constellations with twinkling stars. It is night and the color is a "warm, midnight blue" as Psyche enters from the left with the Zephyrs.[67] The Zephyrs hear Eros coming in and quickly whisk off the still wondering girl. Cupid enters from right as the music changes to Franck's next sequence, "Psyché et Eros." Eros wears white wings of billowing feathers which are attached to a red harness around his shoulders. He wears white arm bands and a spangled white satin brief around his loins. He does not wear tights but white shoes with stockings that are rolled down to below his knees. He circles the stage in a bold flight of leaps and then suddenly stops and kneels. Looking thoughtful he gestures towards the light that is on him and it follows him as he leaves. The sky becomes darker and Psyche reenters with the Zephyrs in great trepidation. They leave her as she lies down stage center in the darkening gloom. The stars in the backdrop suddenly black out and Eros reappears in a solo spot that seems to come from his own being. He moves his hands as if he were pulling wires and Psyche attempts to rise, as if commanded by him. Eros goes to her and she holds on to his shoulder for support. They dance together in a slow and soft *pas de deux* although Psyche never once looks at Eros, since the dance is taking place as if it were in the dark and she could not see him. As the music begins to fade in intensity the lights begin to dim and Eros holds up his left hand. The girl circles the stage and disappears as Eros is left alone in his domain, governing the light of the stars with his own hands. As the stars dim the circle of light around the god narrows to a pinpoint and finally goes out.

It is probably dangerous, as Cocteau implied in his epigraph, to read too much into a simple love story. Many interpreted the actions of the final *pas de deux* as the evolution of Psyche falling in love, losing her lover, and then regaining him.[68] The last section of Franck's music, "Souffrances et Plaintes de Psyché," was not used, so perhaps no punishment and suffering were implied. Whatever the interpretation, Babilée's choreography was given high acclaim by the French critics, who were surprised to see such a lyrical and adagio-styled performance coming from "the angel-thug of the Ballets des Champs-Elysées." Cocteau's pastel designed sets bathed in luminescent light (he had also supervised the lighting) won breathless accolades and were considered one of his finest contributions to stage design. When Babilée and Philippart were guest artists with the American Ballet Theatre in 1951, they brought *L'Amour* with them as well as *Le Jeune homme*. Unlike *Le Jeune homme*, *L'Amour* did not have to be redesigned but used Cocteau's original sets and costumes. Walter Terry thought Cocteau's designs "superb" and John Martin thought they were not only attractive but "in the case of the second one—a simple and spacious panorama of the heavens—eminently evocative."[69] All the critics thought, like *Variety*, that the ballet was a "succès d'estime" and, while very beautiful, would not gain the lasting recognition of *Le Jeune homme*. Terry probably pinpointed the problem, noting the ballet *L'Amour* was "remote, distant, far from reality," and Martin continued, "its legato movements are absorbing to watch but they do not contain the acrobatic savagery that will give *Le Jeune homme* its wider appeal."[70]

The ballet was an excellent showpiece for the French couple, though it did not remain in the repertoire as long as *Le Jeune homme*. Cocteau, despite his divided attention among other projects, gave the couple a beautifully designed work. For once, all the critics agreed that the designs were some of the most elegant and evocative to reach the stage. It is surprising to realize that *L'Amour et son amour* was actually the first ballet Cocteau had ever designed, excepting the costumes and makeshift set for Petit's *Orphée*. This, however, was a growing tendency the poet continued to develop during the last decade of his life. He was less and less the poet of the pen and more and more the poet of the easel. His next two ballets continued this trend.

7

Cocteau and Lifar: The Creations of
Phèdre and *Le Bel indifférent*

*The music, the choreography, the decor, the costumes, the lights: these only
form the piece of paper on which the dancers write their signature in a
style as noble to see as the delicacy of Chinese calligraphy.*
— Jean Cocteau, *Panorama de la Danse*

Cocteau honestly believed that dancers were the central part of any ballet. He
also believed they should be properly framed and his past successes had shown
him as well as the public that he was one of the best framers of talent. Cocteau's
interest in ballet had been stimulated by his work with Petit and Babilée, and
he wanted to continue to contribute to the art form. But, as Cocteau himself
had stated, he was not a choreographer. His role was limited more to producer
or designer. Cocteau liked to mold talents, and this was not always an easy matter with choreographers. As a film director Cocteau could easily control his product through the magic of editing. In many ways his films do dance through
Cocteau's placing of objects and people and the directions and angles he had
his cinematographers take in capturing the underworld of *Orphée* or the enchanted gardens of *La Belle et la bête*. By the late forties, Cocteau was still interested in dance but looking for the right vehicle. This ballet, *Phèdre*, is a product of almost accidental circumstance. It turned out to be Cocteau's last ballet
created in Paris and the first of his works to become part of the Académie Nationale de la Musique, better known as the Paris Opéra.

The Paris Opéra had been rejuvenated during the 1930s by the presence of
the last of Serge Diaghilev's protégés: Serge Lifar. He was still very young and
inexperienced as a choreographer when George Balanchine (1904–1983) became
ill during the rehearsals of *The Creatures of Prometheus* at the Opéra in 1929 and
suggested that Lifar take his place. Balanchine later went to America at the request of Lincoln Kirstein, but Lifar remained in Paris and became both *premier
danseur étoile* and ballet director for the state institution. He gave the dancers

there a new pride and interest in their art and was soon making ballet evenings as important as they had been in the days of Taglioni and Elssler. Now, however, interest was centered on Lifar as the star of his own productions. His new works tended to focus on the principals rather than the *corps de ballet* and his revivals of such classics as *Giselle* or *Le Spectre de la rose* provided him with romantic vehicles to demonstrate his lyrical abilities.

During the 1930s he began to experiment with dance forms in a more radical way. He invented a sixth and seventh position, wrote many treatises on the theory of dance and even presented ballets that used only rhythmic accompaniment such as *Icare* (1935). But soon he abandoned this style for grand, ornate, lavish productions such as *Le Roi nu* (1936) and *Alexandre le Grand* (1937), both of which used the full technical resources of the Paris Opéra and gave Lifar mythohistorical leads.[1]

With the occupation of Paris during World War II by the Nazis, Lifar was faced with a dilemma: close the Opéra and put all the dancers out of work or continue to perform and create—albeit for enemies of France. Lifar had no real political leanings and chose the latter course, even creating some of his best work during these war years, especially *Suite en blanc* in 1943, one of his few abstract creations. Lifar, though, loved publicity, applause and adulation, and to many eyes he was seen to mingle too closely with the upper echelon of the Nazi regime. This lost him his job when the war was over, and he went off to found the Nouveaux Ballet de Monte Carlo in 1945. He was called back to the Paris Opéra in 1947 when it was finally admitted they could not do without him. He alone seemed able to control the backstage squabbles, temperamental dancers and surly stagehands. He returned with one of his most beautiful ballets, *Les Mirages*, but even though dancing played a greater part than usual in a Lifar work the ballet was still dominated by the action and the narrative. Pierre Michaut noted in 1949

> the dancing of the leading roles [in *Les Mirages*] stresses the realistic at the expense of the allegorical and lyrical values of the libretto. For when such a poetical and allegorical fable is transformed onto an outline of a *ballet d'action* confined to *soli*, *pas de deux*, and small *ensembles*; when its conception and development are so forceful and indeed riotous a character, emphasizing the dancer's virtuosity, then its poetry fades and is lost.[2]

This complaint would become general against a number of Lifar's works; this approach would temper any use of a poetical scenario in the style Cocteau was used to producing.

Louis Laloy said Lifar was "far more a realist than a poet."[3] The analysis is apt, but it is also true that Lifar was always *trying* to be a poet—as so many of his own writings attest—and perhaps the poetic vision he was seeking to create was lost among the mass of details and effects that continually laden his complicated scenarios. Lifar was a prolific writer of historical and theoretical works on dance, but he would often try to make these theories work on stage, to the detriment of the piece. He made grand pronouncements and dogmatic statements that he was later forced to revise or even totally reverse. His return to the Paris Opéra seemed to have also coincided with an increase in this erratic and unpredictable nature. He was not the man who had taken control so dramatically in 1929:

> It was not quite the same Lifar as before. He was older. Moreover, he had spoiled his splendid physical gifts. His hair was as thick and black as ever, his face still youthful, but his waistline had expanded and his breath shortened since he had been eating, drinking and smoking without restraint, had given up training and stopped practicing except on stage. His best friends tried to warn him, but in vain. He clung to a few romantic roles, including Albrecht in *Giselle*, and appeared in his new ballets as if to make clear that character roles would never suit him.[4]

Such a man, desperately clinging to his past, would not willingly give in to being supervised, even by such an established theatre man as Cocteau. All of this must be taken into account when detailing the creation of *Phèdre*.

In his book, *Le Livre de la danse*, written in 1954, Lifar states that he had been attracted to the theme of *Phèdre* some years before, in 1938. He had worked out a scenario based on the play by the ancient Greek playwright Euripides and it was to have music by the Italian composer Vittorio Rieti (b. 1898). Circumstances, especially the war, prevented the ballet being presented to the public. He had intended to call the ballet "Hippolyte," thus centering the action around the male protagonist, rather than Phèdre herself. Lifar saw the theme of the story as a contrast between "the pure athleticism of Hippolyte . . . and the tragedy of Phèdre who, with her jealousy, *chez Euripides*, is pierced as easily as a needle pierces the foliage of a plant." Lifar visualized Hippolyte as "the philosopher who is exempt from all imperfection which Euripides has repeated as 'isolated,' a solitary hero detached from vanity and its concessions, a person ideal for theatrical choreography."[5] It was also, one is tempted to add, an idealized vision of Lifar by himself.

In 1965 Lifar claimed that the idea for *Phèdre* was revived when he met Georges Auric at a party given by Comte Etienne de Beaumont sometime in 1947, soon after his return to the Opéra. According to Lifar, Auric's wife Nora asked Lifar to have the Paris Opéra commission a work from her husband. Lifar remembered he "was enthusiastic about the idea and mentioned it to [Georges] Hirsch [director of the Paris Opéra] who said that to his great regret he could not accept the proposition unless Auric would consent to write the score without a fee since the Opéra was very short of money. So it came about that I paid the fee amounting to half a million francs."[6] Other than the improbability of Lifar ever having so much money on hand—he was always in debt—the account does not tally with any other sources, including the accounts at the Paris Opéra and Georges Auric. Lifar never made such a claim in his earlier writings and one must mark this story down to faulty memory since in the same paragraph he also remembered Christian Bérard as designing the costumes and décor. In fact, Bérard had been dead for over a year!"

Georges Auric had received a direct commission from the Paris Opéra administration, though Lifar may have been involved in influencing their decision. It is definite, though, that Lifar did *not* suggest the theme of *Phèdre*, despite the coincidence of his scenario of eleven years before. The origins of this *Phèdre* seems to have come about almost by accident. Auric had the commission for a score but was having trouble deciding what subject to write on. He ran into Cocteau who asked him why he looked so worried. Auric explained that he could not think of a theme for a ballet which the Paris Opéra wanted from him. "What is the height of every actress's ambition?" asked Cocteau. "Phèdre, of course! Why can't it be a ballet, too?"[8] Auric was enthusiastic about the idea and asked Cocteau to devise the scenario and collaborate on the work with him. Cocteau based his version on the Racine play, not Euripides, as Lifar had drafted, though he used elements from the Greek versions. Cocteau felt that *Phèdre*, being a drama from eternal mythology, "needs an atmosphere of menace and blood which only Racine was able to extract from Euripides and Sophocles."[9]

Cocteau also felt that the male dancer most suited for Hippolyte was Jean Babilée whom he was sure he could convince to return to the Paris Opéra for this engagement. For the female lead Cocteau originally wanted Greta Garbo, the motion picture actress, and he entered into a correspondence with her on the subject and even met her in Paris to discuss the role, but this intriguing casting never came off.[10] Instead, Cocteau suggested the arrestingly beautiful and statuesque Tamara Toumanova (b. 1919), one of the original "baby ballerinas" of the Ballets Russes de Monte Carlo and one of the most glamorous of the Russian emigré ballerinas. Free from her professional engagements at the end of 1949 she was willing to be a guest artist with the Paris Opéra ballet for this production.[11]

The Opéra administration was most happy to have Auric and Cocteau developing a ballet for them and when Cocteau indicated he would be willing to design the sets and costumes as well, their pleasure was manifold. Lifar was only brought into discussion on the ballet *after* Cocteau and Auric had developed the scenario and set tentative casting. If this was done in the hopes that Lifar would accept a *fait accompli*, it did not work, since he had his own ideas about the ballet. Cocteau later said he had gone into the work on *Phèdre* hoping he would participate and produce as he had done with Roland Petit on *Le Jeune homme et la mort* but Lifar proved less pliable than the younger and less established Petit.[12] He would not agree to Babilée as Hippolyte but wanted to play the role himself, though he did agree to the casting of Toumanova. The dictates of Auric's score made major changes difficult but a number of minor changes were made which Cocteau had to agree to because of the dictates of choreography.[13] As rehearsals progressed, Cocteau became less and less involved in the ballet, though keeping a close watch on the execution of his set and costume designs. Involved with

Figure 22. Cocteau with Tamara Toumanova during Rehearsals for
Phèdre, 1950
Photograph by Serge Lido.
(Private Collection)

the filming of *Orphée* and *Les Enfants terribles*, Cocteau was very busy, though one can be sure he would have found more time for the ballet if Lifar had wanted him. How much of the final *Phèdre* is Cocteau's and how much Lifar's is difficult to perceive but Cocteau's style and peculiar vision of the myth remain very much a part of the ballet—even in revival today—and Lifar's choreography, while amending this poetry, does not dominate it.

As with most of his works Cocteau stated his theme in the program notes for the audience:

> A myth is a myth because poets have breathed fresh life into it through the ages, thus ensuring its continuance.
>
> None should be unaware of the legend of Phaedra, granddaughter of the Sun.
>
> Let us honour the legend, be it in song or dance.[14]

Following his own ruling, Cocteau took the legend and transformed it into a working scenario which he entitled a "Découpage," a term used for a film script in French cinema. The continuity of the story is episodic and Auric's score follows the outline quite precisely:

> Phaedra forbids her women to adorn her.
> She perceives Oenone standing beside Hippolytus and his chariot.
> Phaedra flees before the friends of Hippolytus.
> Aricia and Hippolytus dance together.
> Phaedra tells Oenone of her love for Hippolytus.
> Phaedra declares her love. Hippolytus, horrified, takes flight.
> Sailors bring tidings of the death of Theseus. Mourning and
> funeral march.
> Oenone urges Phaedra towards Hippolytus. She is not to blame
> for Theseus' death.
> In the far distance Theseus is seen returning.
> The sailors and their followers rejoice.
> Phaedra drives away Oenone.
> Theseus is restored to his son who avows his love for Aricia.
> Oenone is seen to cast herself in the sea.
> Theseus meets Phaedra. Learning that she has a rival, she
> makes false accusation against Hippolytus.
> Theseus invokes the aid of Poseidon. He appears. Waves engulf the scene.
> The dead body of Hippolytus is dragged in by his horses.
> Phaedra, having taken poison, comes to confess her crime.
> She falls dead.
> Apollo has loosed an arrow. On his right, Minos; upon his
> left Pasiphae.
> Minos and Pasiphae step down onto the stage. The mother covers
> her daughter's body with a red mantle.[15]

The plot outline shows how much Cocteau had varied from Racine and, for that matter, from Euripides. Cocteau's scenario, despite the modifications, would still be difficult to convey in dance language and would presume a familiarity with the legend by the audience. This was not unreasonable or unusual of Cocteau to expect from his Parisian audiences, but one can also see why the details of the outline might dismay Lifar. Involved as Cocteau was with his use of Greek myths in his plays, poetry, paintings and films, he may have lost touch with the basic simplicity needed for dance. Lifar was helpful in paring down the symbolism to its choreographic possibilities. At the same time Cocteau, by centering the interest on Phèdre realized that the fallen woman with her inner agony and moral dilemma was of greater dramatic interest than the stalwart but less exciting character of Hippolyte. This helped Lifar channel his energies as choreographer on to the female lead and away from his original focus on his own character of Theseus' son. The weaknesses and strengths of both Lifar and Cocteau balanced each other and played an important part in the ballet's eventual success.

Cocteau's scenario, which involves both humans and gods, was helped by the set he designed to encompass the action. The stage was divided between two planes: the lower front of the stage, used for the "present" action and a small Greek stage backstage center, which was used for the appearance of the gods and to show action that was happening somewhere else. This set was built like a Greek temple with a sky blue curtain which opened to reveal the commentary in frieze action, a *tableau vivant*. The presentation of gods on this higher plane was part of the original Greek tragedies and Cocteau uses the ancient device of the stage within the stage to help convey future, past or concurrent action without the means of dialogue, which was not at his disposal in the silent strictures of the dance idiom as performed at the Paris Opéra.

The use of color for the sets and costumes was striking and, as he had done with *L'Amour et son amour* simplicity and primary colors were the keynote. The stark white temple was backed by the azure Aegean sea and the title of the play was chalked in black on the stage front of the Greek temple. All of the costumes had sun-baked colors and Phèdre was clothed in black with a scarlet red cloak which, when set against the background of yellow, mauve and various grades of orange, made for a striking presentation. It was the one element of the production on which practically every reviewer commented.[16] Cocteau also used the color red in Phèdre's costume symbolically, even to having her covered by her mother with a red cloth at the end of the ballet. Cocteau associated this color with women in many of his works, both stage and literary creations, and used it as a device for agression, sin, carnality, lust and even repentance. He used it in his play *Orphée* and in the previous ballets *Le Jeune homme et la mort* and *L'Amour et son amour*; he would use it again in *La Dame à la licorne*.

The ballet itself received a "sneak preview" in May 1950 at the Maggio Musicale Fiorentino but did not receive its official premiere until 14 June 1950 at the Paris Opéra. The combination of the talents of Auric, Cocteau and Lifar had been talked about for weeks and the ballet opened to a glittering house full of anticipation and, because of the familiarity of the legend, some preconceptions. It was well received, though many critics found the presentation of the plot rather involved and difficult to follow. Irene Lidova thought the performances of Toumanova and Lycette Darsonval (b. 1912) as Oenone particularly outstanding but thought the choreography "seemed a little cold and monotonous, but done with good taste." The settings and costumes she found striking though simple, and Auric's music "made a strong impression."[17] Ivor Guest reviewed *Phèdre* for the English periodical, *Ballet*. He found a number of problems with the production:

> *Phèdre*, termed a "choreographic tragedy" in the programme, contains comparatively little dancing, being a translation of the Racine tragedy into silent movement rather than a ballet. The combination of Lifar, Cocteau and Auric, has produced such a wealth of content that only a tithe is absorbed at first sight; and the plot of the tragedy has been so compressed that a foreknowledge of it is essential in order to fully appreciate the work. Dominating everything is the character of Phèdre, conceived in tones of stark, unrelieved tragedy, and played by Toumanova with a superb authority and the intensity of a Rachel.[18]

These reservations were echoed by the French critics as well but despite such comments the ballet proved to be a success. It was taken to London by the Paris Opéra in 1954 and was still as controversial as it had been four years before, which must have pleased Cocteau.

Peter Williams noted in 1954, "no two people seem to agree about *Phèdre*, those who don't like it say it is too long, and [that] it never gives the feeling of overwhelming tragedy." Williams thought the key to the ballet lay in Cocteau's explanation: "A myth is a myth because poets take it up again through the ages and keep it alive." One had to look at *Phèdre* through the eyes of Cocteau, Williams said, and accept his interpretation:

> More than anyone else in this century, Cocteau has kept classic tragedy alive. In plays, in films, and in the ballet, he has twisted these ancient myths and histories until they fit comfortably into a modern frame. . . . Where Cocteau left off and Lifar started will possibly never be revealed but the programme tells us that the book and designs are by Cocteau, the choreography by Lifar and the music by Georges Auric. If I found it an absorbing and gripping work, I can still see that it has many faults, especially in the unfolding of the narrative. It is not easy to convey in terms of the dance, a woman's burning passion for her stepson who when she finds that he loves another and that her husband (reported dead) still lives, then accuses her stepson of attempted seduction. Nobody other than Martha Graham could realize the full impact of such a tragedy so that the onlooker becomes embroiled in it like in Cinerama. Lifar-Cocteau's characters are like puppets which you look at through a thick wall of glass. But there is no denying that the whole makes very good theatre.[19]

Figure 23. Tamara Toumanova in Costume for *Phèdre*, 1950
Décor and costumes by Cocteau.
Photograph by Serge Lido.
(Courtesy of the Stravinsky-Diaghilev Foundation)

Williams thought that the use of the small Greek stage to reveal tableaux of another scene happening elsewhere or to show the allegorical figures who control the destinies of the characters involved, only confused the issues and those who did not know the story. This complaint was not voiced by many French critics who found the use of the small stage helpful in the explanation of the plot, though they did assume the audience would have a prior knowledge of the story. Most of the French critics had reprimanded Lifar for his weak use of the corps de ballet when the ballet first opened, but Williams found the use of the corps "to reveal by their actions the nature of the principal character" quite effective. However, Lifar's use of the corps as stage effects, such as representing the rising sea at the command of Neptune, was seen by both French and English critics to be not as impressive as it could have been.[20]

It is interesting to record some of the critical reaction to Auric's score, especially in light of Lifar's many pronouncements on the subject. "We do not dance music but only the rhythmic pattern which is its foundation," was one of his most controversial dictums. David Hunt felt that Auric had actually given Lifar more than he had bargained for:

> From internal evidence *Phèdre* would seem to have been created in accordance with Lifar's aesthetic theories first outlined in 1935 in his *Manifeste du Chorégraphe* and the highly organized polyrhythmic ground plan of Auric's fascinating score invented not by the composer, but dictated by the choreographer. Be this as it may, as was the case with the gamelon-like percussive accompaniment for *Icare*, the rich complexity of Auric's rhythmic scheme gives unlimited opportunities for dance invention—far too many opportunities in fact than Lifar has cared to use. And grafted on to this ever-changing rhythmic and metrical framework is an equally highly organized tonal structure. Strong influences are heard throughout of *Le Sacre du Printemps* and the more sadistic sections of Strauss's *Elektra*.[21]

Hunt goes on to compliment Auric on a score that is "powerful, heady stuff, a violent, writhing snake pit of sound that piles climax on dynamic climax." He felt that Auric's music helped give the ballet its tragic quality without hampering pace and momentum. The close conjunction of Auric's music with Cocteau's scenario was of crucial importance in the creation of this ballet. Auric had already done scores for a number of Cocteau's films, notably *La Belle et la bête* and *Orphée*, and the last mentioned was released the same year as *Phèdre* was presented. Cocteau wrote more a screenplay than a ballet scenario—he himself admitted that this was his approach—and Auric wrote his music in very cinematic terms: there are very few places where one can find the typical short dance structures of the traditional ballets. Auric's and Cocteau's work dictated how Lifar could choreograph the ballet since the scenario was episodic and the music was reflective of the principal emotional feelings of Cocteau's *découpage*. It also would limit the use of the corps de ballet, which Lifar probably did not mind. He himself stated it was Cocteau's idea to involve the corps more by using them as commentary on the action, like a Greek chorus. Lifar felt justified in his minimal

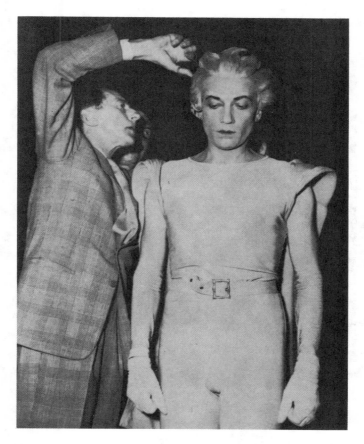

Figure 24.   Cocteau Adjusting and Cutting the Wig on Serge Lifar for
Phèdre, 1950
Photograph by Lipnitzki.
(Private Collection)

Figure 25. The Inner Stage for *Phèdre*, 1950
Designs by Cocteau for the Paris Opéra production.
Photograph by Serge Lido.
(*Courtesy of the Stravinsky-Diaghilev Foundation*)

use of the corps since, within the confines of a Greek tragedy, they would only reflect or comment on the main characters' actions.[22]

French critics have continued to consider the ballet important, both in terms of Lifar's oeuvre and French ballet in general. Jean Laurent and Julie Sazonova in a book published in 1960, *Serge Lifar, Renovateur du Ballet français*, thought that while the *Phèdre* of Racine emphasized pathos, the *Phèdre* of Cocteau and Lifar focused on the erotic and made Phèdre more an egoist. "She plunges into her desires without thought of others," they stated, and they related the scenario with Cocteau's other works, making a parallel between the brother and sister in *Les Enfants terribles*.[23] The authors felt that both Cocteau and Lifar, being "poets," blended their work well together, and they supported this view with a detailed analysis of the connection of certain choreographic combinations with Cocteau's character delineation in his scenario. The book is obviously slanted towards a justification of Lifar and his work, as even the title states, and therefore places much of the blame for the weakness in the ballet on Cocteau's episodic scenario and the difficulty of conveying the inner emotions of the characters through choreography alone.

Pierre Michaut gave a more balanced account and analysis of the production in *Le Ballet contemporain*, published in 1950. Admitting that Cocteau's *découpage* for *Phèdre* was obviously influenced by his work in film and interest in Greek mythology, he did not feel that such influences hampered the ballet. Cocteau, he declared, had constructed a scenario of psychological drama that held great dance potential. The use of the inner stage for "signs from Destiny, messages from the gods to the mortals below" was important not only to clarify the action but to stress the inevitability of human nature. The little temple itself symbolized "unity and harmony, stability and serenity" of the universe, despite human attempts to change the course of events. The vehemence and violence of the myth set against the eternal, both natural (the sea and sky) and metaphysical (the gods or fates). Michaut further noted that the ballet was "incontestably intense and riveting" for the spectator and speculated, as many had, on the division of labor between Cocteau and Lifar. He also wondered how the ballet might have evolved if Cocteau had been given fuller control over the work; as it was, the result was certainly "one of Lifar's better ballets."[24]

And most critics agreed with Michaut on this analysis. The ballet remained in the repertoire, even when Lifar stopped dancing and Toumanova left for other engagements. It was revived in 1959 when Toumanova returned for six more performances and critics were still impressed with the power of the piece. It was revived again in 1977 when the directors of the Paris Opéra decided to honor Lifar with the presentation of three of his works: *Les Mirages, Suite en Blanc (Noir et Blanc)*, and *Phèdre*. Marie-Françoise Christout thought the revival was done very well and that *Phèdre* treated in bold lines, this choreographic tragedy reflects well on that auspicious conjunction of talents [Cocteau, Auric, Lifar]. Today no doubt we see better than then the importance of this or that part of a work which influenced an epoch. As often with Lifar, the corps de ballet is sacrificed to the soloists, all accent being put on the heroes, notably the title part.[25]

The settings and costumes were still considered striking by most contemporary reviewers while the music seems to have suffered with time—one critic called it "bloated though not disagreeable romanticism."[26] There were cast changes in the leads for this revival and many critics noted how much the ballet depended on the right dance-actors in the principal parts, since the demands of the scenario and the choreographic structure made it a *ballet d'action* rather than a *danse d'école.*[27]

Despite Lifar's unwillingness to be supervised by Cocteau, they remained friends and respected each other's work. Cocteau was accustomed to protégés rebelling from his power—witness Radiguet during the 1920s—and easily forgave or forgot, if the other party was willing. As Lifar was neither a protégé nor a young inexperienced choreographer as Babilée and Petit had been, Cocteau was probably not too surprised that Lifar wanted full control of the ballet the moment he was brought in to choreograph it. Although disappointed that he had not been more involved, Cocteau was not resentful. It is not surprising, however, that Lifar and Cocteau did not immediately seek each other out for further collaboration. Their next work together took place nearly seven years later at the request of the ballerina Claude Bessy (b. 1932).

The stunningly beautiful Bessy, a French dancer who quickly became one of the leading prima ballerinas of the Paris Opéra during the 1950s, was asked to perform for H. S. H. Prince Rainier of Monaco at a gala scheduled for November of 1957. Bessy decided that Cocteau's play *Le Bel indifférent (The Handsome Hunk)* had possibilities as a dance-drama and approached the poet in revising the piece for her.

Le Bel indifférent was written in the same mode as *La Voix humaine*, as a showpiece for a particular actress's qualities, except this time the play was tailored for Edith Piaf. In *La Voix humaine* the actress was presented alone on stage talking to her lover on the phone and the implication of the play is the end of an affair; in *Le Bel indifférent* the plot was nearly identical except that the female protagonist speaks to the man directly, who is present on stage, though he never speaks during the woman's entire monologue. Premiering at the Bouffes Parisiens in 1940, it gave "la môme Piaf" one of the most celebrated vehicles, especially as she would usually cast her most recent male companion in the role of the disinterested lover.[28] Cocteau found no problem in shaping his play into a ballet scenario: the jealous, inquiet, amorous and vain girl desiring the man who is muted, indifferent and finally sick of her presence and leaves her.

Bessy asked Lifar to choreograph the ballet, and Max Bozzoni (b. 1917), also a dancer at the Paris Opéra, was asked to play the indifferent man. A special score was commissioned from the young French composer Richard Blareau (b. 1910) and décors were done by Félix Labisse (b. 1900) who had worked mostly in theatre and opera. The set he designed was shaped from a series of folding screens that represented a sordid hotel and, unintentional or not, the color of the chamber was red, Cocteau's favored hue for the presentation of his tortured heroines. The challenge for Lifar as choreographer was considerable since he had to convey the man's taciturnity in the traditionally silent world of dance. The contrast in the original play between the talkative female and soundless male would have to be conveyed in a different way for the dance-drama. Lifar approached the problem by making the female movement aggressive and the male technically responsive though emotionally vapid. For example, when Bessy would lunge at Bozzoni he would catch her, as a partner would do in a ballet, but his demeanor never showed the slightest concern for her; it was the exact reversal of the presentation of the ballerina by the *premier danseur* in the traditional *pas de deux* of classical ballet.[29]

The curtain rose on Bessy smoking and sitting on her bed listening to an Edith Piaf recording—a Cocteau touch in hommage to the drama's original leading lady. She is dressed in a simple dark leotard and fish net stockings, her hair is loose, and she wears no jewelry. She stops the recording and becomes even more impatient; she is obviously waiting for someone who is late. She turns to her telephone and frantically phones to one of the bistros which her lover Jules often frequents. When she hangs up, she goes to the window and looks out, waiting for his arrival. Jules comes in, blasé, his hat cocked jauntily on his head; he is dressed in a dark pinstripe shirt and white tie with dark trousers, his coat is slung over his shoulder. A long extended *pas de deux* then occurs during which the woman pleads, cajoles and reproaches her recalcitrant lover while he shuns her advances and her desperate clinging gestures. Cocteau indicates that her whole feeling should be like a Parisian phrase: *elle se cramponne* [she is like a clinging vine]. He also indicates she is like a "red archangel"—once more using his favored color for his heroines—and by that he means she is very beautiful, though passionate. Lifar's choreography for Bessy gave her much scope for such an interpretation with pictorial emphasis placed on her long legs. At the end of the ballet she clings to her lover's knees in a last desperate maneuver to keep him but, tearing her away, he slings his coat on his shoulders and leaves the room. She is left to her loneliness and despair as the curtain descends "like a mortuary drape on her soul."[30]

Le Bel indifférent has many connections with *Le Jeune homme et la mort*: the lonely squalid room, the smoking figure waiting desperately for the indifferent lover and the final rejection. This time, however, the roles are reversed and the female is the prey of the man, though not to the extent of the onstage suicide in *Le Jeune homme*, though one could assume that this might happen to the desperate girl after the curtain fell on *Le Bel indifférent*. In terms of technique, as well as acting requirements, it was quite a tour de force for Bessy and all the reviews compliment her stunning portrayal and Bozzoni as well; the ballet was called a "danced Utrillo" by one commentator.[31]

Although the ballet was devised as a "pièce d'occasion" it was sufficiently successful at the gala that it was later brought to Paris where it opened, with the same cast, at the Opéra-Comique on 25 April 1958. As a vehicle for Bessy it was much admired, but not looked at as more than a vehicle. Cocteau's involvement had been minimal since he only had to shape a scenario from one of his already existing plays. He did, though, indicate character development, colors, and suggestions for the set in his scenario, which were followed by the choreographer and designer.

Neither *Phèdre* nor *Le Bel indifférent* can be considered outstanding contributions to the balletic repertoire, although they fill the requirements as star vehicles. *Phèdre*, at least, had some interesting stage devices such as the use of the inner stage and the symbolic use of color in the costuming, but much was hampered by a complicated scenario. It was not until Cocteau's next ballet that the potential shown in *Phèdre* was fully realized.

8

La Dame à la licorne

Luxury is now second-class; the luxury of travel. The only really valuable luxury is the luxury of the spirit, which money cannot shackle and which all classes are forever pretending they want.
—Jean Cocteau, *Le Luxe spirituel est le seul qui nous reste*

Throughout the early 1950s Cocteau became less and less enchanted with Paris. It had lost the joy, the life, and the sparkle it had for him before the war. Its new cultural foibles left a bitter taste on his palate. He moved out of the capital and made infrequent trips to the city he had once worshipped and adored. He was further alienated in 1952, when Paris greeted his narration for Stravinsky's *Oedipus Rex* with great hostility. This performance was on 19 May when, according to Cocteau, he was "reconciled" with Stravinsky. Cocteau had originally written the narration and text for Stravinsky's Opera-Oratorio in 1926. It was first performed as a birthday present for Diaghilev at the Théâtre Sarah Bernhardt on 30 May 1927. Diaghilev had not been impressed by the tribute, calling it a "very macabre gift."[1] Cocteau had reserved the part of the narrator for himself, which he performed once again at this 1952 revival at the Théâtre des Champs-Elysées. In honor of the occasion, Cocteau designed settings and masks to be worn by dancers borrowed from Roland Petit's Ballet de Paris, who were to enact a series of seven *tableaux vivants*, while Cocteau recited the speeches from a platform above the orchestra. Originally Petit was to choreograph these sections but Cocteau decided to direct it himself, since he felt his goal was "to avoid killing the ear [Stravinsky's music] by the eye. I had to be violent, paying regard to the monstrosity of the myth."[2] Although he insisted he was not directly influenced by Noh drama for this revival, he did state that the Japanese had shown him the importance of the economy of gesture, which could so enhance a pictorial concept. Also, of course, Cocteau was better able to stage *tableaux*, rather than moving choreographic scenes, and this may have also been an underlying reason for his decision.

Cocteau designed masks so that they could be seen from underneath, "ears, noses, and mouths made of cork and wire, hair of raffia and eyes stuck on at the end of cornets and sticks, as in the *Opium* drawings, the whole contraptions sometimes bristling with Ping-Pong balls painted red. The curtain too was in the style of the *Opium* illustrations, being an enlargement of Cocteau's painting *Le Carrefour des deux routes*, all of which added to the macabre violence of the drama."[3] The dancers did not seem to mind wearing these elaborate masks and enjoyed working with Cocteau. George Reich, an American dancer then with the Ballet de Paris, played Anubis and remembered Cocteau as "a quietly brilliant man, far ahead of his time. He'd make you feel anything you said was something to be taken seriously."[4]

The first night of this semi-staged work went well but on the second night, when they were recording Cocteau's voice for the subsequent album, the audience erupted in a demonstration against Cocteau. There is some debate as to what actually happened, but the incident only confirmed that Cocteau, whether he liked it or not, was still controversial.[5] Rather than accepting the enmity with the glee he would have shown in the 1920s or 1930s Cocteau now left for a tour of Germany with very definite feelings: he was determined that his next creative endeavor would not be premiered in Paris nor would he cater to its xenophobic cultural elitism.

His tour of Germany during 1952 was a pleasant change for Cocteau. The Germans showed great enthusiasm for his plays, his writings, and his drawings and treated him royally everywhere he went. While in Bavaria Cocteau met Dr. Wilhelm Kein, the cultural minister for Bavaria, who asked Cocteau to create a work for one of the Bavarian Staatstheatres. Cocteau accepted, but only on the condition that the piece should be a ballet and that he would be allowed to pick both the choreographer and the dancers. He, himself, would write the scenario, design sets and costumes, choose the composer, and supervise the final rehearsals. What surprised Kein was the name of the choreographer Cocteau chose. It was not a Frenchman like Lifar or Petit but a German working in Switzerland, Heinz Rosen (1908–1972).[6]

This rekindling of interest in ballet was not a spur of the moment decision for Cocteau nor was Rosen's name pulled out of the blue. Rosen, who was born in Hanover and had studied with Rudolph Laban and Kurt Jooss, had performed in such modern classics as *The Green Table* and *The Big City*, dance compositions by the latter choreographer. Germany was closed to Rosen during the war due to his political feelings and he accepted a position as soloist and balletmaster in Zurich, then Basle.[7] Rosen began to choreograph while in Switzerland and his ballets began to be noticed by the European dance world. Cocteau had seen pictures of these works in the magazine *Picture Post* and was immediately struck by the young man's style, invention and pictorial creativity. He invited Rosen to Paris and met him in 1951 during the final rehearsals for his play *Bacchus*. Rosen himself was somewhat in awe at this first meeting with the sophisticated *enfant terrible*:

We sat opposite each other, the shyness—mine—disappeared quickly. This first meeting, which ought to have lasted five minutes, ran to one and a half hours. We wanted to discuss ballet, and we talked of countless things, art, philosophy, politics—Cocteau's statements seemed to me to be the essence of year-long ponderings, seasoned by French *esprit*, bubbling like champagne, yet cool and precise, never allowing the vacuum of an intended vagueness behind which, one would have had to assume, lay an unjustifiable profundity.

Our second meeting—before one of the final rehearsals for *Bacchus*—took place in the Théâtre Marigny. Cocteau directed the production, as well as designing his own sets and costumes. He had just come from a studio outside of Paris where he had spent the morning dubbing one of his films. Casually, he related to me that in the night he had had this basic idea for the ballet and had drawn a few initial sketches. After the rehearsal he stood alone on the stage till 4:00 A.M. and touched up the painting of the sets which seemed to him not to be "just right."

The next meeting was in "Le Grand Véfour" restaurant, one of the oldest in Paris. Robespierre had eaten there, Fragonard died there—Balzac wrote some of his novels there—it was the "regular" bar/restaurant of Bérard, the great painter and designer who was a protégé of Cocteau's. He, himself, sat in a chair on the back of which was emblazoned "Napoleon I," behind my wife's back was written, "Josephine."

Choicest French cuisine; stimulating conversation—ballet was the main topic. Cocteau demanded a piece of paper; he was given a menu, designed by Bérard. Cocteau's unicorns mingled with Bérard's Parisian ladies; the centuries flowed together in an atmosphere that only a genius can create.[8]

Cocteau had obviously had ideas about the ballet for some time, despite his casual presentation to Rosen. He himself admitted there were always a million ideas floating in his head waiting for the right moment to come out. He introduced Rosen to a life totally new to the German dancer, but one in which Cocteau was comfortably at home. Who else would casually sketch unicorns on a hand-designed menu?

Rosen visited Cocteau again after the theatre season and enjoyed a holiday with him in Cape Ferrat and on the Mediterranean. This second meeting took place immediately after Cocteau's first German tour in 1952, when he had received the commission from Dr. Kein. He was very tired but he was enthusiastic about working with Rosen on the new piece. The "holiday" turned into a work session:

Here [in Cape Ferrat], in a few weeks, the ballet libretto grew out of the basic idea. We met every 2nd day. I wrote up the results of our conversations, sent it to Cocteau, his ideas mixed in with my suggestions, and each time we met we exchanged our thoughts about it; whether the work needed further polishing or the story line needed further clarification and continuity. Then each of us would exchange the results of his considerations. From the notes and the meetings I formed the basis for the conversations we would hold the day after. That our conversations did not remain solely with ballet was perfectly natural with Cocteau, whose personality and creativity is so all-embracing that he has no match with any other living poet, painter, director or designer.[9]

Cocteau was the "stimulus" for Rosen but Cocteau's ideas had not been reached on the spur of the moment, despite the traditionally casual attitude that he always showed throughout his life.

The source of inspiration for Cocteau was the famous Cluny tapestries in Paris. Here, in a round medieval-like chamber of the ruined monastary on the Place Luxembourg, a series of beautiful and mysterious 15th-century tapestries depict, in six panels, a young maiden with a lion and a unicorn in a richly embroidered background of flowers, animals, and plants set in a glowing red weave by the Gobelin Factory. The series always went by the name *La Dame à la licorne* and the meaning of all six has always remained ambiguous.[10] The enigma of the lady and her unicorn appealed to the imagination of Cocteau and the mythology of romance was easily transferred to a ballet idiom while the setting appealed to his sense of history, which had recently been awakened to the Medieval and Renaissance worlds. His earlier plays *Orphée* and *La machine infernale* had been set in the ancient worlds, but his most recent works such as *Bacchus* and *Les Chevaliers de la table ronde*, as well as the film *La Belle et la bête* were based on the later epochs. *La Dame* offered the appealing combination of the fairytale world of *La Belle* and the Medieval romance ethos of *Les Chevaliers*.

Before detailing Cocteau's version of the story and its balletic transformation, it is important to investigate both the origin of the legend of "The Lady with the Unicorn" and the mystery of the Cluny tapestries.[11]

Around the end of the 13th and beginning of the 14th centuries, one finds traces of a ballad entitled "La Dame à la Lycorne et du biau Chevalier au lyon" [The Lady with the Unicorn and the handsome Knight of the Lion]. The song may have been based on a legend of the daughter of the King of Friesland who was so good, pure and chaste, that the god of Love—or Christ, depending on the version—granted her a pure white unicorn so she might eternally be known as "The White Lady, Ward of the Unicorn." Though the lady was married she bestows her favors platonically on a knight who has neither fame nor fortune but goes out to win honor and renown in her name. He earns the appellation "the Knight of the Lion" due not only to his brave nature, but his ability to tame and ride a wild lion. After many adventures, in which an evil magician captures the lady and the knight must rescue her, they escape from the villain's castle, the lady riding on her unicorn, the knight on his lion, to search for new adventures and to do charitable deeds. The nature of the two lovers remains, throughout, chaste.[12]

Though the legend is the basis for Cocteau's scenario, the legend is not the story behind the tapestries, which were his visual inspiration. The Cluny tapestries may, according to recent experts, represent the five senses of smell, hearing, touch, taste, and sight, with the sixth anything from dedication to perseverance. In the tapestry entitled "sight" the lady holds a mirror up to the unicorn, who is seen reflected in the glass. Cocteau, who always had a fascination for mirrors and used them constantly as a leitmotif in his plays, movies, and other creations, seized upon this pose and used it as the first view of the lady with her unicorn. He expanded on the theme by incorporating the mirror as a very integral part of the plot when the unicorn later sees his lady—and the knight—in the mirror. The tapestry known as "dedication" was the basis for Cocteau's set, since it is the only one of the six tapestries to have a tent as the focal set piece. This tapestry also included the mysterious dedication in a banner which wraps around the tent: "MON SEUL DESIR V." There are a number of theories as to what "My Only Desire" may mean, as well as the symbolic purpose of the "V" but Cocteau was not concerned with such speculations.[13] He uses the banner as a final drop, an enigmatic statement on the lady, on love, on his ballet. He purposely ends with a question.

In one tapestry there is a young unicorn just sprouting its horn; Cocteau expanded this concept to open his ballet with a flock of the young creatures. The curtain rises on them awakening, then dancing and then pulling aside the flaps of the tent to reveal the lady, the mirror and her white unicorn. The knight appears riding on a lion, as in the legend above, and the unicorns run off, frightened. He finds the lady staring in the mirror and imposes himself on her image, thus entering her world—foisting his reality on her fantasy. The white unicorn runs off and the knight woos the lady in a passionate *pas de deux*. They leave together, embracing. The white unicorn comes on looking for his mistress but does not find her; what he does see is the lady and the knight in his lady's mirror, and within the same mirror two other couples, all dressed alike. The three pairs dance lovingly, much to the animal's horror. Cocteau actually had precedents for such variations on the legend, for in one stanza of the medieval ballad the knight is tempted by the evil magician when three ladies are shown in a magic mirror and the lady is given the same test in the villain's castle. In the Cluny tapestries not one of the six woven women are the same but each is a different lady; there is no continuity of form or figure in the series. Cocteau may have also been fascinated with variations in these art works.[14]

In the ballet the unicorn then thrusts his horn through the mirror and breaks the image. In Cocteau's stage directions the on-stage orchestra—a trio placed on a platform on one side—makes a shattering sound as if glass was breaking. Cocteau also stated that this represented "the deflowering of the maiden."[15] When the lady returns, the unicorn will accept neither food nor affection from his former mistress and after a "dance of death," the mythical beast dies. The knight—who reenters without the lion—cannot regain the lady he has so thoughtlessly seduced and abandoned, and the lady is left alone watching the other little unicorns carry their comrade into the woods. The lady, alone in front of her tent, is frozen in motion as the banner lowers and curls around her head. The lights fade until only the motto "MON SEUL DESIR" and the lady's hand are seen as the curtain slowly descends.

Cocteau was not the first to be inspired by the aura of romance that sur-

Figure 26.   *La Dame à la licorne*, 1953
The Lady (Geneviève Lespagnol) with The Knight
(Boris Trailine) in the Munich production.
(Photograph Courtesy of the Bayerische Staatstheater)

rounded the tapestries, rediscovered by the novelist Prosper Mérimée (1803–1870) in 1847 when he had found them mouldering and abandoned in a provincial chateau.[16] Proust had written about them and Rainer Maria Rilke (1875–1926) had included references to them in his *Sonnets to Orpheus*, published in 1923. Cocteau was a great admirer of Rilke's work (as was Rilke of Cocteau's oeuvre) and the *Sonnets* had already inspired Cocteau's play *Orphée*, produced in 1925. Now Cocteau turned to the same work but for a different reason: Rilke's poetic image of the unicorn which is seen as a pure production of the human soul, freed of all the dross of a curious and frequently chaotic history. In a revealing letter to the Countess Sizzo, Rilke had said "all love is unauthenticated and intangible, all credence in the value and authenticity of what our mind has through the ages created from itself and placed on a pedestal."[17] Cocteau echoed this in his ballet scenario, "where love dies when innocence is lost."[18] Cocteau took this love placed on a pedestal and transformed it in his own fashion, since in neither legend nor tapestry is there any suggestion of the deflowering of the maiden, nor the death of the little white unicorn, although it is part of the general unicorn myth that the animal could only be fed by a virgin. In the Medieval-Renaissance ethos, the virgin was always of aristocratic or royal birth.[19]

Cocteau, though, did not limit himself to the chivalric tone of the legend; there is much in the ballet that belongs to the nineteenth-century ballet tradition which evoked a fairy tale world of German mysticism. At the same time it was a twentieth-century comment on the Romantic approach. Rosen, in an interview at the ballet's premiere, noted the careful romantic strictures Cocteau had placed on the ballet and said his choreography followed these strictures, "in point of view from the scenario—the first romantic ballet since *Swan Lake*. The style of the production I would like to describe as neoclassical. . . ."[20]

For the music Cocteau turned to Dr. Jacques Chailley (1890–1961), Professor of Music at the Sorbonne and editor of the *La Revue internationale de musique*. Chailley took airs and dances of the fifteenth and sixteenth centuries and carefully orchestrated them, piecing them together to fit Cocteau's scenario. In choosing the melodies Chailley tried to fit the themes of the music to the characters involved, even carrying a leitmotif, such as the fifteenth-century chanson "Le Grand Désir" for the Lady, and "Amour de Moi" for the dance of the Lady and the Knight when he intrudes upon her mirror world. The seduction takes place to a sequence of an English pavane and galliarde, while a stately Spanish pavane was found appropriate for the funeral of the White Unicorn. Cocteau also wanted a small stage band which kept the audience aware of the theatricality of the piece and became a reminder of the present, a court orchestra in twentieth-century dress. Chailley had to devise music for this band that, while still composed of the airs and chansons, had a contemporary sound "like musical commentators on the spectacle presented for the audience."[21] Nor is Cocteau's modern symbolism out of place in a period piece since the legend and tapestries themselves are laden with symbolic meaning and hidden references. The courtly ideal of love always included an allegorical approach to the subject with both literate and often political allusions. The Cocteau twist here is the destruction of this world as the Lady loses her power over the mythical beast and her place in the myth itself when she discovers the reality of a sensual appetite that has no place in the platonic ideals of the legend.

With the music written and the sketches for the designs in hand Rosen went to Bavaria to begin work on the ballet. Rosen, of course, was invited as a guest choreographer in Munich and must have been somewhat nervous working with an unfamiliar company in new surroundings. Cocteau, though unable to arrive until practically the final dress week, was still very much in evidence during the rehearsal period. Letters to Rosen were continually arriving, explaining, clarifying his thoughts, directing him from afar. "All the ballet's lighting," one letter stated, "must never be diffuse, *white* spotlights should follow all the characters, others directed upon specific points. The spots—highly concentrated and very lively—should allow the characters to come out of the shadows." On costuming and the realization of his designs Cocteau insisted "the costume material should not be cheap and the colors should be strong. Go to Mme. Frousseau [the head cutter] and refer in everything to my special idea. In no case should silk tricots be used for the unicorns. The material must be dull [non-shining]." Later Cocteau had an idea for the climax of the ballet and quickly wrote to Rosen: "It would be good if the unicorn—after it has seen the knight's face in the mirror—would attack the mirror with its horn; there should be a noise that sounds like smashing glass. The horn bores slowly into the mirror . . . after this the unicorn dances its death—just like the 'Dying Swan.'"[22]

The ballet was scheduled for six weeks of rehearsal beginning the last week in March, and as Rosen was also invited to stage his ballet *L'Indifférent* for the same program, he had to divide his time between the two ballets. Cocteau wanted French dancers for the leads in *La Dame* and sent Geneviève Lespagnol and Boris Trailine (b. 1921) of the Ballet Russe de Monte Carlo to play the Lady and her Knight, while Rosen found a young girl in the corps de ballet to play the little white unicorn, Veronika Mlakar (b. 1935), a young Yugoslavian whose parents were both dancers. Cocteau arrived in Munich on 1 May and immediately began to supervise and rework the ballet, but there were a number of problems and the opening was delayed until they could be ironed out. While all of this was going on Munich courted Cocteau and was excited and honored to have the famous French poet in their midst. One newspaper expressed the hope that his presence "would bring Munich and the Gartnerplaz [the theatre where the ballet was premiering] into the ballet festivals."[23] Cocteau granted a number of interviews while in Munich and explained his concept of the ballet and how it had evolved. He called the ballet "a kind of French Guinevere legend in modern form. As in my film *Orphée* the focal point is a mirror. The image of him who last looked in it remains captured therein." Cocteau also explained that the theme of the piece was "virginity; a virginity that loses its poetic love when it discovers profane love."[24]

Cocteau continued to supervise everything: the cuttings of his costumes, the painting of his sets, the choreography of his story. Unlike the Ballets Russes people, no one in Munich seems to have minded Cocteau's interference, but welcomed his suggestions and encouragement. In Rosen's case the young German seems to have been a willing tool in the Frenchman's hands; he was only a guest choreographer in Munich and the city was honoring Cocteau, not him, so he may have had no choice. However, if he disagreed with any of Cocteau's suggestions or supervision he never said so, even when he had established himself in later years. Later, when Rosen was highly respected as ballet master in Munich, he always expressed his thankfulness to Cocteau for having helped him in his career. Also, whenever he revived or staged La Dame à la licorne he always scrupulously consulted Cocteau even though he no longer needed to do so. Cocteau repaid the compliment by leaving all the drawings, designs and rights to the ballet to Rosen and his family. One must assume that, unlike the relationship of Nijinska and Cocteau, Rosen and Cocteau worked very well together. Ten years after the premiere of La Dame, Cocteau wrote that Rosen "took my plan and gave it its final and moving form" and "his feverish yet calm occupation [for the dance] lends a grace to every sequence of movement. Dance is one of the noblest forms of poetic expression and Rosen gives of himself in the art, throwing his gold dust out of windows of a poor and painful world."[25] Cocteau's direct work on La Dame in those last weeks was probably welcomed by all involved since not only his expertise but his sense of the theatrical would help in making the composition a viable and exciting dance piece.

The ballet finally opened at the Gartner Theatre on 9 May 1953 in front of a gala audience composed of international celebrities. It must have reminded Cocteau of the Diaghilev Ballets Russes openings when the crème-de-la-crème appeared for the Russian impresario. Now they were all appearing for him. All the newspapers reported the event:

> It was an indescribably stimulating evening . . . Jean Cocteau, at present quarreling with his paternal and favorite city—Paris—presented Munich with the world premiere of his ballet La Dame à la licorne. So that a little of Notre Dame remained, he brought his solo dancers with him. . . .
>
> With Cocteau's arrival in Munich, a general, longed for and delightful madness began: the costumes and decor had to be altered, the premiere was postponed, a solo dancer became ill, the fight for first night tickets shook Munich's society to its roots.
>
> The Gartnerplatz Theatre, usually accustomed to the lightest of Muses and grateful bourgeoise audiences, housed, when the great hour came, an international audience; the French and Italian artistic colonies, the stars of the German theatre, and a circle of beautiful Parisian women in very striking gowns. The prize went to the 2nd last row of the orchestra—Dior's mannequins—at present in Munich for a fashion show. [This row of beautiful women reminds one of Diaghilev's

placing of the beauties of Paris as a *corbeille* on the first night of the Ballets Russes some forty years before.][26]

For this gala audience the curtain first rose on *L'Indifférent* and then, after the interval, the event all had been waiting for, *La Dame à la licorne*. The stark but striking set of greens and browns with the blue and red tent placed on a platform in front and the groupings of the white unicorns around the stage was what met the eyes of the expectant public. Every detail was Cocteau's, from the mood changes in the lighting to the makeup of the dancers, which he had designed and applied on them himself. The *Frankfurter Allegemeine Zeitung*, despite being impressed by the audience, had some reservations about the ballet:

> Above all this society brilliance one must not forget the actual event, the ballet of Paris' magician Cocteau. His idea—a white unicorn shimmering with innocence and utter naiveté kept by a lovely Lady [is quite] charming.
>
> The choreographic problems of this poetic gamble with reference to *La Belle et la bête* proved difficult to solve. The unicorn and his little junior unicorns wore spiral spikes on their foreheads, they hopped across the stage with little dog-like steps—more dance-like movements than dance. Most impressive was Veronika Mlakar's mastery of her role as the unicorn. She radiated the gentleness and innocence which the poet attributed to the role. Otherwise the affect of the ballet came not from the movement but rather from the images—the play of colors in the costumes and the transparent forest.
>
> Surprising, but of peculiar charm, was the idea of placing a trio on stage on a wooden platform from which the three bespectacled musicians, along with the orchestra, accompanied the Cocteau-esque *Midsummer Night's Dream*.[27]

The paper noted that everyone was stormily applauded, but Cocteau was the center of attention and adulation.

The *Suddeutsche Zeitung* called the ballet one of the most important events in the city's history and thought Cocteau's ballet "worthy to be called great." It also had some interesting views on Cocteau's surrealistic concept of the romantic vision:

> The ballet . . . has a simple plot which works poetically and convincingly and possesses atmosphere. This ballet will establish itself in stage repertoires like *Giselle* or *Coppélia*. Théophile Gautier's statement that a ballet is all the better "the more chimerical, fairy-tale-like, incredible" its subject is has been added to by Cocteau with one more qualification: the more surreal it is. . . . Seemingly quite natural real and surreal worlds are juxtaposed: here we have the stage musicians visibly one part of the whole, and as long as the red curtain of the tent remains closed and the seven little unicorns remain cowering silently on one side one could believe that this is theatre within theatre. Yet the scenario remains unified: even the stage musicians, the recorder, the gambist, and the harpist, in the midst of the dancers did not disturb me.[28]

The reviewer thought that the music gave the formal basis for the dances while "the sweetness of its harmonies creates the actual atmosphere of the piece." The reviewer also felt that Rosen used his choreographic invention well by limiting himself to a minimum of pantomime and dance formations that reflected the nobility of the characters involved. "The choreographic net is attuned to a delicate minor tonality" highly appropriate to Cocteau's "touching, romantic yet very modern masterpiece."

Helmut Schmidt-Garre in the *Münchener Merkur* thought Cocteau showed the world "a danced Original Sin" [*Sudenfall*] but thought much of the ballet remained "puzzling and mysterious, if not ambiguous" though even here the observer "instinctively senses what is right, when he can find no rational clarity in the happenings and symbols [devised] by Cocteau." The reviewer also felt the musicians underlined "the half-real, half-unreal existence in the legend and unreality of the scenario." As in all the reviews Schmidt-Garre raved about the young Mlakar over the performance of the guest artists. "Her death scene is a highlight of the choreography and the connecting funeral procession, through its silent ceremony, becomes a shattering lament of those creatures driven from Paradise yet ever longing to return." This *Sudenfall* was also symbolized for the reviewer by the "symbolically meaningful red velvet train" of the Lady with Cocteau's settings which were a "refined, atmospheric choreography of color and line." The whole ballet was a feast for the eyes as well as an "important contribution to the dance."[29] Although Cocteau makes no mention of a parallel with the parable of Original Sin and the Fall from Paradise, this meaning can certainly be read into the ballet and its symbolic design.

It is interesting to note that the other ballet of the evening, *L'Indifférent*, was also inspired by a museum piece, Watteau's painting of the same name. The poet Otto Maag had been the scenarist for this ballet, though Heinz Rode thought Cocteau knew how to mold a ballet from essentially static material much better than his German counterpart. Maag had also conceived and designed *L'Indifférent*. However, Rode felt there are problems when a literary poet deals with the visual and kinetic and he pointed this out with Cocteau and *La Dame à la licorne* as well:

> Accuracy is, however, not one of Cocteau's strong points. Whatever goes through his mill becomes literature, is pushed into the realm of refined acting, into the world of the French serial story, that is—to say it straight out—morbidness, which nevertheless can be very striking at moments or even charming, so that only later do we realize the tricks of this great magician. This ballet is the most genuine Cocteau. This friend of Picasso, this nervous, multiple stream man of Parisian cultural life who influences all and is influenced by so much, lights up with this theme of "Virginity." However, the Burgundian tapestry seems to shun choreographic invention and demonstration, within the context of this theme.
>
> The impression is fascinating, but not convincing. It seems as if the temperamental author has completely overridden the choreographer: obviously the intelligent Heinz Rosen (to whom Cocteau dedicates the ballet) would not have come up with [many of] the ideas seen on stage.[30]

The three musicians on stage for *La Dame à la licorne* were distracting for Rode, as well as the "hobbyhorse" lion that the knight had to wear. The white-faced

Figure 27. *La Dame à la licorne*, 1953
The Knight looks on as The Lady mourns her dead
Unicorn (Veronika Mlakar) in the Munich production.
(Photograph Courtesy of Bayerische Staatstheater)

knight, makeup styled by Cocteau after the Japanese theatrical tradition, Rode found out of place. Although the dancing was magnificent the reviewer thought eight white unicorns somewhat disconcerting. All of these observations are interesting as they foreshadow the same feelings from international reviewers when the ballet was taken in by other companies and toured the world.

However, for the German premiere most reviewers were rejoicing that "Cocteau had come to Munich." The *Düsseldorfer Nachrichten* thought that Cocteau's sets, costumes, and makeup were the *"non plus ultra* of good taste":

> Cocteau, who recognizes NO walls between the various intellectual pursuits and who can do without the usual craft codex of the respective artistic departments, sees in Ballet a summary of all the arts and the most appropriate means of expression for the imaginative and sensitive worlds of our day. . . . Cocteau's idea [for *La Dame*] is rooted in the deeper layers of the human psyche and plucks the finest branches of our beings, specifically yearning and sorrow, desire and renunciation.[31]

Walter Eicher, the author of this piece, became even more adulatory in a review for the *Abendzeitung*, noting how Cocteau had made this the "dance event of the season." "The French genius stands high on his victory chariot leading the triumph of art, of the art of the dance, throughout the world." Cocteau is quoted as seeing the dance as the one art with no barriers and the classical unicorn legend as a parable-like background for the world of "ethos and eros" which the poet creates on the stage. Eicher liked the idea of the musical trio on stage "in the middle of a mild yellow-green woodland scene setting on a rough-hewn podium" which created a charming contrast and allowed the stage and the orchestra to relate to one another; not keeping the two art forms separate from each other. Eicher thought the ballet "neoromantic" in tone since it used the German fairy tale tradition in a new and more modern sense: a background for the investigation of the inner workings of the soul, the desires of the heart. Despite all this rather high-flown rhetorical explanation for the ballet, Eicher found it difficult to define the meaning of the work. It is a "world of feeling and imagination with deceptive dance effects which follow upon groupings of moving beauty and spiritualized symbolism."[32]

The *Mannheimer Morgen* was not too concerned with meaning and thought the blending of Cocteau's scenario and Rosen's choreography was perfect, though dividing the credit for the inspiration rather strangely: "It seems to me impossible to imagine a stronger and finer union between the symbolic dance story—derived from the famous unicorn tapestry—and the choreography of Rosen which is derived from the fresco elements in the drapery [referring to the tapestry]." The author, Johann von Kalckreuth, felt that Cocteau had "created here a special dance-poem that, in spite of all metaphysical complications, speaks immediately to our minds and feelings." Cocteau, he wrote, left "unforgettable impressions for the eye, as lasting as a word or music drama." The author saw much symbolism in the colors of the costumes: the black and yellow of the Knight signifying male desire, the white of the unicorn symbolizing purity and the red train of the Lady combined with the white and purple dress a symbol of royalty and innocence conflicting with carnal desire. Kalckreuth concluded that Rilke would have been very pleased with this "poem for the eyes" since Rilke knew how to "laud ever so gently the unspotted animal of legend."[33] Such a parallel must have pleased Cocteau, who always admired the poems of Rilke.

The *Aachener Volkszeitung* stated Cocteau was "not so dependent on atmosphere and milieu as on a classically cool diction, an intellectual clarity of the fable and, at the same time, an aesthetic play of *couleurs et forme*." The author, Klaus Colberg, was actually surprised by the ballet and had expected something much more ornate from the hand of Cocteau:

> There was absolutely no ground for any extravagances which one might expect from Cocteau. He limited himself to a brief, distilled form of the libretto. Nothing more than the fable itself. Even the mirror of the unicorn comes from the tapestry (mirrors have always fascinated this master). He did not decorate this ballet with deeply psychological symbolism. Consequently one saw the ballet as a stylistic, intellectually transparent parable of chastity, around which hovered a gentle melancholy. The strong stylistic intention was noticeable in the music, dance, libretto, and setting. Also in the carefully colored decor and costumes which Cocteau designed himself.[34]

The reviewer was bothered by the on-stage musicians, thinking perhaps they had some symbolic reason for their presence as Orff had done with his *Midsummer Night's Dream*, but that the dancing was beautifully done and tastefully executed.

A Frankfurt reviewer was sent to Munich to see the premiere and he thought Cocteau had given the German ballet world a "new, enervating shot in the arm." This "cynic with the poetic heart has brought back poetry to the dance stage." Noting the strange, melancholic charm of the piece the reviewer, Claus Hardt, thought that by supervising the work Cocteau was able to hold sentiment in check through the extreme austerity of form: both in form of the libretto and form of the design. "The tent contrasted clearly in red and blue, behind which a transparent grey-green forest curtain is seen; there were no tricks or attempts at perspective-illusions." Cocteau himself had stated he wanted the ballet done in bright, primary colors and distinct, clear outlines, so Hardt's analysis is probably correct. Even though, at first glance, "the musicians, the set, the lights, are disconcerting as the ballet progresses they do not disturb but work together as a unit. Quite quickly even the skeptical observer notices the poetic unity—quite quickly Cocteau the magician works his magic."[35]

While all the reviews centered on Cocteau, the contributions of choreographer and dancers did not go unnoticed. What is of interest is the consistency of the reviews about Veronika Mlakar who stole the show from the visiting guest artist from Monte Carlo and was the "overnight" sensation of the ballet. *Der Mittag* from Dusseldorf spent most of its copy on her. Even the title of the article said "Munich ballet girl excelled herself":

> The major portion of the ecstatic final applause was not directed towards the dancers from Monte Carlo, whom Cocteau had brought for the two principal roles [Genevieve Lespagnol and Boris Traline] but rather "little" Veronika Mlakar—whose parents lead the ballet of the Bavarian Staatsoper. This young ballerina, who performed the role of the unicorn, succeeded in entering the secrets of creatures, into the innocence and dependence of animals, its touchingly ignorant blindness and her ability to make visible the genuine animal-like grace. The death of the unicorn . . . was able to move this audience of twentieth-century jades to astonished shock.[36]

Cocteau also saw her incredible ability both in terms of dancer and actress, even though the role required her to perform behind a full facemask of the unicorn. He quickly wrote to Roland Petit in Paris recommending both his ballet and the young girl. "I have included much of myself in the ballet," Cocteau said, "and together with Rosen's work I recommend to you the astonishing little unicorn Veronika Mlakar. It seems to me that this work ought to belong to a ballet company like yours."[37] Already Cocteau saw the possibilities of this work going further than Munich or even Germany and in this he was to be proved right. Mlakar also benefited since Petit did ask her to join his company and a number of works were created for her.

Cocteau was very pleased with both his reception and the welcome given to his ballet. Munich was a refreshing change from the problems and foibles of the Parisian public. From Munich he went to Cannes for the film festival and then returned to Paris. Once there he could not resist writing down his impression of the Munich dance public as compared to the Parisian dance world. The article is pervaded with a sense of bitterness and resignation from an older man who feels not that he is out of touch with the world but that the world is out of touch with him:

> After my return from Cannes and Munich I went to see one of my works featuring Edith Piaf. In the evening at the Théâtre Marigny I was able to establish once again the fact that the audience is split in two; those in the good seats who pay high prices, and those in the gallery who pay less but do not feel that it owes the artists any the less for that.
>
> In Munich, the audience, whether high or low, is the same. They have a reputation of "sitting on their hands" (so at least say the Munich residents), but whenever a work draws them out of this reserve they applaud gratefully. During the countless curtains after my ballet I congratulated myself on having created something for people who are still capable of enthusiasm. The women who were helping me finish the costumes hardly dared to cut the priceless materials. The painters who helped with the sets did not count their overtime, the audience applauded not with their hands but with their souls. I have experienced such a communion between work and auditorium only with *Orphée* in Berlin, *Bacchus* in Dusseldorf, and *Oedipus Rex* in Vienna.[38]

Figure 28.   Heinz Rosen, Cocteau, and Professor Rudolf Hartmann, 1953
Cocteau being welcomed to Munich by the choreographer
of *La Dame à la licorne* and the director of the State
Theaters.
(Photograph Courtesy of the Bayerische Staatstheater)

Of course, Cocteau felt his works were only truly appreciated in the German cities, not in France, just to twist the knife a little deeper in his fickle French public's collective heart.

He also noticed how Dior's mannequins, who had sat so beautifully at his premiere in Munich and were there for a fashion show, were also so warmly applauded by the German public because they and their clothes were so beautiful, not because they were jealous of the models or their outfits. In Paris, of course, it would have been just the opposite. Cocteau then came right to the point:

> I have been asked why, precisely, did I premiere *La Dame à la licorne* in Munich. The answer is simple: here at home [in Paris] the prices are so expensive that a work can never be brought to people who are worthy of it. . . . In the countries where life is not so expensive theatre still is a ceremony, a church open to all.

Obviously, Cocteau felt that Paris no longer went to theatre properly or could see works in their "simplicity . . . an unprejudiced public, a perfectly unbaised audience doesn't only judge the surprising . . . but also the ordinary."[39] Cocteau may certainly be right in his theory but even he could not honestly call the Munich audience "unbiased" when it catered to him and his every wish. It would have been very difficult for Cocteau to have created an out-and-out disaster when the public was so much on his side.

Cocteau still looked at the theatre as a ceremony and a ritual. He wanted to keep the magic of the theatre in the theatre and to do so one must always have a *visual* sense: the poetry of the eyes. To a friend, Milorad Miskovitch (b. 1928), who had sent him a ballet scenario soon after the premier of *La Dame*, he emphasized this ocular aspect of the dance. "It is always an essay of the eyes," Cocteau explained, "You must not ignore this secret of the dance. She is opposed to all intellectualism. A ballet is composed of the hands, the feet, but especially the eyes . . . the head enters a little to form the line of the composition."[40]

La Dame à la licorne proved to be a huge success in Germany and established Rosen as an important European choreographer. He was offered the position of ballet master in Munich and he readily accepted the job. Rosen was also invited to stage *La Dame* in other places around the world. In July of 1954 he presented it in Buenos Aires with an entirely Argentinian cast of young dancers: Irina Borowska (b. 1930) as the Lady, Olga Ferri (b. 1928) as the Unicorn, and Jose Neglia (1929–1971) as the Knight. It was received with great enthusiasm by both the company and the audiences.[41] The Ballet Russe de Monte Carlo, which was always desperately looking for new works to bolster its flagging repertoire, soon asked Cocteau and Rosen for permission to add the ballet to their company. Monte Carlo added the piece in the spring of 1956 before a long tour of the United States. In Chicago the sharp-tongued critic Claudia Cassidy, who rarely gave good reviews to anything, liked it—though with appropriate reservations.

"A most Parisian ballet," she stated, and wrote "Once you get the focus and cut out the irritations, you get a fascinating glimpse of the fecund, febrile mind that is Cocteau."[42]

However, it was not until the summer of 1957 that Monte Carlo finally brought the work to New York to premiere at the Metropolitan Opera House. Irina Borowska repeated her role of the Lady she had danced in Buenos Aires and Igor Youskevitch (b. 1912) played the Knight. The young Polish dancer Nina Novak (b. 1927) was cast as the little Unicorn. Although advance publicity spoke of the ballet as "a rarity for the twentieth-century: a ballet of mood and atmosphere,"[43] the reviews in general were very negative towards the work.

Doris Hering, writing in *Dance Magazine*, thought the ballet started out "promisingly, but soon dissipated into a series of pseudo-Freudian symbolism in place of dance invention." She did not, though, lay all the blame on the choreography. "The ballet's principal problem was its point of view. It was an image of innocence choreographed without innocence, a depiction of a Medieval religious and moral point of view without honest identification with it."[44] Cocteau had stated quite bluntly that he only used the legend as a starting point for his scenario: Miss Hering seems to have expected something that was a direct mental and moral reflection of the period.

P. W. Manchester in *Dance News* was not very happy with the ballet, either, but thought Cocteau should be given his due:

> It is not often that one sees a work which has everything in its favor on paper and yet falls to pieces in performance by reason of its mishandling. A libretto by Jean Cocteau, who also designed the original production, and the French thirteenth- and fourteenth-century Antique Airs and Dances skillfully orchestrated by Jacques Chailley combining to tell the story of the most beautiful of the Gobelin tapestries, make a wonderful foundation for a work which should have been a piece of period stylization.
>
> Unhappily the choreographer, Heinz Rosen, had no idea how to handle the subject and constantly fell back on recognizable clichés of the late nineteenth-century Russian ballet allied to the more sensational lifts of present day Soviet ballet. The result, in its medieval setting, was unsatisfactory to put it mildly, and in addition, the action was strung out interminably so that each situation became boring long before the choreographer had finished with it.[45]

Manchester felt the ballet could work if it was shortened and the action was much more highly stylized. All the dancers, she felt, could do marvels with the parts Cocteau had given them if they were given the right choreographic setting.

Most of the reviews, in fact, hit very hard at Rosen, rather than Cocteau. John Chapman in the *New York Post* thought the choreography was "pretty silly" and *Variety* in a display of verbal histrionics thought it "a sluggish, insipid piece, filled with pleonastic movements and unimaginative choreography." It concluded that the ballet was "an unadulterated flop; a unicorn-fed turkey. . . . Chalk the whole project up as just a big mistake."[46] Walter Terry thought the Cocteau sets, costumes, and story were admirable but Rosen's choreography, despite "flashes of interest" was mostly "undistinguished, repetitious and paced at a funeral tempo" and the funeral march for the little unicorn one of the longest in ballet history, "and there are some notable rivals for this dubious honor." Terry concluded that the Cocteau tale had much going for it but it needed better exploitation by the choreography.[47]

The American reviewers also thought that the "hobbyhorse" lion limited the Knight and that the white mask-headpiece for the Unicorn limited Novak in any visual expression, especially in the death scene. An ironical comment, since Mlakar in the original production was highly praised for her expressive unicorn, and she had to work in the same costume as Novak. All the reviews thought the Cocteau concept admirable, but that it needed a better choreographer. The symbolic and "Freudian-styled" choreography which the American critics snickered at may be considered something of a Germanic trait. Rosen's teachers had been Kurt Jooss (1901–1979) and Rudolph von Laban (1879–1958), whose style of work was very much in this tradition which the Germanic dance world had always appreciated. This is not to say that the American critics were wrong in their point of view, only that the style of dancing was alien to them and perhaps to the dancers. Even today the American choreographer John Neumeier (b. 1942) and his controversial and very Freudian interpretations of the classics are very popular in Frankfurt or Hamburg, but rarely succeed outside Germany, and the same held true for Rosen during the 1950s. Of course, the German reviewers of Rosen's choreography for La Dame à la licorne may have seen the ballet through rose-colored glasses; the American reviews, on the other hand, may have tended to carp due to conceptual dance differences. Clive Barnes, when he saw the ballet revived in Munich in 1963, thought "with Rosen, like so many German choreographers, the virtuosity of classical ballet is more a disease than an instrument."[48] Such a generalized remark is dangerous to make under any circumstances since there are quite a number of German choreographers; at the same time such comments show a general insensitivity to national traits. Obviously, the ballet must have remained popular in Germany for it to last so long in the repertoire.

The real test for Cocteau's ballet would come with Paris. Immediately after the premiere Cocteau had written to Petit and made inquiries in other directions as well, but an even greater honor was in store for the poet. The French government thought that the ballet would be very appropriate for the opening of the remodeled and renovated Théâtre de Château at Versailles, a blue and gold concoction which had originally been built for the rococo theatrical palate of Louis XV. The intimate stage and the elegant surroundings would be perfect for Cocteau's balletic legend and plans were made to bring the ballet to Paris for the scheduled October 1957 opening. However Cocteau's joy soon turned to bitterness when a stagehands' strike forced the cancellation of the intended premiere. How well Cocteau must have remembered his remarks in 1953, when he said that Paris had become too expensive for the production of anything of quality there anymore.[49]

Two years after this setback, the Paris Opéra decided to take the ballet into its repertoire and this time the scheduled opening for January 1959 took place as planned. Due to the demands of the larger stage Rosen had to increase his corps of unicorns from six to twelve and Cocteau had to redesign the sets on a larger scale though the colors and main design remained essentially the same. Although Cocteau was too ill to attend the opening, he watched and guided many rehearsals and even dictated orders from his sickbed at Cape Ferrat. Claude Bessy was cast as the Lady, with Michel Renault as the Knight and Liane Daydé as the Unicorn. Although Cocteau thought Bessy and Daydé "adorable" he had reservations on the latter since he still remembered Mlakar's dancing "like a creature from another world." "Personally I thought the production [at the Paris Opéra] very moving," Cocteau wrote when he finally saw his work soon after the premiere, but he also said that he was not happy with the lighting which he was unable to supervise himself, not only because of his illness but due to the rules of the stage unions, whose strictures and expensive grievances have annoyed many producers before and since Cocteau. "I was unable to supervise the lighting," Cocteau remarked in resignation, "but beauty loves shadow," he added with some irony.[50]

The Paris production received generally favorable, though mixed reviews. Marie-Françoise Christout thought the grand dimensions of the Opéra theatre worked against the production and that it needed more intimate surroundings; something the Versailles theatre could have given it. She also thought the ballet "an inconsequential trifle which suffers by inevitable comparison with two earlier works: the very original *Phèdre* which is also by Cocteau, and with the Medieval *Chevalier et la demoiselle* (Gaubert/Lifar/Cassandre), whose music and choreographic themes are similar." Christout thought Cocteau's choice of theme "a poetic one" and his set design of green, blue and red lovely, though the costumes were uneven. "His happiest choice is that for the Knight, which is black and yellow, with a white makeup which reminds one of the Oriental mask." But the Unicorn suffered from the design of its mask which "while certainly ingenious, lacks any expression." The Lady's mauve and purple costume was "undoubtedly too long at the back and too short in the front. While its train dangerously impedes her movements, the skirt, which is so short as to be almost nonexistent, hardly suggests a pure young maiden, but rather a somewhat flamboyant courtesan." Christout then rhetorically asked, "whatever has happened to the master touch of he of whom Diaghilev once begged: 'Jean, étonne-moi!'?"[51]

While Christout's criticisms must not be disregarded, it may not be fair to put all the blame on Cocteau. Daydé, from all accounts, was an excellent Unicorn technically but did not have the *body* expression of Mlakar. The mask may be an incumbrance to a dancer only if he or she does not know how to use it as part of the character. The same may be said for the train—which is also used in Balanchine's *L'Enfant prodigue* for the Siren—it can be used as part of the choreographic movement if the dancer knows how to manipulate it. A courtesan can also be expressed by the use the dancer makes of a costume, not the other way around, and account should be taken of the kinetic and personal factors involved in the presentation of a theatrical piece. In dance the same steps on different dancers can give a totally different perspective on a piece, sometimes to the ballet's advantage, oftentimes not.

Jean Silvant in *La Musique* was somewhat kinder, although he presented some terrifying remarks on the state of dance in Paris and the probable fate of *La Dame à la licorne*:

> It is not proper to speak of [*La Dame*] as a great work, but it does give us many beautiful moments, without doubt due to excellent interpretation by the artists and in spite of the choreography of Heinz Rosen, who does not show that he has any great knowledge of choreographic structure. . . . This hybrid work, despite the presence of Cocteau, who, as we know, is a remarkable catalyzer, is a graceful work that is interpreted beautifully today. Unhappily, at the Opéra (and the Opéra-Comique) it is not possible to keep a ballet as fresh and interesting as the creators first conceived it. And to be more precise, *La Dame à la licorne* will finally be lost due to lack of interest.[52]

What Silvant is talking about is a problem many state theatres have within their own repertory system: the ballet usually has many less performances and rehearsals than the opera, and suffers accordingly. *La Dame* is lost, even though revision work could improve and help the piece, because other productions and a lack of interest finally force the work to be dropped from the repertoire.

Perhaps the most perceptive and interesting review of the ballet was by Antoine Golea in *Musica Disques*. Golea had seen both the Munich premiere and the Paris opening and was able to compare what had happened in the transfer—the loss of intimacy, the radical choreographic adjustments Rosen had to make to cater to the French dancers, the extension of the corps, and even the lighting and technical problems. He also saw it as Cocteau's last testament to the dance theatre, a final homage from a visual poet, and in this analysis he was quite correct:

> *La Dame à la licorne* which has just entered the repertoire of the Paris Opéra is one of the great poetic acts of our time. All of it was conceived by Jean Cocteau; he conceived every angle of the poetry [of the ballet], he transcended poetry into some domain of art where the artist is the active poem itself . . . inspired by the magnificent tapestries of another age Cocteau has given us subtle and profound moving figures that are modern souls clothed in Medieval garb.[53]

Golea saw Cocteau as giving us a parable on human destiny where the Unicorn represents a pure love which the Lady always sees reflected in her mirror until the Knight brings change and flux into a basically stable world. Golea detailed the difference between the Munich and Paris interpreters: Mlakar died a death of resignation while Daydé's death was a death "without pity." Claude Bussy added a suavity to the role of the Dame that, perhaps, made her too worldly and Michel Renault an almost "too Parisian knight" for this fable. Perhaps, Golea felt, the Munich *poème lyrique* evolved into too much of a tragedy in the vast hall of the Paris Opéra.

The ballet, as Silvant predicted, did not last very long in the Paris repertoire, though it was revived many times and with great success in Munich. On its tenth anniversary, in 1963, Cocteau was still giving notes, even from his death bed. He wrote Rosen that he was "happy every time the *Unicorne* is successful—please insist that the dancers NEVER use red lipstick—that is hideous."[54]

For all its problems and difficulty in transferral from Munich to the rest of the world, *La Dame à la licorne* was obviously a work which Cocteau cared about and which had taken much work, thought and care. Perhaps both music and choreography may have been weak, but it is unfair to lay all the blame at Cocteau's feet. All were agents of his ideas and ideas change the moment they leave the creator's hands. At the same time one must hold Cocteau responsible for the work's concept, though circumstances may have forced adjustments and changes in the ballet that proved unsatisfactory in its travels abroad. All the critics, however, thought Cocteau's concept, both visual and narrative, was of intriguing interest and an excellent idea for a ballet. The least that can be said about the ballet is that it was a bold and interesting project and the last important gift from a poet to the dance-theatre he loved so much. It may be the last ballet or dance composition where the choreography and dancers were overshadowed by the scenarist and scenographer. Perhaps, too, the Lady frozen in eternal time at the end of the ballet with her mysterious motto: "Mon Seul Desir" is Cocteau's final word to us all, a final sanguine expectancy. In the end we are left alone but, hopefully, we will be remembered; perhaps that is Cocteau's only desire.

9

The Reluctant Muse

Every poet is posthumous. This is why it is very difficult for him to live. His work hates him, it eats him, it wants to get rid of him and live alone as it pleases. If he comes to the fore, his voices leave him.
—Jean Cocteau, *Beauty Secrets*

The final years of Cocteau's life were not dominated by any important balletic work although he did not lose interest in the art. Cocteau continued as an inspiration after his death, not only in the posthumous transformation of some of his literary output into dance productions, but also for his theories concerning balletic art and its potential.

Cocteau was a poet who realized that he could not hold onto his works once they were finished. This did not stop him, however, from trying to control the production of his creative output. As he grew older, his body lost the mobility to contribute to and be active in the dance and theatre environment. Cocteau then spent more time on his poetry—notably his *Requiem*—and in illustrating some of his themes in permanent fashion by murals executed in the south of France, in London and in the chapel where he was finally laid to rest, Saint-Balise-des-Simples. This type of work he could control. *Phèdre* and *La Dame à la licorne* were his last major contributions to the ballet, though he did work on some other ideas, only one of which reached fruition during his lifetime.

After collaborating with Rosen on *La Dame* in 1953, it was only natural that Cocteau would want to do something again with the young and enthusiastic choreographer. During the late 1950s he began to draft a scenario for a ballet entitled *Le Fils de l'air*, in which a young boy is stolen by gypsies from a dreamy mother and turned into a funambulist, for "stolen children know how to walk in the air."[1] But the drafting was delayed as Cocteau became involved in other occupations and the scenario was transformed into a poem which concluded with a warning:

Vast is the world, and new, and dark, and troubling.
Mothers beware of windows, of doors,
Of sons bewitched by those who bear them off
And of dwellings drawn by four white horses.[2]

Cocteau was still thinking of this poem as the pretext for a ballet in the last year of his life, due mostly to the insistence of Rosen, as this letter from Cocteau to the choreographer discloses:

It is correct: my first idea for [the poem] "Fils en l'air" was that of a ballet, i.e. a dance-libretto. But the ideas changed gradually . . . it seems to me impossible to attract this or that composer simply with the goal of a choreographic work. That would mean to demand of Brecht that he do without Kurt Weill. The work will be (or will not be) a mime-drama, wherein dance will take up very little space; more important are words and gestures.

Thanks to you this work is promised to [Hans Werner] Henze, admittedly without setting any definite dates, and if I am not able to realize this work, should Henze give up on the idea to write it, [then it probably won't get done].

Neither my age nor my style nor our Time seem suitable for a so-called "pure classical ballet." On the contrary a visual [plastique] and musically tight work is expected by the youth of to-day whom I don't wish to disappoint after the catastrophe of The Two-Headed Eagle.[3]

Dated 11 December 1962, exactly ten months to the day before his death, the letter reveals a man who feels he is getting old but does not want to be out-of-touch with anything that is new. Always afraid that he would not be in the forefront, Cocteau became more wary in his later years of doing anything that would not raise controversy. The play The Two-Headed Eagle, which had been written for the actor Jean Marais (b. 1913) in 1946 was released as a film in 1949. Its reception had not been what Cocteau had wished for the film; after Orphée and La Belle et la bête, it was considered old-fashioned. Obviously, Cocteau was still disturbed by this criticism fourteen years later. He was now hesitant before committing himself to projects, and Le Fils de l'air never got any further before his death.

The poem did finally reach the stage as a ballet, but not until nearly ten years after Cocteau's death. On 14 April 1972 Maurice Béjart (b. 1927), director and choreographer for The Ballet of the Twentieth Century, had students from his school, Mudra in Belgium, present a dance visualization of Cocteau's poem as the opening ballet in a three-part program honoring the French poet. It was presented at the Royal Cirque in Brussels. The students were allowed to choreograph the poem themselves and performed this collective creation in the way Cocteau's letter to Rosen had dictated. Le Fils de l'air was a mime-drama, acted, sung and danced. It began with a joyous parade of gypsies leading in their queen on a Sicilian cart. Following the text of the poem the gypsy queen steals away the child of the too dreamy mother and makes him fly above the houses—an effect aided by the flywires of the Cirque itself. Marie-Françoise Christout reviewed the evening, and thought Cocteau would have been very pleased, especially with the presentation in one of his favorite performance areas, the circus:

> Coordinated with skill, entries and exits, individual improvisations and mass movements follow each other, while the mother walks around plunged in her reading and then in her grief [at the loss of her son]. Although one may find fault with details, such as the realistic style in which the child-stealer's poem is sung, this mime drama finally shows rhythm and cohesion and sensitively translates Cocteau's poem.[4]

Familiar with Cocteau's wishes for a mime drama of this poem, Béjart allowed his students to improvise but still keep Cocteau's words and his indicated gestures as the groundwork for the piece.

Cocteau, of course, never saw this ballet, but he did write one more scenario for a ballet which he did see, three years before he died. Soon after his seventieth birthday, Cocteau witnessed the premiere of *Le Poète et sa muse* in July 1959 at the Festival of Two Worlds in Spoleto, Italy. The scenario was requested by the composer Gian-Carlo Menotti (b. 1911) who also directed the festival and who wrote the music for the ballet. Cocteau designed the costumes and decor, though he was unable to supervise them to the extent he had for *Phèdre* or *La Dame à la licorne*. Cocteau's scenario reads like a tortured amalgamation of a number of his previous scenarios:

> A young American poet appears tormented by his searchings. His muse appears in a ball dress and from behind her fan dictates him a poem in an unknown language. . . . In order to assure his fame, this muse, with the gestures of Tosca, makes him lie down and simulate suicide, and herself places funeral candles to the left and right of his face. A revolver shot attracts a group of young people in blue jeans who go into transports of hysterical admiration. After the departure of these young aesthetes a champagne cork, to celebrate the adventure, simulates a revolver shot and recalls the troupe. Thinking that they have been fooled, they torture the poet and insult the muse.
>
> The muse throws the trampled manuscripts out of the window and disappears without glancing at the poet who commits suicide by following the route by which he came and leaping from some skyscraper into space.
>
> The curtain falls as one hears the screaming of the police sirens.[5]

One can see in this ballet elements from many of his other works: the Muse as death (*Le Jeune homme et la mort*), the group versus the poet (*Orphée*), the ending in death which pervades so many of his later works. The ballet is also very much a final personal statement: "Every poet is posthumous. This is why it is very difficult for him to live." The muse has to present the poet as dead so his work will be admired by the public, and when they later find out they have been deceived, they abandon his work. One hears echoes of Cocteau's comment to Rosen on "the youth of today" and their reaction to his plays and films; the tired poet making one last stand of defiance. The designation of the poet as American had its purpose as well, as Cocteau had pointed out ten years earlier in his "Letter to Americans":

> It is true that your enterprises of the same order [books, poetry] find it extremely difficult to materialize and the U.S. can more easily find billions to organize a great catastrophe than the little sum which would make a true birth possible. It is true that beauty in all its forms remains accursed and slips in surreptitiously, while things which last don't come into the world with the ease of things that don't. But you are the people who consecrate the dangerous enterprises of Europe. Your power is without limits. My last request therefore is to ask yourself to pay attention to novelty which has not proved itself. . . . [6]

The ballet *Le Poète et sa muse* was a reiteration of that request: recognize the poetry before you lose the poet. One cannot think Cocteau meant the ballet as a reference only to himself but as a statement for future reference, for the poets that would come after him. The ballet has never been produced since this festival.

Jean Cocteau's death on 11 October 1963 did not prevent others from using his works as inspiration for balletic presentations. On the same program as *Le Fils de l'air* in Brussels in 1972, Béjart choreographed another one of Cocteau's poems, *L'Ange Heurtebise*, published in 1925 and Cocteau's tribute to his beloved Raymond Radiguet. Originally Béjart planned the ballet as a dialogue between the narrator/poet, played by Cocteau's friend and companion during the 1940s, Jean Marais, and his dancing angel, played by the young Argentinian dancer Jorge Donn (b. 1947). As the ballet evolved in Béjart's mind, he expanded his concept to include three other angels, all played by dancers in his company: Cegeste (Bertrand Pie), Dimanche (Iukiko Sakai), and Elziver (Jean-François Bouchard). All three angels had been used or invented by Cocteau for his works, though Heurtebise always remained the dominant spirit. Béjart added to this cast a group of soldiers and a Dantesque circle of malevolent demons.

The score by Manos Hadjidakis included a number of strange instruments, such as the bouzouki, which added to the eerie quality of the spectacle. The costumes by Joel Roustan and Roger Bernard had a diaphanous quality, what Marie-Françoise Christout called "pre-Raphaelite robes of chiffon" which suggested "an underwater fairyland for Heurtebise and fruits for the other flower-crowned angels."[7] Christout also praised the contrast between the "plastic authority and broken voice" of Jean Marais which perfectly expressed "the tragic force whose monumental nature stands opposite the mobility and bounding ease of Jorge Donn as a fascinating angel of stunning beauty, whose virile grace contrasts with the floating robe in the style of Dante Gabriel Rosetti." Béjart included a number of stunning effects to enhance his concept, including blood-red shackles which suddenly hold the black-clad poet immobile in the center of the arena and the flight of Heurtebise and Cegeste to heaven, the hoisting being done by the Cirque wires attached to the angels' upthrust fists. Christout found the effects impressive and felt that they corresponded "to a dream or theme dear to Cocteau."[8] The program was rounded out by a revival of *Les Mariés de la Tour Eiffel*, though without the recreation of the stunning original designs by Jean Hugo. The Béjart presentation is interesting for its combination of words, music and dance in all three ballets—an effect Cocteau had pioneered with *Les Mariés*, though he had tried earlier and failed to gain Diaghilev's approval for dialogue in *Parade*. It may be paradoxical to note that 1972, the year of the Béjart tribute, also marked the centenary of Diaghilev's birth.

Another choreographer, Glen Tetley (b. 1926), used a Cocteau piece for the basis of a ballet for American Ballet Theatre. Taking the scene between the sphinx and Oedipus from the play *La Machine infernale*, Tetley centered on this confrontation and the *deus ex machina* role of the Jackal-headed god Anubis, also in the Cocteau play. Using the Concerto for Two String Orchestras, Piano and Timpani by Bohuslav Martinů with scenery by Rouben Ter-Arutunian (b. 1920) and costumes by Willa Kim, the ballet, entitled *Sphinx*, premiered in Washington, D.C. at the Kennedy Center on 9 December 1977 with Martine van Hamel (b. 1945) as the sphinx, Clark Tippet (b. 1953) as Oedipus and Kirk Peterson (b. 1951) as Anubis. The dance outline followed the plot of the play though the involved nature of the three participants may have seemed bewildering to those who were unfamiliar with the text. In both play and ballet, the sphinx allows the womanly part of her to take control of herself when she meets Oedipus, though Anubis warns her of the consequences. She is instructed by him to ensnare Oedipus, "wrapped in the hold of a reptile / Numb as an arm you have slept on" and then destroy him.[9] However she weakens in her love for him and lets him go, while she returns to her position as the cold and calculating sphinx with Anubis as her mentor. All of this could not be conveyed in the ballet, but the intricate and angular choreography, enhanced by the Martinů score and metal-structured platform of the sphinx's perch did convey a feeling of a strange and foredoomed meeting parallel to the opening scene in the play.

Transformations of works from one medium to another, especially when the author himself has no voice in the matter, are often discouraged out of respect for the original work. One cannot imagine Cocteau, however, complaining about Tetley's use of his play since he himself had done the same with his own *Le Bel indifférent* and *Orphée* as well as with Racine's *Phèdre*. Nor probably would he have minded Béjart's use of *L'Ange Heurtebise* since he had allowed Lifar to use his poem *Plein Chant* for a ballet in 1943.

Cocteau's own life was the inspiration for a full-evening ballet entitled *Poppy*—so-called because of Cocteau's association with opium. The work was choreographed by Graeme Murphy for the Sidney Dance Company and premiered in Australia in 1978. An ambitious project that used the whole company, the ballet was divided into two sections: biographical and philosophical. The commissioned score by the young Australian composer Carl Vine reflected this concept, with the first section using orchestral music inspired by the compositions of "Les Six," and the second half using electronic music, "the music of the mind and emotion," according to Vine.[10] The first section showed Cocteau growing up, going to school, and becoming intrigued with Nijinsky, who is seen in three guises, as the Dancer, the Soul, and the Choreographer. Then Cocteau meets and falls in love with Raymond Radiguet, who is taken away by the Angel of Death, as the first half closes.

The second half opened with Cocteau undergoing treatment in the detoxification clinic and then continued with a series of images that touched upon a variety of Coctelian subject matter, both real and imaginary. Murphy cast many dancers in dual roles so that one saw Radiguet transformed into Cocteau's imaginary angel Heurtebise and Isadora become Jocasta, linked by a red scarf. With so many images intermixed and so much material it was difficult for the audience to relate to, unless one had really taken the time to research Cocteau's life. Murphy reworked the second section over the next few years, before bringing the ballet to New York in the spring of 1981. *Poppy* received generally favorable reviews for its daring and its intriguing theatricality, since Murphy used slides, films, puppets, special lighting effects and nudity to convey Cocteau's life and ideas. The second section had been tightened, but still remained a metaphysical exercise where, as Julinda Lewis in *Dance Magazine* said, "symbol, dream, and reality become inseparable as the cast of characters—boyhood friends, lovers, the Angel of Death, Orpheus, Oedipus, Babette, Merlin, and more—pass in and out of an opium-filled mind with calm logic and breathtaking imagery." Lewis thought the ballet had "unbelievably spectacular visual effects" and was "the most impressive piece in the [Sidney Dance Company] repertoire."[11]

One of the most impressive aspects of Cocteau's work in ballet is not just his transformation, or allowance of transformation, of literary works into the dance idiom but the general diversity of styles within his total balletic oeuvre. From the exotic *Le Dieu bleu* he proceeded to the surreal world of *Parade* and *Le Boeuf sur le toit*; he then experimented with text and dance in *Les Mariés de la Tour Eiffel* and *Roméo et Juliette*, with acrobatics and circus technique in *Le Train bleu*, accidental synchronization in *Le Jeune homme et la mort*, and the transformation of legends, such as *Orphée*, *L'Amour et son amour* (Cupid and Psyche), and *La Dame à la licorne*. In fact, it is extremely difficult to try to give a general classification to Cocteau's ballets because of their eclectic nature and because he himself gave each of his ballets subtitles that purposely stretched the accepted definitions of a dance presentation.

It may be that Cocteau, like his Orpheus, insisted on his right to be different. It is also the artist's naturally selfish desire to mark a work as "his" and give it his personal touch so that it may be recognized as such by the public. In ballet this was difficult for Cocteau because of the other contributions involved in its eventual presentation: designer, composer, choreographer and dancers. He was more than a scenarist: he was a producer, though the former occupation was still part of his domain. But unlike any scenarist before or since, Cocteau wanted firmer control of his work. One does not read of Scribe dictating the choreography of *Robert le Diable* to Filippo Taglioni in 1830, or Gautier telling Perrot and Coralli how to stage *Giselle* in 1841, or even Cocteau's contemporary Kochno standing up to Diaghilev as often as Cocteau tried to do with his co-workers. Cocteau, on the other hand, would give out sheets of notes to Massine, Babilée, Petit, Nijinska and Rosen. He would attend rehearsals and make suggestions, welcome or not. Later in his career when he designed his own sets and costumes he would insist on total supervision and attend lighting rehearsals, changing settings continually until they suited his concept. Even the small niceties of a ballet were not given to anyone else—he wrote the program notes, drew the posters, made up the press releases, granted interviews. Often his aggressive possessiveness aggravated the artists involved, often it hampered the production, but all were marked with Cocteau's style.

What is the Cocteau style? Can one make a general statement and find a similar theme running through all his ballets from 1912 through 1959? Walter Sorell in an obituary notice published in 1964 thought Cocteau's central theme was in no way different from any other important artist of any time: the probing and recreating of man:

> He [Cocteau] felt that "every man is a night, and the artist's task is to bring this night into daylight." In his sentence: "To be reborn one must burn oneself alive," lies the key to the understanding of his genius. And this thought of rising like a Phoenix from one's own ashes was echoed in a later statement: "My discipline consists in not letting myself be enslaved by obsolete formulae."
>
> In retrospect it becomes altogether clear that Jean Cocteau was a pioneer in transferring the reflection of everyday life onto the dance stage. Instead of the spectacular sequence of heightened unreality, the fairy tale atmosphere on which ballet has fed for so long, he broke with the cliché and he offered the gesture of heightened reality. What we have accepted as avant-garde in dance in the fifties and sixties has been built, in more ways than one, on Cocteau's living and dying, and living again.[12]

The key phrase in this appraisal is "transferring the reflection of everyday life onto the dance stage." Except for *Le Dieu bleu*, in which Cocteau was purposely trying to imitate the exotic Ballets Russes style, all of his dance compositions fit into this definition. Who else would have thought to present the suicide of an artist on stage as he did in *Le Jeune homme et la mort*, the American prohibition in *Le Boeuf sur le toit*, a wedding party on the Eiffel Tower in *Les Mariés de la Tour Eiffel*, swimmers performing acrobatics at the beach in *Le Train bleu*, or circus performers trying desperately to entice an audience through their street *Parade*? In his transferral Cocteau heightened the reality and gave it a peculiar twist through the use of props, sets, or costumes in unusual ways—the large head-masks in *Les Mariés* and *Le Boeuf*, the black and white costuming of *Roméo*, the color scheme in *L'Amour* and *Phèdre*—or surprise effects such as the orchestra on stage for *La Dame*, silent film action in *Le Train bleu*, the tableaux in *Phèdre*, the everyday noises in *Parade*.

In many ways these could be considered the affectations of a social dilettante who was still following Diaghilev's dictum of "Astonish me!" But while this remark can be considered the catalyst that helped launch Cocteau on his varied and diversified career, it was not the overriding factor. He was simply trying out different ways of expressing himself while remaining true to his theory that everything could be poetry, it only depended on the presentation. "Poetry borrows astonishing contrasts by chance, it transplants things, it accidentally sets up a new order."[13]

This new order often looked puzzling to Cocteau's contemporaries. He wore various masks throughout his life, and one cannot help but feel that he played these magician tricks on purpose and his facility of execution in so many fields deceived the audience into thinking that it was all so very easy. But behind all this exhibitionism and seeming inconstancy of purpose worked a very organized and disciplined genius whose madness shows much more method only now in retrospect. In many ways he used art, discarding this or that form when it did not suit him and returning to it when it was the most viable means of expression. Thus ballet for him was an instrument of expression to be wielded like the film camera or his brush or pen, if it became too frustrating for him to work in the balletic idiom, he turned to another with as much ease as a driver shifts the gears on his car.

He loved dance because of its universality. Time and again in his career he reiterated this important aspect of the art: "Dance is the universal language where the corps is charged to express themselves and make darkness light for the waiting audience." Through its language *plastique* Cocteau felt that dance could reach "a superior realism, a higher expression which speaks more than traditional pantomime." Speaking of dance in the female gender, which he did with all his muses, Cocteau said "she is an 'esperanto' in the contemporary babelism. She traverses the wall of idioms. She gives, in addition, the direct translation of a poetry which abandons all terms."[14] The appeal of the idiom was its ability to reach further since it was not bound by the laws of language; its drawbacks for Cocteau were his own technical inability to choreograph the picture as he saw it.

This aspect of ballet probably frustrated Cocteau the most, though he eventually found another way to become a choreographer. This was as film director. Although it is beyond the scope of this work to investigate the dance-like compositions of so many of his films, even a layman can observe how Cocteau makes his camera turn his decors and actors into balletic presentations: Beauty floating down the Beast's hall in *La Belle et la bête*, the travels in the underworld by the bewildered *Orphée*, the "celestial ceiling" in *Le Sang du poète*. In all of these instances, and many more besides, Cocteau becomes the choreographer he could not be for stage dance.[15]

Film provides a permanent record of Cocteau's contribution to that art and the printed page is the guardian of his poetry, plays and essays. One can investigate Cocteau's paintings and murals through pictures or travel to view the originals, but dance, by its very nature, loses something even after its first performance. How, then, can one make a definitive judgment about a work that has not been seen for twenty, thirty or even forty years? The historian of dance is confronted with contemporary accounts, reviews, some faded pictures, and the memories of those involved in the production. Not always does even this meager evidence agree, as has been seen with *Parade*, *Le Dieu bleu*, *Le Train bleu*, and *Les Mariés de la Tour Eiffel*. Contemporary reviews have often contradicted both Cocteau's account and the later reflections of artists involved in the various enterprises. No judgment should be made about the latter, perhaps, except to say that memory often deceives and changes faster than the printed word. The contemporary reviewer, even considering prejudices of the era, will have more immediacy than the memory of a performer some years later. Of course, critical assumptions must be taken into account when using them as evidence, but personal memory often exaggerates the speaker's importance or the details of the production. Cocteau himself is a case in point as his writings on *Parade* do not always tally with the evidence available—in his desire to create a scandal like *Le Sacre du printemps*, Cocteau's dramatic account of the opening night may be attributed to his own insecurity and ego. Every piece of evidence used must be placed in both a personal and general artistic and historical perspective. As Cocteau became less defensive and insecure, his writings about his later ballets become more reliable, although even here he tends to let the poet in him color the details with symbolic or philosophical explanations. This convoluted prose style often makes it difficult for the historian to sift the facts out from under the poetic embellishments.

At the same time that Cocteau had to strive less to prove himself in his later career he began to be treated as an "institution" by many members of the press. This can color critical reception: either they criticise him for not being as innovative as they felt he was before or they seem afraid to make any overt negative comments, like the reviews of *La Dame à la licorne* in Munich. His personal reception in Munich may have contributed much to the success of that ballet. Are, therefore, the less enthusiastic reviews of *La Dame* in Paris and America more truthful? Or was *La Dame* that much worse in production when it left the confines of Germany and changed casts? One cannot really make such black and white qualifications with a clear conscience as the Parisian perspective and the American perspective of *La Dame* will be formed by different preconceptions and ideas than the German mind. Even in this age of supranationalism, theatrical productions do not always travel well across national boundaries, even when the two cultures are closely united. How often has an English stage success turned into an American fiasco or vice versa? And who is to say that this decade's prejudices or concepts have denied some of Cocteau's ballets a present place in the international repertoire?

In 1946, *Le Jeune homme et la mort* was considered a strong and emotional work with a definite impact. Later many critics felt the dramatic and traumatic effect no longer concealed its technical address. The revival of the work by Roland Petit in 1983 may have reestablished its popularity, despite its dependence on the right interpreters, such as Patrick Dupond. Does Dupond have more affinity with Cocteau's original intentions because he is French, as opposed to Baryshnikov's Russian heritage? How much does a dancer have to know about the background of a work to interpret it well? One of the major complaints by the Joffrey dancers involved in the revival of *Parade* in 1974 was the absence of this understanding of the period and people that created the work and the need to develop a rapport with the collaborator's original intentions.[16]

Despite these reflections on the difficulty of producing certain Cocteau ballets today or the difficulty of putting on paper the facts about their original creation, it is important to recognize the major influence of Cocteau on the dance. His writings continually reiterate his loathing of repetition, monotony and boredom. His work in ballet reflects this mental mobility and dextrous versatility. No generalizations can be made on how he worked in ballet since his role as *causeur* could contract or expand at will, depending on his collaborators or his own interests. What Cocteau gave to the dance is easier to define. Cocteau continued the work of Diaghilev and his collaborators in the extension of the thematic material for dance, but took it one step further. Cocteau's particular abilities to transform everyday action into heightened reality could make the most mundane situations look attractive, amusing or surprising. His particular vision of dance as theatre centered around the presentation of these commonplace actions as "poetry of motion" which focused on the entire stage picture, rather than one element of the ballet. Cocteau showed that art could survive in terms of the present and ballet could reflect this reality and even comment on it without destroying the accepted codes and conventions of established practice. Though he was no dancer or choreographer in the accepted sense of the word he was far from being just a scenarist for the ballet. He showed choreographers that the historically formulated and rigidly structured codes of ballet technique could be used for a dramatic revolution in dance which did not depend on conventional stage practices. The versatility of his approach is still an indirect influence on dance production today. Ten years after Cocteau's death, Carl Wildman made mention of this important aspect of the poet's career:

> His contribution to the ballet had been crucial, diverse, his action catalytic; the veins which he explored are still being mined. Though a number of his works have a place in theatrical history rather than in repertoire, it is by the ramifications of his influence that his presence is chiefly known.[17]

These ramifications cannot be denied, even when the artists involved do not always know where or with whom they originated. Cocteau's spirit still presides over every controversy, every surprise, every new device or idea that choreographers today test out on the dance stage of the world. "Astonish me," he tells them, "but always make it poetry."

Appendix

Major Writings of Jean Cocteau on the Ballet

1 "Le Ballet Russe"

This is a marvelous season.

Like the spring, the summer, the autumn, she [referring to the Ballets Russes] displays splendor that is always the same but ever changing in the use of color and light.

Though she is unrecognized, like a Phoenix bird in the center of Paris, she is there: an eddy of magic in an uproar. She is mystery and pleasure, and we feel impregnated with her unknown splendor. All hearts should follow her soft flutter; all eyes should look at everyday images suddenly turned into intense decors.

And then suddenly the season is over and she is gone.

One suffers a little, one tries not to own up to the loss, one fears its impression will diminish and one will try to hold on to a souvenir of those magnificent things that are now gone. But suddenly, it is announced they are back! And they approach, burdened with precious stuffs, with jewels, with flowers, with gems, with perfumes and with music, like a fabulous procession of the Magi.

In the suite of Serge de Diaghilev one finds Mme. Ida Rubinstein. She walks with stately grace. Each of her steps are like glides as she indolently throws her head back in this forward motion. The long, slim body with the long slim legs and parallel to this her long slim arms which rest slightly at the elbow on her hips. There is the round arrogance of her shoulders between which is embedded her neck, reminding one of the Ibis bird stalking with closed wings.

She is very beautiful, with a special essence that leaves a lingering impression on the mind. Her left hand, held against her heavy robe, plays with a blue lotus while her right hand—like the broken edge at the end of her arm—points and gesticulates like a long, golden arrow. She holds our city by the insignia of these roles. [At the time of writing Cocteau wanted Rubinstein to play the Lotus goddess in his ballet *Le Dieu bleu*, tentatively scheduled for the next season, and thus the reference to the lotus. The Ibis refers to her portrayal of the lead in *Cléopâtre*.]

And now—Vaslav Nijinsky. In him is reincarnated the mysterious child Septentrion, who died dancing on the shores at Antibes. Young, erect, supple, he walks only on the ball of his foot, taking rapid, firm little steps; he is compact as a clenched fist with his neck long and massive as a Donatello, and his slender torso contrasting with his overdeveloped thighs. He is like some young Florentine, vigorous beyond anything human, and feline to a disquieting degree. He upsets all the laws of equilibrium, and seems constantly to be a figure painted on the ceiling; he reclines nonchalantly in midair, defies heaven in a thousand different ways, and his dancing is like some lovely poem written all in capitals.

Let me speak of him in *Schéhérazade!*
What negro sumptuousness! Voluptuousness! His mocking laughter!
Let me speak of him in *Les Sylphides!*
What poetic romanticism! His gracefulness! His vaporous quality!

[In *Schéhérazade*] he reels from the joy of the orgy, springing from the mute cries of all in the decadent scene which the spectator has just witnessed; he then falls on the gold cushions where his golden trousers make him resemble a fish who flops in the sun and then immediately he jumps into the center of the demonic dance. Finally he recoils from the slice of the sabre in his chest and he falls . . . extending and contracting like an arc in midair, he dies in spasms . . . and, a few minutes later, reappears, pale and blond, in white tights, black vest, and a peasant blouse. [This is *Les Sylphides*] in which ballet his soul becomes quiet and falls under the antique charm of Chopin, adrift among the stalks of dahlias and tutus of gauze.

Now, [with this season] he goes from these past works into new triumphs. [Cocteau now describes a composite picture of Nijinsky's new roles, as he did earlier for Rubenstein.]

His left hand holds a Narcisse [*Narcisse*], his right hand holds a rose [*Spectre de la rose*], a reptile wraps itself around his waist [*Le Dieu bleu*]. These new images will be added to the illustrious ones he has shown us so far.

Here is Tamara Karsavina and she resembles a little girl. Softly and with a distracted air she skims the surface with her *pointes* as she exits [during *Les Sylphides*]. Her arms are crossed over her breast. Beneath her luminous tresses appear timid eyes which sparkle with joy underneath her long eyelashes. She enters in the suite of the somber Sophie Fedorova who also has in her train—like an agitating Tyse with a touch of flame—[Vera] Fokina the Flexible, [Lydia] Lopokova the precocious, Ludmilla Schollar the turbulent, and Natalia Trouhanova, who enters in a manner so unforeseen and so radiant in this farandole of beauties that all her cohorts respond like bending stalks of swaying flowers [this refers to the dance movements of the soloists and corps during *Les Sylphides*].

Here is Fokine!

His wings are animated by the sound of the violin [often used for rehearsals as Cocteau has now moved from a performance to a *répétition*] and feeling the tempo he flutters from one group to another. He gives an order, he executes a gesture and all array themselves, prepare, coordinate their movements. His eye is everywhere and notes every detail with exactness; his voice is calm and implacable. He goes around the troupe with an active but genial zeal. This is Mercury!

Around him repose an encampment of young athletes and adolescents with pale faces. [Adolph] Bolm, [George] Rosay, [Alexander] Orlov, [Leonide] Leontiev, etc. They all get up very calmly to take their places for the rehearsal and then, suddenly, with a veritable frenzy but with one accord, they dance briskly, starting and stopping exactly together and with the cleanest precision before returning to the harmonic repose they held at the start of the rehearsal. They are like quicksilver which scatters in so many directions before returning to its accustomed shape.

And finally there is Leon Bakst. A man of gigantic, spicy, silky, and thrilling surprises! You will see [this season] the pool where the tragic young *Narcisse* discovers the nymphs of the woods, the monsters who are charmed by the *Dieu bleu*, the window from which surges the *Spectre de la rose*, the street-fair booths of *Petrushka*, the many-colored talisman of the *Péri* [this last ballet was never performed by the Ballets Russes, though scheduled for that season].

All this from Leon Bakst! And also from Alexander Benois, [Alexander] Golovin, [Nicholas] Roerich, and [Boris] Anisfeld—because they must prepare a dignified cage for the immense bird [the Ballets Russes] which resembles a living tapestry from the *Thousand and One Nights*. These artists have created the beautiful setting for an enterprise which will be over all too soon and only leave behind a memory of the divine soul which we have been privileged to glimpse with stupified wonder.

Source: the printed article from *Comœdia illustré*, 1911. Originally translated by the author, with commentary, in *Dance Scope*, Vol. 13, No. 4, (1979), pp. 7–11. All translations in the appendix are by the author unless otherwise indicated.

2   The Scenario for *Le Dieu bleu*

A monstrous scene of festooning serpents, the sacred lotus in a dark pool on whose edge stands a giant tortoise. An inner shrine in a deep fissure of the rock is barred by massive gates. Overhead through a cleft shines the deep blue Indian sky—it is the background for the supernatural story of the "Blue God." A young neophite is initiated into the rites of the priesthood by curious ceremonial dances. In the crowd who minister to the ceremonial of his initiation is a young girl whose love the neophite has won, but suppose he has put away from himself. Her eager face makes him pause an instant, but recovery quickly follows and he goes on his way through the prescribed ritual. Wilder dances follow as self-intoxication rises to its climax in the breasts of the devotees. As the neophite pauses a second time before his deserted love, she breaks from her place and casts herself at his feet. The priests endeavor to draw her away, but her agony causes a revival in the youth of all his old affection, and tearing off his priestly garments the two endeavor to escape in flight. Priests and fakirs interfere; they are separated, the young man carried away, the girl confined in the cavern by the lotus pool. Awaking from this first stupor she passes from the cavern to a darker den, peopled by hideous monsters. Here her terrors multiply, until she makes appeal to the deities of the place, and out of the lotus in the pool arise the god and goddess who rule here. The Blue God steps from the lotus and raises the prostrate girl to a sitting posture, while before her he executes a dance that vivifies for the beholder the postures of Hindu sculpture. The monsters are thus subdued, and the girl's trepidations are further allayed when the goddess joins in the subduing rhythms. Their blessings are scarcely uttered when the priests return to find her not devoured by the monsters, but bathed in a radiance that overwhelms them. The young man for whom all has been dared is brought in and the union of the lovers is effected before the deities fade from the astonished vision.

Source: Ballets Russes Souvenir Program, 1912. In a private collection.

3   Program Notes from the English Program for *Parade*

PARADE
A Merry Display
Theme by JEAN COCTEAU Music by ERIC SATIE Choreography by LEONIDE MASSINE
Curtain, scenery, and costumes by PABLO PICASSO

SYNOPSIS.   The original idea of Parade dates from the eighteenth century. When wealthy courtiers were indulging their taste for entertainment in the Palaces, it was customary for a few performers to entertain the common people outside. In the same way at County Fairs it is usual for a dancer or an acrobat to give a performance in front of the booth in order to attract people to the turnstiles. The same idea brought up to date and treated with accentuated realism underlies the ballet "Parade."

The scene represents a Sunday Fair in Paris. There is a traveling theatre, and three music hall turns are employed as Parade. These are the Chinese conjurer, an American girl and a pair of acrobats.

Three managers are occupied in advertising the show. They tell each other that the crowd in front is confusing the outside performance with the show which is about to take place within, and they try in the crudest fashion to induce the public to come and see the entertainment within, but the crowd remains unconvinced. After the last performance the managers make another effort, but the theatre remains empty. The Chinaman, the acrobats and the American girl, seeing that the managers have failed, make a last appeal on their own account. But it is too late.

Source: [English] Souvenir Program. In a private collection.

4   Jean Cocteau's Letter to Paul Dormée, Editor of the Review *Nord-Sud*[1]

MY DEAR FRIEND,

You ask me for some details about "Parade." Here are some too quickly written down. Excuse the style.

Every morning new insults reach me, some from very far away, for critics assail us without having seen or heard a work; and since abysses cannot be bridged, and it would be necessary to start at the very beginning, I considered it more dignified never to reply. I therefore read with equal surprise articles which are insulting or contemptuous, articles in which the amusement is mingled with indulgence, and congratulatory articles which are based on misunderstanding.

Before this pile of shortsightedness, crudeness, and insensibility, I think of those admirable months during which Satie, Picasso and I lovingly invented, sketched and gradually put together this pregnant little work, where modesty consists precisely in not being aggressive.

******

I first had the idea of it during a period of "leave" in April, 1915 (I was then in the Army), on hearing Satie play his "Morceaux en forme de poire" for four hands, with Vines.

A kind of telepathy inspired us simultaneously with a desire to collaborate. A week later I returned to the front, leaving with Satie a bundle of notes and sketches which were to provide him with the theme of the Chinaman, the little American girl and the Acrobat (there was then only one acrobat). These indications were not in the least humourous. They emphasized, on the contrary, the prolongation of these characters on the other side of our showman's booth. The Chinaman could there torture missionaries, the little girl go down with the "Titanic," and the acrobat win the confidences of the angels.

Gradually there came to birth a score in which Satie seems to have discovered an unknown dimension, thanks to which one can listen simultaneously both to the "Parade" and the show going on inside.

In the first version the Managers did not exist. After each music hall turn an anonymous voice, issuing from a kind of megaphone, sang a type-phrase, summing up the different aspects of each character. When Picasso showed us his sketches, we realized how interesting it would be to introduce, in contrast to the three chromos, unhuman or superhuman characters who would finally assume a false reality on the stage and reduce the real dancers to the stature of puppets.

I then conceived the "Managers," wild, uncultured, vulgar and noisy, who would injure whatever they praised and arouse (as actually happened) the hatred, laughter and scorn of the crowd by the strangeness of their looks and manners. During this phase of "Parade" three actors, seated in the orchestra, announced through speaking-trumpets, as loudly as posters, the names of advertisements such as Pears Soap, etc., while the orchestra was settling down.

Subsequently in Rome, where I went with Picasso to join Leonide Massine, in order to unite scenery, costumes and choreography, I perceived that one voice alone, to represent each of Picasso's Managers, even though reinforced, jarred and constituted an intolerable error of equilibrium. We should have had to have three timbres for each manager, and that would have led us far from our principle of simplicity. It was then that I substituted for the voices the rhythm of footsteps in the silence. Nothing satisfied me so much as this silence and these stampings. Our manniquins quickly resembled those insects whose ferocious habits are exposed on the film. Their dance was an organized accident, false steps which are prolonged and interchanged with the strictness of a fugue. The awkwardness of movement underneath those wooden frames, far from hampering the choreographer, obliged him to break with ancient formulae and to seek his inspiration, not in things that move, but in things round which we move, and which move according to the rhythm of our steps.

At the last rehearsals the thundering and languorous horse, when the stage carpenters had finished his badly made carcass, was metamorphosed into a cabhorse of Fantomas. Our wild laughter and that of the stagehands decided Picasso to let him keep this fortuitous silhouette. We could not have supposed that the public would receive with such bad grace one of the only concessions made to it.

We now come to the three characters of the "Parade," or rather four, since I had altered the one acrobat to two.

Contrary to the belief of the public, these characters are more Cubist than "our managers." The managers are a sort of human scenery, animated pictures by Picasso, and their very structure necessitates a certain choreographic formula. In the case of these four characters, the problem was to take a series of natural gestures and to metamorphose them into a dance without depriving them of their realistic force, as a modern painter seeks his inspiration in natural objects in order to metamorphose them into pure painting, but without losing sight of the force of their volume, substance, colour and shade.

FOR REALITY ALONE, EVEN WHEN WELL CONCEALED,
HAS POWER TO AROUSE EMOTION.

The Chinaman pulls out an egg from his pigtail, eats and digests it, finds it again in the toe of his shoe, spits fire, burns himself, stamps to put out the sparks, etc. . . .

The little girl mounts a racehorse, rides a bicycle, quivers like pictures on a screen, imitates Charlie Chaplin, chases a thief with a revolver, boxes, dances a ragtime, goes to sleep, is shipwrecked, rolls on the grass, buys a Kodak, etc. . . .

As for the acrobats (shall I confess that the horse was ridden by a manager, and that when this manager fell off we suppressed him for good and all at the very last moment?), the poor, stupid, agile acrobats—we tried to invest them with the melancholy of a Sunday evening after the circus when the sounding of "Lights out" obliges the children to put on their overcoats again, while casting a last glance at the "ring."

Eric Satie's orchestra charms without the use of pedals. It is like an inspired village band.

It will open a door to those young composers who are a little weary of fine impressionist polyphonies.

Listen to it emerging from a fugue and rejoining it again with a classic freedom.

I composed, said Satie modestly, a background for certain noises which Cocteau considers indispensable in order to fix the atmosphere of his characters.

Satie exaggerates, but the noises certainly played an important part in "Parade." Material difficulties, however (amongst others the suppression of the compressed air), deprived us of those "ear-deceivers"—with dynamo, Morse apparatus, sirens, express-trains, aeroplane—which I employed with the same object as the "eye-deceivers"—newspapers, cornices, imitation woodwork, which the painters use.

We could hardly enable the typewriting machines to be heard.

And this is the history, though superficial and lacking in form, of a disinterested collaboration which, in spite of universal indignation, was crowned with success, the truth being that for centuries one generation has handed down a torch to another over the heads of the public, whose breath has never succeeded in extinguishing it.

Source: *Le Rappel à l'Ordre*, trans. Rollo Meyers.

5   *Parade*: **Ballet Réaliste**

Parade: Ballet Réaliste
In Which Four Modernist Artists Had a Hand

No ballet of recent years has created the discussion—not to say fury—that was aroused by the first production of "Parade," a ballet by Jean Cocteau, the French poet, and editor of "Le Mot." The music for the ballet was composed by Eric Satie, the leader of the futurist musicians in Paris; the curtains and costumes were designed by Pablo Picasso, the leader of the cubist school of painting in Europe; the choreography was by Leonide Massine, and the entire production was under the direction of M. Diaghileff. This brief article by the poet-author of the ballet will convey to our readers a slight idea of the artistic aims which inspired the artists in the production of "Parade."

M. Diaghileff's Ballets Russes company has at last produced our ballet entitled "Parade." This work was the result of several months of close collaboration between Pablo Picasso, Eric Satie, M. Diaghileff and myself. It was produced at the Chatelet Theatre, in June, under the vivid rays of a newly discovered artificial light. Picasso painted the curtain and scenery and designed the costumes; Satie wrote the music; and I contributed the story. It was quite impossible for us to foresee the tumult which transformed this entertainment into a *scandale* which turned one half of the artistic public of Paris against the other. I listened to the storm from behind the scenes, on the first night, and it raged so fiercely that the players actually had difficulty in following the music. At certain times they were unable to hear the music at all and were obliged to dance by counting the measures of the conductor's baton.

The plot of "Parade" is supposed to take place on a street in Paris, on a Sunday. Certain music hall artists show themselves in the street, outside of a music hall, in order to draw a crowd. This is always called a "parade," among the traveling circuses in France. The headliners are a Chinese magician, a little American girl, and two acrobats. The managers, in their atrocious language, try awkwardly to attract the crowd, but are unable to convince the people sufficiently to draw them into the theatre. The Chinaman, the American girl, and the two acrobats come out onto the street from the empty theatre, and seeing the failure of the managers, they try the power of their charms; but all their efforts are to no avail. In short, the story of "Parade" is the tragedy of an unsuccessful theatrical venture. Simple—innocent enough.

Picasso's curtain aroused no protest. By its irreproachable calm and grace it astonished those who came to hoot and hiss it. His scenery had the same effect. It was calm and beautiful where an unnameable extravagance had been expected of it.

The entrance of the first gigantic "manager" passed without any remark—probably because he danced beautifully to the music; but, after a while the audience whistled and clapped and hooted, and their clapping and hooting drowned the orchestra.

Massine, who played the Chinaman, had a great ovation. Few people realized with what care the role of this ferocious Chinese magician had been written. Among his minor accomplishments, he could produce an egg from his pigtail, spit fire and put out the eyes of missionaries. Everyone applauded the marvellous technical skill of the great comic dancer, and his brilliant costume caused enthusiastic comment.

The little American girl was played by Marie Chabelska. Of her role, I had aimed to make a union of grace and agility,—a sort of uniting of the outdoor world with the music hall. The little girl mimicked one thing after another, jumped on a moving automobile, flew in it over a road, swam a river, trembled like the flickering of a "movie," chased a robber with a revolver and imitated Charlie Chaplin. These are but a few of the feats she performed. Her performance charmed many but revolted others. Many people thought her really a small girl—Marie Chabelska is twenty years old—and they accused some of the actors of maliciously bruising her knees when she swam.

When Picasso's horse made its entrance, I feared that the hall would collapse. I have heard the cries of a bayonet charge in Flanders, but it was nothing compared to what happened that night at the Châtelet Theatre.

Swerien and Lapokowa [sic], the acrobats, so sad and awkward, delighted almost every one. The public did not, however, appreciate that we had combined in their act the accidental art of the circus with the happy remembrances of childhood.

The Finale in which the whole company breaks loose and collapses, resulted in a renewed and prolonged tumult. Seven enthusiastic calls drowned the hissing and the protestations. Through a hole in the drop curtain I watched the audience, which for a long time continued its arguing and disputations.

We expected the unusual hilarity, but not the bad humor, which Abel Hermant has so cleverly explained is the result of the habitual seriousness peculiar to adults who dislike being entertained by a "Punch and Judy" show, with all its traditions and perspectives. No symbolism is hidden in it. The subtitle of "Parade"—"Ballet Réaliste," is no impertinent fantasy. I long considered the selection of this subtitle. I wanted to give true realism its place in the ballet. What has been known, until now, as realistic theatrical art is a sort of absurdity, as that sort of realism consists in putting on the stage real objects which lose their reality as soon as they are introduced into artificial environments. The theatre is the art of illusion and should always remain so.

In all of Picasso's work there is true realism: that is to say, the world is weighed, measured, verified and felt, with a love and respect for its volumes, its material aspects, its movements, its shadows. He often declares that he goes along the street armed with a foot-rule, measuring objects before putting them on canvas.

In "Parade" the dances are not the result of an effort to achieve decorative effects, but of a desire to amplify the real, to introduce the detail of daily truths and rhythms into the vocabulary of dancing; for truth can always arouse the highest emotions.

Leonide Massine saved the dances. Without his marvelous technique and the amplitude which he always gives to the slightest suggestions of a poet, it would have been impossible for us to produce many of the ideas which inspired us all.

To show that it was not our intention to surprise the public but, on the contrary, to follow in the path of the masters, Picasso and Satie opened the spectacle with a curtain and a fugue of a classic nature, from which all the scenery and all the music that followed seemed to flow as a natural development. Satie's orchestration was wholly free. The utter absence, in his music, of slurring of pedals, of all evidences of the melted and the hazy, resulted in the unfettering of the purest rhythms and frankest melodies.

Certain motifs of a serious character in Satie's music gave to "Parade" its ambiguous charm. In it two melodic planes are superimposed. Without causing the slightest dissonances, his music seems to marry the racket of a cheap music hall with the dreams of children, and the poetry and murmur of the ocean.

"I only composed," says Satie modestly, "a background to throw in relief the noises which the playwright considers indispensable to the surrounding of each character with his own atmosphere. These imitated noises of waves, typewriters, revolvers, sirens, or aeroplanes, are, in music, of the same character as the bits of newspapers, painted woodgrain, and other everyday objects that the cubist painters employ frequently in their pictures, in order to localize objects and masses in nature."

Source: *Vanity Fair*, September 1917.

6 Jean Cocteau's Preview Article on *Les Mariés de la Tour Eiffel*

A VOL D'OISEAU sur "LES MARIES DE LA TOUR EIFFEL"

I have barely enough time to speak to you about *Les Mariés de la Tour Eiffel* because of the work which I am always engaged in. I am not just a poet who *seeks out musical talent* but who seeks out the best set designer, and a costume designer who can execute the costumes at the last minute for a work that must be rehearsed over and over.

My friends and I have found air that is as envigorating as a sea voyage, we are always together. We thrive on each other, dine together, we telephone each other, we each give each other nicknames, it is possible for us to discover a million adventures together from *The Italian Straw Hat* to *Around the World in Eighty Days*.

This harmony is naturally rent by the usual fights, disputes, arguments, dramas, and bickerings that make up every really compatible group.

A work of the theatre or for the theatre should be written, designed, costumed, composed [music made for], and played as well as danced by one man. This "man-orchestra" does not exist so he must be replaced by individuals who can do the most that individuals can do within their respective talents, thus I speak of an amicable group as the one creator.

There are many churches, but very few religions. There are many theatres but very few who can really create as a group. I have, by chance been able to form an interesting, intriguing, sometimes exasperating group with some young musicians, painters and poets. The particular nature of our group has made us seem like a dangerous band of extreme left artists, but in reality I think we have the etiquette of the *extreme right [lieu vierge ou personne ne se trouve]* though they evidently think of us as avant-garde and look horrified at our audacity. In *Les Mariés de la Tour Eiffel*, my contribution has been an image of a state of poetical spirit. My first idea was to call it a comedy-ballet, but this did not work. It is not proper to call this spectacle anything that has been used before, since it is a poem of a very nebulous nature.

Poetry is most real when it shows what is real. It is mistaken to think poetry casts a haze over everything it touches, on the contrary it makes things clearer, more real, more alive so that mankind can recognize things more clearly, sometimes more painfully. It enables us to see and hear at the same time for the first time.

[What is The Wedding Party on the Eiffel Tower?] Ballet? No. Play? No. Tragedy? No. Rather a sort of secret marriage between the antique tragedy and the modern review, between the ancient chorus and the music hall turn. Everything is seen from afar, in perspective,—modern antiquity, people of our childhood, wedding parties that are dying out—an episode on the Eiffel Tower which, having been discovered by the painters becomes again what it should never have ceased to be—a charming person in mittens whose one function was, formerly, to reign over Paris and who has now become a telegraph operator.

What happens? Nothing is described. People such as we always meet on Sunday move about while two human phonographs, to right and left of the stage, comment on their movements. Thanks to Jean Hugo, these people, who would usually be too small, too pitifully real on the stage to stand out from the luminous and decorative mass of the scenery, are constructed, stuffed out, rectified, repainted, led by artifice to a resemblance and a scale which do not flame like straw in the fire of the footlights and the spotlights. Thanks to Irène Lagut, our Eiffel Tower brings to mind those Parisian postcards at the sight of which I have seen even little Arabs sigh in Africa.

I have been asked if the text is satirical. Wherever there is reality there is satire, and I cannot endure a work which, however far from the subjective reality it be carried, has not its deep roots in the reality about us. I have tried to avoid tinkering with style, to avoid originality; I have tried to write freely.

Georges Auric's overture, "The Fourteenth of July," evokes the powerful charm of the streets, the people on a holiday, the little band platforms that look like guillotines and about which drums and cornets incite clerks and girls and sailors to dance. His soft trills accompany the pantomime in the same way that a circus orchestra repeats a tune interminably during an acrobatic act. This atmosphere circulates also through "The Wedding March," "The Bathing Girl," and the "Quadrille" of Germaine Tailleferre, Arthur Honegger, Francis Poulenc, and Darius Milhaud. While the little boy, armed with ingratitude from his birth in the camera, slaughters his people with balls, the cries of his family mingle with the sound of a fugue by Darius Milhaud in which the ancient imprecations are faithfully translated for orchestra.

Source: *La Danse*, June 1921. Courtesy of the Stravinsky-Diaghilev Foundation.

7   Letter from Jean Cocteau dedicated to Jean Börlin after the Opening Night of *Les Mariés de la Tour Eiffel*, June 1921

In *Les Mariés de la Tour Eiffel*, we employ all the popular sources of Parisian life which France will have none of at home, but will always approve whenever a musician, native or foreign, exploits them from the outside.

I have never known a summer à la *Die Fledermaus* (Chauve-Souris), but do you think, for example, that a Russian can hear *Petrushka* in the same way we do? Other than the charms of this musical masterpiece, he finds there his childhood, his Sundays in Petrograd, his lullabies sung to him in his nursery.

Why should I deny myself this double pleasure? I assure you that the quadrille of Germaine Tailleferre, the "chrome" of Poulenc, the overture of Auric, the nuptial march of Milhaud, the funeral march of Honegger—moves me much more than any number of Russian or Spanish dance (variations). It is not a question of musical valour nor the establishment of patriotic precedence. I think I have sufficiently exalted Russian, German, and Spanish musicians and even Negro orchestras to permit me this opinion which some may (wrongly) see as chauvinistic.

It is curious to observe the patriots on the one part, and the internationalists on the other, repulsing bitterly whatever is truly French and embracing unreservedly the local alien spirit. It is curious, too, that in the case of *Les Mariés* an audience at a dress rehearsal should have been outraged by a classic blockhead character whose presence in the wedding cortege was neither more nor less controversial than the presence of the commonplace in the text.

For the rest, in Paris, the combination of so much good and bad humor makes the atmosphere of this city the richest, most invigorating, the most exciting of our time. Serge de Diaghilev said to me one day (some time ago) that he had felt nothing like it in any other capital city.

Every work of the poetic order contains what Gide, in his preface to *Paludes*, so aptly calls "God's share." This share, which can allude the poet himself, often surprises him as much as the public. This or that phrase, such and such a gesture, which originally meant no more to him than the third dimension means to a painter, has a hidden meaning that each person will interpret in his own way. The true Symbol is never planned by the author. It emerges by itself, so long as the bizarre, the unreal, do not enter into the reckoning. *Terra firma*, a certain *terra firma*, is always of the first importance. In a fairyland, the fairies do not appear. They walk invisibly there. They only appear to mortal eyes in those places where their appearance is least expected, the most mundane: the food, a hallway, the bedroom.

The unsophisticated mind is more likely to see fairies than others, for it will not oppose to the marvelous the resistance of the hardheaded realists.

It is in *Les Mariés de la Tour Eiffel* that an infant is more appalling than any other personage in the ballet. I always like to see that which was most appalling [*plus gros*]. The public, which likes to interpret everything literally, demanded of me exactly the reason for such an inclusion. I can give the answer I overheard from a machinist during the rehearsal, who said to one of his fellow workers: "Look at that brat! Is he not clumsy? Just like all little brats." I am content with that admirable observation. In fact I can say that the Chief Electrician, with his reflections, has illuminated my own piece for me more than the lamps he works.

A remark of the Photographer might do well for my epigraph: "Since these mysteries are beyond me, let's pretend that I arranged them all the time."

In *Les Mariés*, "God's Share" is quite large. To the right and the left of the stage the human phonographs, like an antique chorus, like the *compère* and *commère* of the music hall stage, describe, without the least sounding like "literature," the absurd action which is unfolded, danced, and pantomimed between them. I say absurd [Ridiculous] because instead of trying to keep this side of the absurdity of life, to lessen it, to arrange it as we arrange the story of an incident in which we played an uncomplimentary part, I accentuate it, I push it forward, I try to paint more truly than the truth. Is this not a good definition of poetry? raising the clouds of mist and haziness? The poet must disengage his objects and ideas from these veiling mists and hazy clouds, and then display them suddenly and so quickly that they are scarcely recognizable. It is then that they strike us with their youth, as though they had never become aging officials.

This is the case with the commonplace, old, powerful, generally esteemed after the manner of masterpieces, but whose original beauty, because of long use, no longer surprises us.

In our spectacle, I rehabilitate the commonplace. It is my concern to present it in such a light that it recaptures its teens.

A generation devoted to obscurity, to jaded realism, does not give way before the shrug of a shoulder. I know that my text may seem too obvious, that it is too *readably written*, like the alphabets in school. The music which accompanies it provokes a misunderstood analogy. It employs a clarity, a simplicity, a marvelous sense of humour, that are new. It is naivity that triumphs. One seems to be listening to a cafe concert orchestra. The ear is deceived, though, much as an eye which could not distinguish between a loud garish material and the same material copied by Ingres.

Hisses and ovations. A terrible press. [Terrible Press notices]. Some articles. Surprise. Three years later the scoffers are applauding and cannot remember having once hissed—Such is the history of my *Parade*, and of any other piece that alters the rules of the game.

When one hears Georges Auric's overture one sees regiments which are always marching on the 14th of July, marching bands whose music blares out at the street corner and moves away—there then is a roll of the drum and the scenery of Irène Lagut is revealed, and reminds one of forget-me-nots and the bright etchings of a picture postcard; then there are the sculpted costumes, built up and constructed by Jean Hugo with every device of artistry to a likeness on an epic scale; then there are the phonographs which speak with voices more exaggerated than natural; you rebel against this, my audience! they do not understand the double use of these phonographs. You do not understand you have been insulted!! And then, only after weeks and weeks, after we have been working day and night for your pleasure.

Source: *Les Ballets Suédois dans l'art contemporain* (Paris, 1931).

8 Scenario for *Le Train bleu*

Scene I

The chicks and their gigolos.

A fashionable beach, in the sunshine. Running in place after bathing, the gigolos do physical gymnastics rapidly while the chicks scatter and freeze into groups of cute poses as is seen in color picture postcards. The effect should be given by the "ensemble" by their gestures and their ridiculousness of the illusion of an operetta chorus at the rise of the curtain. (*Does one not know a certain pomposity which is always taken for style?*) It is as if one could almost hear the chorus singing: "We are the gigolos, etc. . . . "

But there is a certain stupidity in the poses of these beautiful statues.

The silliness of the operetta, in marble, so chic, so sportive which is formed so beautifully by all, melts and then molds into one.

Perhaps it would look good to make each man and woman, two by two, form in a line in front of the ramp, and to obtain by the gesture of each couple the discord between the voices of the women and the bad singing of the men. (*Combine as one the distracted air of the chicks who sing in ensemble and the smiles they use in the bedroom.*)

The ensemble are now in military formation.

Scene II

The door of the cabin opens. Out comes a male bather (in a swimsuit). Poses in front of the cabin. The chicks group themselves on the right in seductive attitudes. (*One motions with her breasts, the other with a finger on her mouth, another lays down and swings her legs in the air.*) It reminds one of groups which have just finished the quadrille at the Moulin-Rouge. The gigolos come over to the swimmer and carry him in triumph. (*As one sees the photos of boxers carried in triumph after the match.*) They deposit him in the wings and reenter. The chicks stretch across the first level, downstage right. The gigolos arrange themselves one against the other facing the public, in front of the cabins, to cover the placing of the trampoline. They turn all their figures to the stage right wings.

Enter the swimmer, slowly and in great strides; arriving in the middle of the stage he quickly jumps on the trampoline throwing himself up in the air and disappearing in the wings, stage left. His passages and his jump are watched by the gigolos in profile, after the jump all turn their profiles to the left.

Before the beginning of the next section of the musical score, the orchestra stops and the dancers, stopping in the position they hit on the final note, form an immobile tableau. (*Between each end of each reprise by the orchestra the dancers hold poses as if they were having their photograph taken.*)

Scene III

The *danseuse* enters by the first wing, stage left. She has been swimming. The gigolos mass together and mount on each others shoulders. They form a pyramid to prove their prowess for the male swimmer. The chicks wrap the female swimmer in a bathrobe, she dries herself off and is conducted to cabin #2 and she enters and closes the door.

Scene IV

Reenter the male swimmer by the first wing, stage left. (*He is shaking his head to remove the water from his ears, he shakes out his hair, passes both hands over his body, etc. . . . .*)

The gigolos give him a bathing robe. He reenters cabin #1 and closes the door.

Scene V

The chicks and gigolos shake the cabins. One of them locks them with a key. The male swimmer and the female bather get very angry. They raise their heads over the skylight. Everyone dances around the cabins. Everyone then stops suddenly. All the "band" are immobilized and look up into the sky (*grimacing because of the sun*). A cloud covers the scene, it is a plane. The chicks and the gigolos, trying to follow it with their eyes, curve themselves backwards and knock over each other. (*At this point each person should put on their sunglasses for a few moments during which yellow lights should reflect off the glasses and glisten for the audience.*)

The airplane throws off a cluster of colors, all the colors of the rainbow, upon the scene below. The first time this color should be seen stage right, a second time about the middle of the stage, the third time on the extreme left. Chicks and gigolos gesticulate and wave their many-hued and gaudy handkerchiefs and leave through the last stage left wing, upstage, running after the airplane.

The two cabins stir. The male swimmer and the female bather shake the door knobs which still have the keys in their respective keyholes.

Scene VI

The tennis champion enters stage right. (*Her walk, her attitude, her dances, her entire role is inspired by the snapshots one sees in magazines of such people. It is also the same for the golf player, when he enters.*) This type walk as if they were in a race with a photographer, always with their feet in the air, marching in front. These type of people love to have their photo taken and they pose, jump, turn, reverse, even pick up balls for the camera. . . .

She looks at the time on her wristwatch, using a classical gesture that reminds us of the important looking gestures seen on greek bas-reliefs.

The male swimmer pushes his figure further through the narrow skylight of his cabin and swings his arms, calling for help.

The tennis champion frees him.

A duet between the two based on sport themes. The pas de deux should always be facing the audience and is inspired by the pantomime of those singers who swing round and round the couplets and then take the entire refrain.

(*Hand in hand, gestures of affection between the two, etc.*)

The duet continues to be a sportive duo.

All of a sudden, the tennis champion turns and becomes very frightened.

This is because she sees her lover, the golf player, who is approaching. (*The public should not see this happen.*) The male swimmer looks for a place to hide and pushes the tennis champion into the cabin while he hides behind it.

Scene VII

The golf player enters from the second wing, stage left.

All his mannerisms and his type of sportive walk should become a sort of slow dance which the music accompanies, "without sticking" too close to one another [without his moving too closely with the musical phrase and rhythm].

He lights his pipe.

The female bather calls to him and pleads with him to let her out of her cabin. She raises her figure through the skylight and waves her arm, like the male swimmer did before. The golf player frees her.

Flirtation.

A "dancy" waltz.

(*This is inspired by the waltz professional ballroom dancers perform with kisses to each other, high leg throws, kicks in the air, etc. . . .*)

The bathing beauty pretends to see the arrival of her lover. She pushes the golf player into cabin #2 and closes the door.

Scene VIII

Beau Gosse [the male swimmer] and Perlouse [the bathing beauty] return to center stage and dance together, laughing at the tennis player and golfer who appear in the skylight with furious expressions.

They call back in the chicks and gigolos.

Scene IX

All the ensemble run in with their Kodaks and portable cameras.

The chicks and gigolos sit down with their backs to the audience, against the ramp.

Perlouse opens the door of Cabin #1 and lets out the champion of tennis and Beau Gosse does the same for the golfer in cabin #2.

Fugue between the tennis champion and golfer during which they bawl each other out.

Here is the gesticulation for this pas de deux:

When one of them gesticulates, the other crosses his arms and listens with impatience while looking up into the air. (*Using almost total immobility side by side, except when the man swings the toe of his foot while eyeing the sun during the tennis champion's speech and when the woman shrugs her shoulders during the man's speech, etc. . . .*)

Their exasperation finally brings them to blows. This should develop like a silent film with turns in place, pivots, jerky gestures, etc. (*like one sees Charlie Chaplin do*).

The chicks and gigolos take pictures of this fighting, at the instant the two fighters freeze in their battle, they then turn the film and the fighters move again and stop each time their picture is taken.

Beau Gosse and Perlouse try to separate the two combatants and add their dance of love to this dance of battle.

Finally the tennis champion tries to reason with the golfer. She turns her back on him and fixes her hair. She turns back but cannot resist asking the golfer for explanations, why he did what he did, etc., etc., and frustrated he stalks off while the tennis champion is left alone, facing the company.

Scene X

Beau Gosse puts on his dressing gown and a straw hat.

Perlouse and Beau Gosse look to see if they are observed and approach one another for a romantic embrace in the middle of the stage (*just like one sees at the end of an adventure film*) but at that moment a gust of wind comes up and makes Beau Gosse's straw hat fly off and disappear into the sea at the back of the set.

Beau Gosse goes over onto the trampoline and prepares to jump after the hat.

Perlouse follows him.

The curtain falls as she plunges in after him.

Source: The original notes in Cocteau's handwriting, in the collection of the late Sir Anton Dolin. A somewhat different version of this scenario can be found in the published piano score, Heugel and Co., 1924.

9   Cocteau's Articles (Appreciations) of *Les Biches* and *Les Fâcheux*

BEAUTY ONCE AGAIN COMPROMISES HERSELF WITH US

Hazard arranges things well. On January 6 and 19, 1924, it invited Francis Poulenc and Georges Auric to come and triumph at its own headquarters. For Serge de Diaghilev was giving his festival of French music at the Casino at Monte Carlo.

Of course everyone knows that Monte Carlo is a very ugly town, Venice a very beautiful one, and Lourdes a very impressive one. But Lourdes may shock, and Venice disappoint you, and I confess that I like Monte Carlo. There you see the sun shining on gold, and the Café de Paris resembles Saint Marks. The sky-blue chairs are exquisite; the white pastry-like facades stimulate our appetites for life, and the pigeons which the shooters have missed come and settle on Massenet's head. There is one thing wanting, however, and that is a bust of Pascal, to whom we owe Roulette, in the middle of the terrace.

The tourist in Greece turns to his Homer. Here I am guided by Fantomas. The systems are in full swing, and the pilgrims enter their losses on registers. There they are, licking their pencils while the roulette is still slowly turning under its coat of many colors, reminding one of racehorses coming back to the paddock. Moving about between the tables are a few of the fairies who bring good and ill luck: charming, mad old Englishwomen, who sleep standing up, and walk about without ever having undressed since the reign of Queen Victoria. It was in this illustrious spot that I was to win what I had staked upon the two young musicians, with whom my friendship is well known.

LES BICHES

I think, to begin with, in order to emphasize the significance of what I am going to say, I had better confess that I do not like the choreography of "Noces." I admire it, however, without liking it, for although I may blame the form of a piece of furniture I can respect the skill of the cabinetmaker.

Perhaps my severity is due to a too whole-hearted admiration of the purely musical part of this ballet. It is an oratorio, any addition to which I should find disturbing.

In the music of "Noces" I discern a very important feature: in it Stravinsky de-ridiculizes the sublime, just as you are going to hear Poulenc de-ridiculize grace. The spirit of "Sacre" here finds its orchestral formula.

The "Sacre" still preserved some shadow; in "Noces" the mystery takes place in full daylight and at full speed. I consider that the conscious striving after grandeur and the mystery in the choreography is ill adapted to the spontaneous mystery and grandeur of the bare orchestra that has no drapery, and never raises its eyes to heaven. It wears its grandeur underneath, and to emphasize it on the stage is almost like making it seem to be worn outside.

But after all, in order to find fault we have to start from a very high level. This work is a masterpiece of its kind, but I should have preferred the music to have been only a pretext for them, and to have watched the heads being piled one upon another, and the groups being built up and dissolved, in silence.

In "Les Biches," Mme. Nijinska has succeeded in attaining grandeur without premeditation. This was made possible by the absence of subject and the apparent levity of the musical style. For the beauty and melancholy of "Les Biches" are not the product of any artifice. I doubt whether this music knows it hurts. I suspect it of being as hard-hearted as Youth, which spatters passers-by with impertinent scorn. Its rhythms have a sporting distinction. They are like splendid girls going by, covered with sweat and a racquet under their arms, who throw a shadow over us as they pass. After it is over, I go home feeling humiliated. I want to impart emotion to a contemptuous body. I recall my solitude when I was twelve and used to visit the Palais de Glace. I measured the distance that separated me from the celebrated *cocottes*. They would be limping round the warm passages, and then, suddenly, out there in the rink in the cold (reminding one of the ice is a surprise omelette), I would see them bowing and gliding about like ships in full sail.

Yes, Poulenc's music is distant. It is haughty, exhibiting itself half naked, and by failing to understand itself, producing the same effect as perversion.

It only wanted Marie Laurencin. Her scenery and dresses are as apt as can be. They frankly underline the point of everything. This painter's pictures always make us feel sad at the thought that plants and animals do not like us, and are not interested in us. Perhaps a kiss would be enough to break the spell. But who would dare place one upon those muzzles?

Think what a combination of naive luxury and cruel freshness we get from such a painter as this and such a musician! Look at that bouquet, and those ribbons in the florist shop! We flatten our noses against the window; we dare not go in and ask the price.

With an instinct, surprising in a Slav, Mme. Nijinska slips into her place without striking a false note. What Poulenc—like a young animal trying awkwardly to make love and—Laurencin—girl-flower or girl-beast—needed, was just this kind of saint.

Mme. Nijinksa lives shut up in her work. She never stops. Scarcely does she pause to do her hair or fasten her dress. By dint of jumping, and pirouetting, and working her muscles, she ceases to be a worker and becomes a tool. Looking at her sturdy legs, her hair, and her angel's eyes, one admires her as one would a pickaxe or a carpenter's plane.

How will she hold a fragile fan, or proffer beribboned hoops for poodles to jump through? But her brother's blood runs in her veins—a blood that has wings. She does not try to discover what there is at the back of Poulenc or Laurencin. She is guided by intuition. Without the slightest calculation, and by simply obeying the rhythm, and the exigencies of the frame she has to fill, she is about to create a masterpiece: the Fêtes Galantes of her time.

To have thought about Fêtes Galantes, to have thought about the hidden audacities which specialists discover in a Watteau tree, to have thought about the author's names—so redolent of the Isle-de-France—to have thought about art—in short, to have thought at all, would have meant losing the game.

The poetry of these dances was not expressly written down. The dances in "Noces" oblige us to recognize a poem of sacrifice, a Russian poem of maternity, birth, marriage and death. Here nothing forces us. We are free. There is no poetry except the poetry that resides in figures and clear outlines.

I shall not attempt to describe "Les Biches." When the curtain goes up you would think you were at the photographer's. A carping critic will think the frocks are too pink. That is the result of the fever brought on by playing hide-and-seek. A sofa plays the part of star dancer and tenor. One can hear, in imagination, its celestial voice. It is rolled about and jumped on, and when everybody is tired out they collapse upon its cushions. The characters come on and off. Here we have an up-to-date park, and a tea party that might have come straight out of the "Bibliothèque Rose"—a flesh colored rose.

I recommend to you the following: the laughing women near the footlights, and then the entry of the men down the steps. What are these wild creatures, these champion swimmers, these Sports Club prizewinners, these heavenly bullies? They speak along the ground. Their voices come out of the orchestra. Their stout, naked legs leave the young ladies quite unmoved. The latter belong to an age in which couples dance on the beach in bathing costume, and their wreaths are woven on the football field.

Look! . . . There are our fine fellows locked together for an Apotheosis tableau: the Wrestling Match. The ladies unlock them, follow them about, and whisper mocking words into their ears. And I can assure you our heroes are not lacking in self-confidence! The way they swagger about is positively preposterous.

These garden parties, cotillions, and plastic poses prepare us for the entry of Mlle. Nemotchinova.

How right Stendhal is in his use of the word "sublime"! The entry of Nemotchinova is, in the true sense of the word, sublime (no Wagnerite will be able to understand what I mean). When this little lady issues forth from the wings on her toes, in an excessively short jerkin, with her long legs, and her right hand in its white glove raised to her cheek as if in military salute, my heart beats faster, or stops beating all together. And then, with unfailing taste, she presents us with a combination of classical steps and quite new gestures. The most difficult sums solve themselves all alone on this slate, with the aid of the pupils' colored chalks—white, blue, and pink.

Next the two pigeons make their appearance. Two young girls in grey, side by side, but facing one another. One holds the other by the neck; the other places her companion's hand on her own heart. They are profoundly actuated by a singular friendship. They perform their disdainful dance. To the accompaniment of a stormy roll of drums and swallow-like twitterings, the dance increases in intensity, and finally leaves them crossed one behind the other, like a pair of steel scissors, and then they part—but not without exchanging, as they go off, one on the left and one on the right, a brief glance—proud, full of complicity, and unforgettable; the glance of the young girls of Proust.

Marie Laurencin, were you looking for a horse? Here is one: it is Mme. Nijinska. A circus horse with a plum on its head, or, if you prefer, a champagne-colored person who has been drinking champagne, and who plunges on the stage alone, with her cigarette and her pearls, to the rhythm of a Rag-Mazurka. Poulenc's music jumps round her like a poodle.

You must look with all your eyes, for this is a sight you will never see again. Mme. Nijinska accomplishes a *tour de force*: she escapes from the domain of the dance and its judges; when she enters, it is the theatre itself which enters; and as for her dance, which looks so easy, so sketchy, and so nonchalant, she could never teach it to anyone. For here a single look, the teeth pressed on the lower lip, a gesture of the shoulder or elbow are just as important as an *entrechat cinq*, or her brother's famous leap.

See how she maintains her balance on the brink of caricature without falling into it, just as the musician, in spite of his easy manner, never lapses into mere facility. Watch her sit down, stretch out her hands towards the dancers, lead them by a movement of her eyelashes and shoulders towards the screen, and bring the work to an end on a note of confusion provided by three persons whom the fall of the curtain has taken by surprise.

In conclusion, what do you think this ballet reminds us of?

From the house opposite a most mischievous, cunning, and skillful hand is flashing a ray of sunlight from a pocket mirror on a woman's face.

LES FACHEUX

[In the first part of the article Cocteau discusses the music by Georges Auric and compares it to Poulenc's score for *Les Biches*. He then goes on to discuss the settings by Georges Braque and the choreography of Bronislava Nijinska.]

From the moment the curtain goes up, Braque, in one stride, and without effort, "gets over" the footlights, hand-in-hand with Molière. His faun-colored, lion-like elegance is dangerous, as is proved by the fact that he devours the choreography without making the slightest movement. There is too much bustling about, but Braque gets the better of it, like a very calm man having an argument with a very talkative one.

I said that Braque got the better of the choreography; I ought to have said that he was the real choreographer and Mme. Nijinska could only follow him. All the real dancing in the "Fâcheux" is done by the colors—beiges, yellows, browns and greys. The girls who play at battledore and shuttlecock, whose faces, thanks to certain shades of yellow and mauve, seem abnormally pink, fill our field of vision without the aid of any artifice other than that of having a wall or tree as a background.

Orphise, handsome in a flat sort of way under her hat, which is too big for the window from which she watches Eraste, if she wants to express herself, merely has to turn her back in order to disappear like those insects which know how to assume the color and shape of a dead leaf. If she turns round, why bother to run on her toes? if she stands on them it will be enough. Her costume affords us a surprise equivalent to that of an ingenious step. The entry of the bowls players is enough to change the whole lighting, and plunge the scene in moonlight.

When they all run away the decor rocks like a boat. Eraste becomes half as big again, and the houses come nearer. These strange stage effects accompany a pantomime which ought to have been discreetly outlined. No doubt Mme. Nijinska, on account of the restraint imposed upon her by the fact of having such an artist as collaborator, will be blamed for the tactful way in which her dancers hesitate between the Russian Ballet and the Comédie française.

In my opinion, there are few scenes as noble as the massing of colors at the end, merging together, as Renan would say, like those on a dove's neck, while a military call on the trumpets, torn from the orchestra, announces the fall of the curtain.

Source: (Paris: Editions de Quatre Chemins, 1924), and Cocteau's original handwritten notes from a private collection, Paris. The order of this translation follows these source notes, rather than the published edition.

10 The Scenarios for *La Dame à la licorne*

Below are two plot outlines for this ballet, both written by Cocteau. The first was written for the program itself. The second is the final draft copy given to Rosen and used by the choreographer as his "working script."

Program Synopsis

The famous wall tapestries with the red background—the so-called "with the Unicorn"—inspired this ballet. Its theme is virginity. According to the legend, the unicorn accepted its food only from the hand of a virgin. The mirror, with which the lady—or virgin—shows the unicorn its face, contains the reflection of another face: that of the knight—who brings her profane love. The unicorn sees this and dies. The knight meanwhile does not remain faithful. He repents his inconstancy and returns, but the lady will not look at him any more.

She mourns her unicorn. The knight forsakes her forever. Without the unicorn and without the knight, the lady remains alone—with her famous, puzzling "motto"—"Mon seul desir."

The Complete Scenario (Final Draft)

The decor is inspired by the tapestries with the red background, but with the simplicity of a forest cottage.

The tent, to the left, advances or recedes on a mobile platform. To the right, three musicians in dress coats which are quite practicable in the woods; they emphasize that in the ballet which the legend cannot recount. Their music stands remain lighted even when a scene is over with.

The little unicorns awaken in the forest. They open the flaps of the tent and reveal the lady on a divan; next to her is the white unicorn.

There then follows the dance of the Lady with the mirror; she gives something to eat to the unicorn, who sees his image in the mirror. A bugle sounding from afar frightens the unicorns. They become wild. The lady goes into the tent with the white unicorn.

The knight enters, mounted on a heraldic lion with a tournament skirt around the beast. He prances. He raises the flaps of the tent. The white unicorn runs away. The lady is seated in front of her mirror. The knight imposes himself on her image and makes himself part of her world. Dance of love. The lady and the knight embrace and go off together.

The white unicorn reenters, looks for the lady, finds the mirror; but the mirror shows the little animal the knight, with a second knight who looks like the first, and then a third. He also sees three ladies who resemble his Lady. Within the mirror the three couples perform an amorous dance.

The unicorn destroys the mirror with his horn ("the deflowering of the Lady"). A musician from the small stage ensemble visibly breaks a real glass at the same moment. The unicorn carries, suspended on his horn, the mirror, which frames entirely his masked head.

The couples [in the mirror] disappear. The lady reenters. The unicorn refuses to eat from her hand. The unicorn's dance of death. The lady collapses over the cadaver of the small mythological animal.

The knight reenters and sees nothing of the on-going scene. He disappears into the wings, backwards.

The knight reenters, without the lion, just as the other unicorns transport the little white unicorn on their shoulders out into the opposite wing. The lady weeps as she watches the funeral cortège.

The lady disregards the knight and he leaves. She is without the unicorns and without the knight and only stares after the funeral cortege disappearing into the woods.

She advances to the front of the stage. She raises her right hand while a banner descends slowly and curves itself around her. It carries the poetic inscription "MON SEUL DESIR." The lights fade until only the hand[2] of the lady and the poetry of the banner are the only things seen.

CURTAIN

Source: Archive, München Staatsoper; trans. Kenneth Griffiths from the original notes in German.

11   "Danse"

Nothing is more mysterious than figures, mathematics and dance. She is a universal language where the corps is charged with expressing themselves in the darkness and bringing it into the light of day. She raises the theatre onto that ideal stage where the dialogue and the gesture which underline a text are no longer needed. Throughout the long years of her existence she has escaped from the conventional style which she was first held as a prisoner in her early decades. She appears to us now by another road with that intense expressiveness which is as expressive as the dance of the planets and like unto the dance David did in front of the Ark. It is not a behavior that is regulated by simplicity and graciousness alone—it is now a religious ceremony.

In our epoque where the secrets of religion and science are now divorced, she [Dance] has now worn out her old pantomime language in order that she can obtain a superior realism, a higher language *plastique* which does not have to speak in the old fashion. It is probably that these efficacious expressions touch us lightly when they disengage themselves from all the geometric figures which the dance continually inscribes in space, as the spectators applaud with enthusiasm but without understanding exactly what it is that is touching them—though thinking it is only the music which can raise the senses to such heights.

In *Le Sacre du printemps* of Nijinsky or *Le Jeune homme et la mort* with Babilée, all the dances that worked were those that seemed to penetrate the public through the pores of the skin, playing to the eye and the ear while unconsciously entering the system by another means: creating a confusion in the *mode equilibrium*, a mode that is artificially balanced when it should be always in disorder.

In addition, in this contemporary babelism, dance represents an "esperanto." She traverses the wall of idioms. She gives, in addition, the direct translation of a poem which does not need any terms, which abandons them.

When Nijinsky was acclaimed after *Le Spectre de la rose* he gave the audience a sour look because they had not received his choreography for *Le Sacre* as well. And in a single night he played both ballets, trying the justices and injustices of the actuality and inactuality, the triumph of the merely charming over the innovative. These are always the obstacles that all poets and painters must face with audacity.

One finds one shaking oneself, torn between two extremes. One finds one does not comprehend that because of the intervention of the mute language of dance these extremes conjugate themselves in the same verb, the same person with equal force.

In our day a public is capable of applauding side by side the charming and the audacious. They have grown up since Nijinsky danced. And I have seen dancers carry themselves with the same success from the classical piece to the modern composition. Because the eyes *prime* the ears—I repeat it—eyes and ears give to the human machine that chance for the art to enter the system like waves on the skin.

Vive la Danse! Not only does she traverse the wall of all languages, but she also seems able to master the tiresome rights of both peasant and prince and appeals to all. We are offered a spectacle of humanity that is less ponderous but more meaningful than our own.

Source: *Prestige de la danse,* eds. Jean Gueritte and Monique Lancelot (Paris: Charles Portal, 1953).

12   Index to the Ballets of Jean Cocteau

Le Dieu bleu. Ballet in one act by Jean Cocteau and Frédéric de Madrazo. Music by Reynaldo Hahn. Choreography by Michel Fokine. Décor and Costumes by Leon Bakst. First performance: Théâtre de Châtelet, Paris, 13 May 1912. Principal dancers: Nijinsky, Karsavina, Fokine. For the Ballets Russes.

Parade. Realistic ballet in one act by Jean Cocteau. Music by Eric Satie. Choreography by Leonide Massine. Curtain, décor, and costumes by Pablo Picasso. First performance: Théâtre de Châtelet, Paris, 18 May 1917. Principal dancers: Massine, Zverev, Chabelska, Lopokova. For the Ballets Russes.

Le Boeuf sur le toit. Ballet-farce in one act by Jean Cocteau. Music by Darius Milhaud. Décor by Guy-Pierre Fauconnet and R. Dufy. First performance: Comédie des Champs-Elysées, Paris, 21 February 1920. The Fratellini Brothers were featured.

Les Mariés de la Tour Eiffel. Ballet-farce in one act by Jean Cocteau. Music by Auric, Poulenc, Milhaud, Honegger, Tailleferre. Décor by Irène Lagut, costumes by Jean Hugo. Choreography by Jean Börlin. First performance: Théâtre des Champs-Elysées, Paris, 18 June 1921. With C. Ari, J. Figoni, K. Vahlander. For the Ballet Suédois.

Les Biches. Ballet with songs, in one act. Music by Francis Poulenc. Curtain, décor, and costumes by Marie Laurencin. Choreography by Bronislava Nijinska. First performance: Monte Carlo, 6 January 1924. Principal dancers: Nijinska, Nemtchinova, Vilzak. Cocteau worked on the first draft of the ballet, but was given no credit. For the Ballets Russes.

Les Fâcheux. Ballet in one act by Boris Kochno, after the comedy-ballet by Molière. Music by George Auric. Choreography by Bronislava Nijinska. Curtains, décor and costumes by Georges Braque. First performance: Casino, Monte Carlo, 19 January 1924. Principal dancers: Dolin, Krassovska, Nijinska (taking over for Idzikowski). Cocteau devised the first book before it was handed over to Kochno. For the Ballets Russes.

Roméo et Juliette. A pretext after William Shakespeare. Décor, mobiles, and costumes by Jean Hugo, music for the scenes arranged from popular airs of the time of Shakespeare by Roger Desormières. With Marcel Herrand, Andrée Pascal, Jean Cocteau. Conceived and directed by Jean Cocteau for Comte Etienne de Beaumont's *Soirées de Paris*. First performance: Théâtre de la Cigale, Paris, 2 June 1924.

Le Train bleu. Opérette dansée in one act by Jean Cocteau. Music by Darius Milhaud. Choreography by Bronislava Nijinska. Décor by Henri Laurens, curtain by Pablo Picasso, Costumes by Gabriel "Coco" Chanel. First performance: Théâtre des Champs-Elysées, Paris, 20 June 1924. Principal performers: Dolin, Nijinska, Sokolova, Woizikowsky. For the Ballets Russes.

Plein Chant. Pas de deux based on the poem by Jean Cocteau. Choreography by Serge Lifar for Colette Marchand and Serge Perrault. First performance: Paris, 1943.

Orphée. Scenario by Jean Cocteau from his play of the same name. Choreography by Roland Petit. Music by César Franck. Costumes and décor by Jean Cocteau. Performed as a *pas de deux* by Janine Charrat and Roland Petit. First performance: Paris, Salle Pleyel, 15 February 1944.

Le Jeune homme et la mort. Ballet in two scenes by Jean Cocteau. Choreography by Roland Petit and Jean Cocteau. Music by Bach. Décor by Georges Wakhevitch after ideas by Cocteau. First performance: Théâtre des Champs-Elysées, Paris, 25 June 1946. Principal performers: Nathalie Philippart and Jean Babilée. For the Ballets des Champs-Elysées.

L'Amour et son amour. Ballet in one act. Scenario, sets and costumes by Jean Cocteau. Music by César Franck. Choreography by Jean Babilée. First performance: Théâtre des Champs-Elysées, Paris, 13 December 1948. Principal performers: Babilée and Philippart. For the Ballets des Champs-Elysées.

Phèdre. Lyrical tragedy in one act by Jean Cocteau. Music by Georges Auric. Décor and costumes by Cocteau. Choreography by Serge Lifar. First performance: Opéra, Paris, 14 June 1950. Principal performers: Toumanova and Lifar. For the Ballet de l'Opéra.

Oedipus Rex. Opera-oratorio in two acts, after Sophocles. Music by Igor Stravinsky. Text and narration by Jean Cocteau. Originally performed on 30 May, 1927 at the Théâtre Sarah Bernhardt. For the revival at the Théâtre des Champs-Elysées on 19 May, 1952 Cocteau set *tableaux vivants* on dancers from the Ballet de Paris. Settings and masks by Jean Cocteau.

La Dame à la licorne. Ballet fantasy in one act by Jean Cocteau. Music composed from fifteenth- and sixteenth-century songs by Jacques Chailley. Décor and costumes by Jean Cocteau. Choreography by Heinz Rosen. First performance: Munich, Gartnerplatz-theater, 8 May 1953. Principal performers: Mlakar, Laspagnol, Trailine. Mounted for the Paris Opéra with the same décor and choreography on 28 January 1959.

Le Bel indifférent. Ballet in one act based on the play by Jean Cocteau, adapted by the author. Music by Richard Blareau. Choreography by Serge Lifar. Décor by Felix Labisse.

First performance: Monaco, Monte Carlo Opera, 19 November, 1957. For Claude Bessy and Max Bozzoni.

Le Poète et sa muse. Scenario, décor and costumes by Jean Cocteau. Music by Gian-Carlo Menotti. First performance: Spoleto, Italy, Festival of Two Worlds, July 1959.

Posthumous Ballets

Le Fils de l'air. Based on the poem and (unpublished) scenario of Jean Cocteau. Music by Hans Werner Henze. Choreography by the students of Mudra under the direction of Maurice Béjart. First performance: Brussels, Cirque Royale, 14 April 1972.

L'Ange Heurtebise. Ballet based on the poem by Jean Cocteau. Choreography by Maurice Béjart. Music by Manos Hadjidkas. Décor and costumes by Joelle Rousten and Roger Bernard. First performance: Brussels, Cirque Royale, 14 April 1972. Performers: Jean Marais, Jorge Donn, Bertrand Pie, Iukiko Sakai, J.-F. Bouchard.

Sphinx. Based on the play by Jean Cocteau. Choreography by Glen Tetley. Music by Martinů. Sets by Rouben Ter-Arutunian, Costumes by Willa Kim. First performance: Kennedy Center, Washington, D.C., 9 December 1977. Performers: van Hamel, Tippet, Peterson. For American Ballet Theatre.

Poppy. Based on the life and works of Jean Cocteau. Choreography by Graeme Murphy. Music by Carl Vine. Sets and costumes by George Gittoes, Gabrielle Dalton, Kristian Fredrikson, Joe Gladwin and Terrance Jable. First performed in 1978 by the Sydney Dance Company in Sydney, Australia, revised in 1981 by the same company for New York performances, City Center, New York. Performers: Robert Olup, Carl Morrow, Paul Saliba, Ramli Ibrahim.

Notes

Chapter 1

1. In 1955 when Cocteau was made a member of the Académie française Cartier made his Academy sword for him, after his own design. See Hans Nadelhoffer, *Cartier, Jewelers Extraordinary* (New York: Harry N. Abrams, 1984), pp. 279–81.

2. Jean Cocteau, *The Difficulty of Being*, trans. Elizabeth Sprigge (London: Peter Owen, 1966), p. 148.

3. *Portraits-souvenir* (Paris: Bernard Grasset, 1953), p. 61: "J'assistais à la toilette de ma mère."

4. *Difficulty of Being*, p. 37.

5. Ibid., p. 39.

6. Ibid., p. 41.

7. *Portraits-souvenir*, p. 81.

8. Ibid., p. 89: "Brusquement, le cake-walk vint disperser et décolorer tout."

9. Ibid., pp. 90–91: "Ils dansaient, maigres, crochus, enrubannés, scinitillants d'étoiles, éclaboussés de lumière blanche, le chapeau sur l'oeil et sur l'oreille, les genoux plus haut que le visage renversé en arrière, les mains agitant une canne flexible, arrachant leurs gestes d'eux-mêmes et martelant un plancher artificiel des claquettes de leurs souliers vernis. Ils dansaient, ils glissaient, ils se cabraient, ils se caissaient en deux, en trois, en quatre, ils se redressaient, ils saluaient. . . . Et derrière eux toute une ville, toute l'Europe, se mettait à danser." This delightful book of Cocteau's memoirs is also filled with sketches of the circus and the performers whom he most admired. Another team were the clowns "Footil et Chocolat" who were also the inspiration for other artists of the period, including the young Pablo Picasso.

10. For an interesting survey of the European dance mania before World War I see Peter Buckman, *Let's Dance* (New York: Paddington Press, 1978), pp. 104–56.

11. Marcel Proust, *Lettres à Reynaldo Hahn*, ed. Philippe Kolp (Paris: Gallimard, 1956), p. 203.

12. As quoted in Nigel Gosling, *The Adventurous World of Paris, 1900–1914* (New York: William Morrow, 1978), p. 65. For a further analysis of this period in France and the origins of the Avant-Garde see Roger Shattuck, *The Banquet Years* (New York: Random House, 1955, 1968).

13. For further information on the Paris Opéra ballet see Ivor Guest, *Le Ballet de L'Opéra de Paris* (Paris: Flammarion, 1976), pp. 127–69. A chart of the ballets included in his Appendix shows the sharp decline in new productions after 1860.

14. Stéphane Mallarmé, *Oeuvres complètes* (Paris: Mondor et Jean Aubrey, 1945), p. 307.

15. *Portraits-souvenir*, pp. 127–28: "De cette foire confuse et poussiéreuse de conserve une seule image vivante et flamboyante: Mme. Loïe Fuller. . . . Est-il, en revanche, possible d'oublier cette femme qui trouve la danse de son époque? Une grosse Américaine, assez laide et à lunettes, debout sur une trappe-lentille, manœuvre avec des perches des flots de voile souple, et sombre, active, invisible, comme le frelon dans la fleur, brasse autour d'elle une innombiable orchidée de lumière et d'étoffe qui s'enroule, qui monte, qui s'évase, qui ronfle, qui tourne, qui flotte, qui change de forme, comme la poterie aux mains du potier. . . ."

16. Ibid., p. 149: "J'aimerais paraphraser Nietzsche et Wilde: Elle a vécu le meilleur de sa danse."

17. Ibid., p. 151: " . . . qu'elle bravait et s'obstinait à mettre."

18. There are many books that contain information on Petipa but few that discuss his contributions in great detail. The best is a collection of documents and essays, *Marius Petipa, Materiali Wospominanija Stati* (Leningrad: Verlag Iskusstwo, 1971), which has yet to be translated into English. Fokine's theories are included in the Appendix to Cyril Beaumont, *The Ballets of Michael Fokine* (London: Beaumont Press, 1933). There was no animosity between Petipa and Fokine and the former expressed admiration for Fokine's ideas.

19. For further information on the Ballets Russes see the opening chapters of Richard Buckle, *Nijinsky* (London: Weidenfeld and Nicolson, 1971) and *Diaghilev* (New York: Atheneum Press, 1979). Bronsilava Nijinska, *Early Memoirs* (New York: Holt, Rinehart, Winston, 1981) gives a superb account of the training and schooling in Russia under the last years of Imperial government and Nesta MacDonald, *Diaghilev Observed* (New York: Dance Horizons Press, 1976), includes reviews from the New York and London tours of the Ballets Russes.

Chapter 2

1. Authors who make this mistake include Richard Buckle, *Nijinsky* (London: Weidenfeld and Nicolson, 1971), p. 80; Francis Steegmuller, *Cocteau* (New York: Atlantic, Little, Brown, 1970), p. 68; Frederick Brown, *An Impersonation of Angels* (New York: Viking Press, 1968), p. 81. See n. 4 below for the evidence against Cocteau's being at the *répétition générale*.

2. "Le Théâtre et la Mode," *Masques*, 1, No. 1 (1945), p. 16

3. Jean Cocteau, *The Difficulty of Being*, trans. Elizabeth Sprigge (London: Peter Owen, 1966), p. 32.

4. Quoted by Margaret Crosland, *Jean Cocteau* (New York: Alfred A. Knopf, 1956), pp. 23–24. If Cocteau's recollection is correct it would have been the 2 June 1909 performance or one of six later performances. Anna Pavlova did not arrive in Paris until the season was well under way and did not dance *Pavillon* until 2 June.

5. More detailed information on Misia's relationship with Diaghilev, as well as Stravinsky, can be found in Vera Stravinsky and Robert Craft, *Stravinsky in Pictures and Documents* (New York: Simon and Schuster, 1978), Appendix B. See also Arthur Gold and Robert Fizdale, *Misia* (New York: Alfred A. Knopf, 1980).

6. *Difficulty of Being*, p. 32.

7. Misia Sert, *Two or Three Muses* (London: Museum Press, 1953), p. 111.

8. Jean Cocteau, *Dessins* (Paris: Librairie Stock, 1923), plate 53.

9. Sert, p. 112.

10. *Schéhérazade* lasted for five issues. Its contributors were mostly society artists and writers despite Cocteau's later claims to have included works by Braque and Picasso—there is no trace of these artists in the magazine or any of the avant-garde writers. See Steegmuller, pp. 43–49.

11. Tamara Karsavina, *Theatre Street* (New York: E. P. Dutton, 1931), p. 239.

12. Alexander Benois, *Reminiscences of the Russian Ballet* (London: Putnam and Co., 1941), p. 378.

13. Prince Peter Lieven, *The Birth of the Ballets Russes* (London: George Allen and Unwin, 1936), p. 121.

14. *Difficulty of Being*, pp. 45–46.

15. Ibid., p. 44.

16. Ibid.

17. Quoted by Robert Phelps, trans. by Richard Howard, in *Professional Secrets* (New York: Farrar, Straus, and Giroux, 1970), p. 49.

18. Quoted by Margaret Crosland, *Cocteau's World* (New York: Dodd, Mead, 1973), p. 259.

19. In the article from *Masques*, quoted above, Cocteau reiterates this fascination for Nijinsky, "this contrast between the Nijinsky smiling and bowing after *Spectre* and the poor athlete who, after each curtain call, collapsed against the proscenium arch . . . an example of extraordinary force and weakness combined in one man."

20. *Dessins*, plates 49–57.

21. Ses also the drawings in *Portraits-souvenir* and the Ballets Russes programs for 1910, 1911 and 1912.

22. Some of the drawings have never been published and are in private collections. The author was able to view some of these through the courtesy of the late Leonide Massine.

23. *Difficulty of Being*, p. 45.

24. Jean Cocteau and Paul Iribe, *Six Dessins à V. Nijinsky* (Paris: n.p., 1911). The book is extremely rare.

> Apollon tient le fil au bout dequel il pend.
> Nègre de la Sultane, il vole en s'échappant,
> Et le décor a l'air de la traine d'un paon.
>
> Il lance, Hermès rempli de mystérieux zèles,
> Des fleurs qu'on ne voit pas pour courir après elles
> Et charge tous les cœurs sur d'invisibles ailes!

25. Lieven, p. 122.

26. *Difficulty of Being*, p. 33.

27. The author is grateful to the late Anton Dolin for allowing him to look through the "black book" before its sale at Sotheby and Company, London, on 5 June, 1975. For a detailed discussion of the problems involved with the entries in this book and the dating of the material see Sotheby and Company, *Ballet and Theatre Material* [Sales Catalogue] (London: Sotheby and Company, 1975), pp. 71–75.

28. Richard Buckle, *In Search of Diaghilev* (London: Sidwick and Jackson, 1950), p. 95. The post card has a printed address: "Restaurant Le Grand Vatel, 275 Rue St. Honoré, Paris," and the postmark is 27/10/10. By this date all the dancers had left for Russia, and Buckle states that

Nijinsky and Diaghilev had gone to Venice for a holiday but returned to Paris to consult about this particular ballet.

29. Astruc papers, Dance Collection, New York Public Library at Lincoln Center. There are four drafts of the contract before the final, typed version.

30. Marcel Proust, *Lettres à Reynaldo Hahn*, ed. Philippe Kolp (Paris: Gallimard, 1956), p. 203.

31. Astruc papers.

32. The Society was founded by another "homme des lettres" involved with balletic activities, Eugène Scribe. It protected writers of any theatrical presentations, including ballets and operas, and guaranteed the issuance of a fee per performance.

33. "Le Ballet Russe," *Comoedia illustré* (Paris: n.p., 1911). The entire text is translated in Appendix A.

34. Arthur King Peters, *Jean Cocteau and André Gide: An Abrasive Friendship* (New Brunswick: Rutgers University Press, 1973), p. 28. The probable date of the letter is sometime in early August 1912. It was common to refer to Nijinsky as Vestris.

35. George Painter, *Marcel Proust, A Biography*, vol. II (Boston: Atlantic, Little, Brown, 1965), p. 176.

36. See Painter, pp. 174–78, for an analysis of Proust's use of Cocteau's characteristics for Octave.

37. Buckle, *Nijinsky*, p. 175.

38. Ibid.

39. Pictured and detailed in Buckle, *Nijinsky*, plates 35–38, and discussed in his *In Search of Diaghilev*, pp. 93–96.

40. Souvenir program for the 1911 season, Dance Collection, New York Public Library at Lincoln Center.

41. Proust, *Lettres*, p. 182. Hahn noted the importance of the color blue in "Eastern" ballets in his review of *Schéhérazade*, *Le Journal*, June 1910.

42. Benois, p. 346, and Lieven, p. 170.

43. Proust, *Lettres*, p. 171; Igor Stravinsky, *Memories and Commentaries*, with Robert Craft (London: Faber and Faber, 1960), p. 32.

44. Buckle, *Nijinsky*, p. 186. See also Philippe Jullian, *Prince of Aesthetes* (New York: Viking Press, 1968), pp. 240–46, which discusses the creation of *Martyrdom* in some detail.

45. S. L. Grigoriev, *The Diaghilev Ballet* (London: Constable, 1953), p. 72.

46. Ibid., p. 78; Peters, p. 17. Steegmuller claims that Cocteau was at all dress rehearsals but does not give any sources. It is possible that Cocteau was at some early rehearsals, but his correspondence shows he was in Algiers at the time the final dress rehearsals were in progress.

47. Reynaldo Hahn, *Le Dieu bleu*, piano score (Paris: Hengel et Cie., 1911), n.p. Cocteau's scenario from the piano score and that published in *The Art of Leon Bakst* (London: Fine Arts Society, 1913) are very similar though more details are included in the piano score. The sequence of numbers follows Cocteau's scenario carefully:

> Prélue
> Première Danse
> Danse des Porteuses d'Offrandes et des Musiciennes
> Danse des Bayadères du Lotus
> Danse des Yoghis

Scène de la Jeune Fille (Supplication)
Danse des Souvenirs
Colère des Prêtres
Clair de Lune [accompanied the lighting change from day to night]
Monstres et Démons
Le Miracle [appearance of the gods]
La Déesse Parait
Le Dieu bleu (danse et scène)
L'Enchantement divin
Les Amants se Réunissent
Danse et Scène
L'Escalier d'Or et le Montée du Dieu
Hahn dedicated his score to Lady Ripon.

48. Compare with this quote from *Potamak:* "Nourished on mandragoras and montgolfier ballons, the Potamak . . . unfolded his paws and slid near me." Cocteau, *Oeuvres complètes*, vol. I (Lausanne: Marguerat, 1946–51), p. 76. Written in 1914, the book did not appear in print until 1919.

49. All quotes are from the piano score, unless otherwise noted. See also the program.

50. *Le Théâtre*, May 1912, p. 32.

51. *Mercure de France*, 15 May 1912.

52. *Le Figaro*, 14 May 1912, p. 8.

53. This is not correct. According to the scenario and contemporary descriptions this was the *final* view of Nijinsky. He was first seen rising from the lotus pool.

54. Lydia Sokolova, *Dancing for Diaghilev* (London: John Murray, 1960), pp. 36–37.

55. Ibid., p. 37.

56. Ibid.

57. Buckle, *In Search of Diaghilev*, p. 95. Stravinsky thought Cocteau was never serious about *Le Dieu bleu* which he discusses in "On Music and Other Matters," *New York Review of Books*, 14 March 1968.

58. *Daily Mail*, 28 February 1913. Reviewers of the time are very frustrating to read as they did not know how to critique dance, and there are few remarks of pertinent information; most describe the sets and costumes and state whether the dancing was "good" or "bad." In terms of the reviews for *Le Dieu bleu* all the newspapers did note the dated look of the piece. See the *Observer*, 2 March 1913, and the *Daily Telegraph*, 28 February 1913. *The Times*, 1 March 1913, did have something more to say by remarking on the history of ballet and its continual use of the East for inspiration (where China and Asia were easily interchangeable). "It was regarded then and is still regarded as a kind of halfway house to fairyland."

59. Nesta McDonald, *Diaghilev Observed* (New York: Dance Horizons, 1975), p. 201. See also the Souvenir program issued by the Metropolitan Opera Company in New York for the 1916 tour and the Valencia Theatre program, San Francisco, January 1917.

60. However, it seems Fokine did revive the ballet in America for Paul Haakon (b. 1914) in 1928. Haakon's father recreated the original Bakst designs (cf. John Gruen, "Paul Haakon," *Dance Magazine* [November 1977], pp. 60–67. The article includes one picture of Haakon as the blue god on p. 67. The ballet also inspired a number of *objets d'art*, such as the Malvina Hoffman statue of Nijinsky in bronze, presently in the private collection of Robert L. Tobin.

Chapter 3

1. Jean Cocteau, *A Call to Order*, trans. Rollo Meyers (London: Faber and Gwyer, 1926), p. viii.

2. Francis Steegmuller, in *Cocteau* (New York: Atlantic, Little, Brown, 1970), discusses the various stories of Cocteau's meeting with Stravinsky, pp. 83–84.

3. *A Call to Order*, p. 42.

4. Ibid., pp. 46–47.

5. Ibid., p. 48.

6. Steegmuller, p. 89.

7. *A Call to Order*, p. 49.

8. Ibid., p. viii.

9. Igor Stravinsky, *An Autobiography* (New York: Steuer, 1958), pp. 39–40.

10. Steegmuller, pp. 93–100. The manuscript letters were lent to the author by Igor Stravinsky.

11. Some of the letters obviously went through a number of drafts and were looked over by Cocteau's friends. Those printed in Sert's memoirs (see below) are only a few of a large series, now in a private collection in Paris.

12. Paul Morand, *Journal d'un Attaché d'Ambassade* (Paris: Gallimard, 1953), p. 43.

13. Margaret Crosland, *Jean Cocteau* (New York: Alfred A. Knopf, 1955), p. 43.

14. Jean Cocteau, *My Contemporaries*, trans. Margaret Crosland (London: Peter Owen, 1967), p. 75.

15. *A Call to Order*, p. 46.

16. Frederick Brown, *An Impersonation of Angels* (New York: Viking Press, 1968), p. 125.

17. Gabriel Astruc, *Le Pavillon des Fantômes* (Paris: Grasset, 1929), pp. 112–13.

18. See Steegmuller, p. 135, for the letter from Satie to Valentine Gross [Hugo].

19. For more information and the debate on whether Satie meant these for Cocteau's ballet, see Pierre-Daniel Templier, *Eric Satie* (Cambridge: M. I. T. Press, 1969), pp. 86–91, and James Harding, *Eric Satie* (New York: Praeger Publishers, 1975), pp. 133–41. Although it cannot be proved, it would seem likely to have been written for Cocteau as Satie told Valentine Gross he wanted to use only new music and to ask Cocteau not to use his older compositions.

20. Steegmuller, p. 136.

21. Ibid., p. 154.

22. Ibid.

23. Misia Sert, *Two or Three Muses* (London: Museum Press Ltd., 1953), p. 117.

24. The final score does not carry a dedication to Sert. Only the printed piano score is dedicated to her.

25. Sert, p. 147.

26. Douglas Cooper, *Picasso Theatre* (New York: Abrams Press, 1968), p. 16. Cocteau's version is found in his essay on Picasso. Cooper discusses the sources in detail. Varèse sailed for America on 18 December 1915.

27. See Cocteau's essay on Picasso included in *A Call to Order*, quoted above.

28. *A Call to Order*, p. 226.

29. *My Contemporaries*, p. 78.

30. Pierre Cabanne, *Pablo Picasso* (New York: William Morrow, 1977), p. 176.

31. *My Contemporaries*, p. 78.

32. Ibid. Telegram quoted in Cabanne, p. 180.

33. *A Call to Order*, p. 23.

34. Cocteau's notebooks for *Parade*, hereafter referred to as *Parade*, were the personal property of the late Leonide Massine. Two of the pages were photographed and printed as an appendix in Cooper. The present author studied a holograph of the complete original through the courtesy of Leonide Massine.

    Cocteau's *Cahier roman*, a notebook kept by Cocteau during the rehearsals of *Parade*, came after the notebooks sent to Massine. The *Cahier roman* has been reproduced in full in Richard Axsom's *Cubism as Theatre* (New York: Garland Publishers, 1979). Further information can also be found in "The Ballet *Parade*: A Dialogue Between Cubism and Futurism," by Marianne Martin, *Art Quarterly*, n.s., Spring 1978.

35. *Parade*, n.p. This was originally written to Eric Satie.

36. Ibid.

37. Brown, p. 129.

38. Cooper, p. 19.

39. Ibid., p. 333.

40. Ibid., p. 334.

41. Ibid.

42. *A Call to Order*, p. 51.

43. Ibid. See also Appendix 5.

44. The texts of the contracts are quoted in full, but only in English translation, in Richard Buckle, *In Search of Diaghilev* (London: Sidwick and Jackson, 1953), p. 93.

45. Gertrude Stein, *An Autobiography of Alice B. Toklas* (New York: Harcourt, Brace, 1933), p. 108.

46. Georges Auric, in an article on the revival of *Parade* in 1930 for *La Nouvelle revue française*, noted that Diaghilev asked Satie if he knew Rome. The composer replied, "Only by name, sir, only by name." "Chronique sur Parade," *La Nouvelle revue française* (February 1921).

47. *My Contemporaries*, p. 79.

48. W. A. Propert, *The Russian Ballet in Western Europe* (New York: John Lane Company, 1921), p. 85.

49. Letter in the Dance Collection, New York Public Library at Lincoln Center.

50. André Fraigneau, *Entretiens avec Jean Cocteau* (Paris: Jalard, 1965), p. 22.

51. Leonide Massine, *My Life in Ballet* (London: MacMillan Company, 1968), p. 101.

52. *Parade*, n.p. From the notes Massine developed the order of action for the Chinese conjurer's dance: a deep bow to the audience and sides of the stage, making an egg disappear in his

mouth and coming out of his foot, blowing fire, sword swallowing, fanning himself, running leaps about the stage and a final bow and exit. Cocteau indicates for five and six that these actions should be performed with a minimum of movement.

53. Massine, p. 103.

54. Cocteau, *A Call to Order*, p. 52. Also see Appendix 4.

55. Massine, p. 103.

56. Appendix 4.

57. Some writers have seen the little American girl as an imitation of Pearl White serials. Massine told the author that the dance was a reflection of Mary Pickford based on Cocteau's suggestion. There is no reference in the notebook, though the last line of a poem Cocteau wrote about the little American girl coming out of the theatre after a performance of *Parade* says, "Allons, Marie." *Poésies*, 1920.

58. *A Call to Order*, p. 237.

59. Steegmuller, p. 169.

60. No place, no date, but seems to have been sent from Italy. Courtesy Stravinsky-Diaghilev Foundation: "Serge était bien inquiet de me voir laisser le travail en panne. Je crois que vous serez contente. Le Chinois est fait—Massine devait jouer l'acrobate mais il indique le chinois avec un tel talent que je l'ai prié de prendre ce rôle."

61. Stravinsky-Diaghilev Foundation.

62. Sert, p. 119.

63. Stravinsky-Diaghilev Foundation. In both letters he tells stories about "the old man" and makes jokes about his work.

64. *A Call to Order*, p. 237.

65. *My Contemporaries*, p. 79.

66. Letter is at present in the Stravinsky-Diaghilev Foundation. No date, but postmarked from Rome.

67. For an interesting discussion of the effects the Futurists may have had on Picasso at this time (as well as Larionov, the designer of *Contes Russes*), see "Kubismus und Theatre" by Ina Stegan in the *Neue Zuricher Nachrichten*, 5 March 1967, p. 10. "The cubist costumes of *Kikimora*, stiff, geometric, cardboard dummies, were the first of their kind." *Kikimora* was the first version of *Contes Russes* and premiered before *Parade*, although all were in rehearsal at the same time.

68. Douglas Cooper has proved beyond a shadow of a doubt that most of the work was done in Paris. However, this does not exclude the building of the models and frames in Rome.

69. Letters from the Stravinsky-Diaghilev Foundation.

70. On tour the sound effects had to be cut totally and Ansermet, the conductor, had to substitute orchestra sounds. Letter from Ansermet to Diaghilev on this is quoted in Boris Kochno, *Diaghilev and the Ballets Russes* (New York: Harper and Row, 1970), p. 120.

71. *A Call to Order*, pp. 238–39.

72. Program, Théâtre du Châtelet. A copy of the opening night program is presently in the collection of the author. The quotes are taken from this copy.

73. Ibid. This essay is also quoted in full in Kochno and Steegmuller.

74. Ibid.

75. A discussion of the various figures in this curtain is included in Nesta MacDonald, *Diaghilev Observed* (New York: Dance Horizons, 1975), p. 242.

76. This reconstruction of opening night is based on the personal observations of Valentine Hugo and Georges Auric. Some plot outlines still include the dummy Negro, which is correct according to Cocteau's original notes, but not to the performance on stage.

77. See Appendix 3, 4 and 5 for further information. Cocteau also claimed that he never watched the ballet from out front because he was too upset about the changes Picasso, Satie, Massine, Diaghilev, et al., had made in his production. See Fraigneau, p. 23.

78. See Appendix 5.

79. See Appendix 5.

80. Massine, p. 111.

81. S. L. Grigoriev, *The Diaghilev Ballet* (London: Constable, 1953), p. 131.

82. Morand, p. 243.

83. For the reviews, see Harding, pp. 176–80.

84. Huntly Carter, "Newest Tendencies in the Paris Theatre," *Theatre Arts* (December 1917), p. 35.

85. MacDonald, p. 238.

86. Propert, p. 119. Cyril Beaumont, *The Diaghilev Ballet in London* (London: A. and C. Black, 1940), p. 149.

87. Grigoriev, p. 158.

88. Lydia Sokolova, *Dancing for Diaghilev*, ed. Richard Buckle (London: John Murray, 1960), p. 103.

89. Grigoriev, p. 158.

90. Steegmuller, p. 261.

91. Ibid., p. 232.

92. *Comœdia illustré* (21 December 1920), n.p.

93. Ibid.

94. Sokolova, p. 104.

95. Douglas Cooper, "*Parade*, a Report on its Revival by the Joffrey Ballet," *Dance and Dancers* (June, 1973), pp. 20–25.

96. *The New York Times*, 23 March 1973, section C, p. 14.

97. *New York Post*, 23 March 1973, p. 15.

98. *New York Post*, 1 April 1973, p. 12.

99. *The New Yorker*, 11 November 1974, p. 92.

100. The author talked to Gerald Arpino and members of the company in the spring of 1976 while they were performing *Parade* in Bloomington, Indiana. Arpino mentioned how spontaneous and enthusiastic the applause was, the horse always being a big hit (this also proved true in the London provincial tours for Festival Ballet). Gary Chryst, who danced the Chinese con-

jurer, mentioned how fascinated the company was with the ballet and even in the midst of a gruelling twenty-three week tour he had not grown tired of his part but always found something new in it.

101. *Dance and Dancers*, April 1974, p. 35.

102. Most of the works start from the premise of the "scandal" of opening night. Neal Oxenhandler's book *Scandal and* Parade (New Brunswick: Rutgers University Press, 1957), centers on the *Parade* opening. If one would look at the *Sacre* opening as the real start of Cocteau's need to "astonish," the *Parade* problems would take on a better perspective.

103. Fraigneau, p. 23. Also see Kenneth E. Silver, "Jean Cocteau and the *Image d'Epinal*," in *Jean Cocteau and the French Scene* (New York: Abbeville Press, 1984) pp. 81–105. Silver discusses some of the sources for Cocteau's ideas for *Parade* and *Le Boeuf sur le toit* noting especially the use of the Alphabet Grotesques des Cris de Paris. Childhood imagery was certainly a part of Cocteau's "reality" for both these ballets.

Chapter 4

1. Jean Cocteau, *A Call to Order*, trans. Rollo Meyers (London: Faber and Gwyer, 1926), p. 3.

2. Margaret Crosland, *Cocteau's World* (New York: Dodd, Mead and Company, 1973), p. 301.

3. Francis Steegmuller, *Cocteau* (New York: Atlantic, Little, Brown, 1970), p. 217.

4. Darius Milhaud, *Notes without Music* (New York: Alfred A. Knopf, 1953), p. 97.

5. Ibid.

6. Francis Poulenc, *Moi et mes Amis* (Paris-Genève: La Palatine, 1963), p. 20.

7. Arthur Honegger, *I Am a Composer*, trans. W. O. Clough (London: Faber and Faber, 1966), p. 104.

8. "Auric Speaks of Then and Now," *The New York Times*, 25 June 1978, sec. G., p. 2.

9. Jean Cocteau, *Entretiens avec André Fraigneau* (Paris: Michel-Claude Jalard, 1965), p. 28.

10. Milhaud, p. 97.

11. Georges Auric, "On the Diaghileff Ballet and Jean Cocteau." *The Ballet Annual* (London: A. and C. Black, 1956), p. 76.

12. Milhaud, p. 102. Steegmuller discusses the origin of the title, p. 218, n. 4.

13. Ibid., pp. 102–3.

14. *Entretiens*, p. 29.

15. Steegmuller, p. 240.

16. A translation of the scenario is in Margaret Crosland, *Cocteau's World* (New York: Dodd, Mead and Company, 1973), pp. 163–68.

17. *Comoedia illustré*, 21 February 1920, n.p.

18. Ibid.

19. Ibid.

20. Ibid.

21. Milhaud, p. 103.

22. *Comœdia illustré*, n.p.

23. Ibid.

24. Ibid.

25. Ibid.

26. Jean Cocteau, *Order Considered as Anarchy*, in *Cocteau's World*, trans. Margaret Crosland (New York: Dodd, Mead and Company, 1973), p. 389.

27. Milhaud, p. 104.

28. Jean Cocteau, *La Jeunesse et le Scandale*, Vol. IX of *Oeuvres complètes* (Lausanne: Marguerat, 1950), p. 326: "Le scandale est très vivant, mais il dérange les artists, l'orchestre, et empêche les quelques personnes sérieuses de voir les milles nuances d'un travail de plusieurs mois. Je l'évitai en apparaîssant devant le rideau et en prononçant quelques paroles qui rendaient le public mon complice. S'il sifflait, il se sifflait. Je ne broncha pas."

29. Jacques-Emile Blanche in the *Comœdia illustré* article quoted above.

30. *Le Journal*, 22 February 1920, p. 12.

31. Ibid.

32. *Paris-Midi*, 22 February 1920, p. 20.

33. Ibid.

34. Ibid.

35. Ibid.

36. *The Matinee*, 23 February 1920, p. 4.

37. Ibid.

38. Ibid. The dialogue of "The Neutrals" contrasts remarks for them against Cocteau. The underlying complication in the review is the fact that Cocteau has sold out to his fame rather than creating something worth while which might not have the same sensational appeal and publicity value that *Le Boeuf* had. This is also implied in the last remark about Satie since Bastia considered that composer's music a self-indulgence.

39. *Comœdia illustré*, 23 February 1920, n.p.

40. Ibid.

41. Ibid.

42. *Paris-Midi*, 25 February 1920, p. 21.

43. Ibid., p. 22.

44. *Le Ménestrel*, 12 March 1920, p. 9.

45. Ibid.

46. *Musical Standard*, 13 March 1920, p. 46.

47. Milhaud, p. 104.

48. Ibid.

49. Elizabeth Sprigge and Jean-Jacques Kihm, *Jean Cocteau: The Man and the Mirror* (New York: Coward McCann, 1968), p. 78.

50. Milhaud, p. 117.

51. Ibid., p. 118.

52. Milhaud claims Ruth Draper followed the presentation of *Le Boeuf*, but all the reviewers speak of Grock's act following the ballet. Milhaud may have been thinking of a later change in the program during the next two weeks.

53. Milhaud, p. 180. The ballet was also performed in Ba-ta-clan, a club of dubious respectability. Not much information is known about this production.

54. *The Stage*, 15 July 1920, p. 3.

55. *The Times*, 13 July 1920, p. 8.

56. *Sackbut*, August 1920, p. 50.

57. *Musical Standard*, 17 July 1920, p. 46.

58. *New York Herald Tribune*, 25 April 1930, p. 20.

59. *The World*, 25 April 1930, p. 17. Critics found *Antigone* even less enjoyable than *Le Boeuf*. The cast of *Le Boeuf* included: Francis Fergusson as the Barman, Emily Floyd as the Lady with Red Hair, Marion Crowpe as the Lady in the Low-cut Gown, Karl Swenson as the Policeman, William D. Post as the Negro Boxer, Charles Kradoska as the Bookmaker, T. Renick Hayes as the Gentleman and W. Robert Spruill as the Negro Billiard Player.

60. Both Milhaud and Cocteau mention the confusion over the bar and ballet in many of their writings.

61. Milhaud, p. 108.

62. Ibid., p. 109.

63. *Les Ballets Suédois* (Paris: Editions du Rianon, 1931), pp. 149–50.

64. Cocteau published a poem on *Les Six* in his *Poésies* (*Oeuvres complètes*, Vol. III) which purposely excluded Durey's name from the list. By the 1950s all of *Les Six* had been reconciled.

65. Jean Hugo notes this name change in his "Pages de journal," *Cahiers Jean Cocteau* (Paris: Gallimard, 1975), Vol. 5, p. 19.

66. Jean Cocteau, *The Difficulty of Being*, trans. Elizabeth Sprigge (London: Peter Owen, 1966), p. 20.

67. Jean Cocteau, *Les Mariés de la Tour Eiffel*, in *Oeuvres complètes*, Vol. VII, p. 21. All future references to *Les Mariés* come from this edition. An English language translation is available in *Jean Cocteau: The Infernal Machine and Other Plays*, trans. Dudley Fitts (New York: New Directions, 1963), pp. 151–78. The translation is idiomatic and does not capture Cocteau's style. The book, however, also includes the complete 1922 preface to the play.

68. *Les Mariés de la Tour Eiffel*, introduction. All future references come from the *Oeuvres complètes*.

69. Ibid., pp. 29–30.

70. Ibid., p. 31.

71. Ibid., p. 35.

72. Ibid., pp. 45–46.

73. Ibid., p. 50.

74. *La Danse*, June 1921, n.p. The text is translated in full in Appendix 6.

75. Darius Milhaud made a recording of the music in France. I am grateful to David Leonard of Dance Books, Ltd., in London, for obtaining a tape of this recording.

76. In *Les Ballets Suédois*, Milhaud said "The music of *Les Six* for this ballet blended so well that even we were surprised, considering how little we have in common." In his *Notes without Music* published in 1953 Milhaud thought only Poulenc's selections truly outstanding.

77. *Les Ballets Suédois*, p. 125.

78. *Les Mariés de la Tour Eiffel*, introduction.

79. Jean Hugo, p. 22.

80. Ibid., p. 20.

81. Ibid., p. 22.

82. *Les Ballets Suédois*, p. 35.

83. Jean Cocteau, *La Danse*, June 1921, n.p.

84. Jean Hugo, p. 21.

85. *La Danse*, June 1921, n.p.

86. Ibid.

87. Ibid.; also printed in the souvenir program.

88. Jean Cocteau, *Order Considered as Anarchy*, in *Cocteau's World*, p. 384.

89. This is noted by both Hugo and Milhaud as well as Maré in *Les Ballets Suédois*.

90. This was on 22 June.

91. Crosland, *Jean Cocteau*, p. 65.

92. Quoted in full in Appendix 7.

93. *Order Considered as Anarchy*, in *Cocteau's World*, pp. 394–95.

94. Cocteau, *Entretiens*, p. 32.

95. Ibid., p. 32.

96. *Order Considered as Anarchy*, in *Cocteau's World*, p. 391.

97. *Les Ballets Suédois*, p. 56.

98. In the first season there were 10 performances followed by 8 in the second season, 9 in the third, 3 in the fourth, and 20 in the fifth, making a grand total of 50. (Tableau des Représentations, *Les Ballets Suédois*, 1931.)

99. Edmund Wilson, Jr., "The Aesthetic Upheaval in France: The Influence of Jazz in Paris and the Americanization of French Literature and Art," *Vanity Fair*, February 1922, pp. 94–96.

100. Ibid. He said in 1975 that Cocteau was always upset since many non-French though him a "dadaist." Even Wilson had called *Les Mariés* a dada review in 1922 (*The New Yorker*, 28 April 1975).

101. *Les Ballets Suédois*, p. 118.

102. See n. 75. The recording is now out of print. Angel Records in the United States released Poulenc's two contributions on S–36519, under the direction of Georges Prêtre. The costumes

and set designs for *Les Mariés* are now divided between the Paris Opéra museum and the Theatre Museum in Stockholm. They were originally in the *Archives de la Danse* founded by Maré and directed by Pierre Tugal in Paris from 1931–1950. When the center closed in 1950, the contents were divided between the above-mentioned museums. In 1983, the twentieth anniversary of Cocteau's death, there were performances of *Le Boeuf* and *Les Mariés*, but obviously without a reconstruction of the original choreography, since this had been lost after the original performances.

103. *Professional Secrets*, in *Cocteau's World*, p. 377. In the same essay Cocteau said: "In *Les Mariés de la Tour Eiffel*, I claim to have at last succeeded in producing something of this kind [referring to poetry as truth]. The author gives the public twenty years before they feel the poetry it contains. Until then the piece will rank simply as a rather feeble and more or less comic dialogue. His aim was too true, his weapon too perfect. The bullet goes clean through; in spite of his groans the adversary feels nothing" (p. 354).

Chapter 5

1. Jean Cocteau, *Entretiens avec André Fraigneau* (Paris: Michel-Claude Jalard, 1965), p. 60.

2. Ibid.: ". . . sa mort m'a coupé les mains."

3. Cocteau once said that life and death are two sides of the same coin separated only by the thickness of the metal, although they cannot know one another. At Giraudoux's funeral, for example, Cocteau grew so depressed by the oratory and display that he said to a friend he was with: "Let's leave. He didn't come." ("Allons-nous-en, il n'est pas venu.") Wallace Fowlie, *Jean Cocteau* (Bloomington: Indiana University Press, 1966), p. 4.

4. The original manuscripts of both scenarios are in the Francis Poulenc Collection, Paris. A study by the author, through the permission of the Poulenc estate, shows how similar Cocteau's sketches were to the final form of the ballet. However, they are still very rough drafts and probably had much input from Diaghilev, Poulenc and Auric.

5. Anton Dolin in an interview with the author in 1975 thought that Kochno probably wanted to write the scenarios from the first. It seems, though, that Diaghilev only gave him *Les Fâcheux*, as there is no credit on *Les Biches*. The latter, however, was very much Poulenc's child and when Cocteau could no longer work on it the composer finished the outline for his music himself. For a discussion of Poulenc's involvement in this work, see James Harding, *The Ox on the Roof* (London: MacDonald and Company, 1972), pp. 147–52.

6. Although there is no physical reason why men cannot dance *en pointe* (there are a number of lithographs from the 1820s of men doing such), it has usually been considered aesthetically unacceptable. For the part of the fop in *Les Fâcheux*, however, the effect was exactly right.

7. See Appendix 9 for a full translation of these introductory essays. Two variations on these essays on both ballets are translated in *A Call to Order*, trans. Rollo Meyers (London: Faber and Faber, 1926).

8. Opening night program, Monte Carlo. In the author's collection.

9. *Entretiens*, p. 60.

10. Francis Steegmuller, *Cocteau: A Biography* (New York: Atlantic, Little, Brown, 1970), p. 322.

11. Jean Hugo, "Roméo et Juliette," *Jean Cocteau et son Théâtre*, Vol. V of Jean Cocteau, *Cahiers Jean Cocteau* (Paris: Gallimard, 1975), p. 24.

12. Steegmuller, p. 328.

13. Jean Cocteau, *Roméo et Juliette, Théâtre* (Paris: Grasset, 1957), p. 56: "J'ai cru devoir laisser quelques indications sommaires de mise en scène qui se trouvaient sur le manuscript. Il n'existe malheureusement encore aucune écriture qui permette de conserver le détail chorégraphique d'un mécanisme ou rien n'était livré au hasard."

14. Hugo, p. 25.

15. Ibid., p. 26.

16. Steegmuller, p. 328.

17. Hugo, p. 25.

18. Hugo, pp. 26–28. The cast list includes such dancers as Joyce Meyers, Hewitt, and dance-trained Yvonne George, though she played the nurse. Male dancers included Segur, Brasseur, Steletski, Baikow, and de l'Hoste.

19. *Roméo et Juliette*, p. 63: "Leur démarche réglée sur une musique de danse qu'on suprime après."

20. *Roméo et Juliette*, p. 59: "Tous les jeunes gens élégants de Vérone auront une certaine démarche agressive, la main sur la garde de l'épée."

21. Neal Oxenhandler, *Scandal and* Parade (New Brunswick: Rutgers University Press, 1957), p. 54.

22. *Roméo et Juliette*, p. 53: "Un vrai directeur de théâtre m'eut-il laissé carte blanche? J'en doute."

23. Serge Lifar, *Serge de Diaghilev* (New York: G. P. Putnam and Sons, 1940), p. 228.

24. Steegmuller, p. 326. Mr. Dolin noticed this version of *Le Train bleu* in the book and asked Steegmuller about it when they later met in Venice. The author admitted he had only intereviewed Lifar in reference to Cocteau's ballets.

25. Boris Kochno, *Diaghilev and the Ballets Russes* (New York: Harper and Row, 1970), p. 216; Serge Grigoriev, *The Diaghilev Ballet* (London: Constable, 1953), pp. 197–207; Lydia Sokolova, *Dancing for Diaghilev* (London: John Murray, 1960), pp. 220–24.

26. Anton Dolin, *Divertissement* (London: Low, Marston, and Company, n.d. [1932–33]), p. 64.

27. Darius Milhaud, *Notes without Music* (New York: Alfred A. Knopf, 1953), p. 159.

28. Ibid.

29. Darius Milhaud, "Diary," unpublished. Private collection, Paris.

30. This is confirmed by Milhaud's diaries and W. A. Propert. See n. 59.

31. Kochno, p. 216.

32. Deidre Pridden, *The Art of the Dance in French Literature* (London: A. and C. Black, 1952), p. 124. The fixation on youth is a facet of Cocteau's dance work upon which even Miss Pridden fails to comment.

33. Kochno, p. 216.

34. See Appendix 8 for Cocteau's detailed instructions.

35. Interview with Anton Dolin. See the scenario in Appendix 8 for further details.

36. Darius Milhaud and Jean Cocteau, *Le Train bleu* (Paris: Heugel and Co., 1924). The handwriting of Diaghilev has been affirmed by Sotheby and Co., which sold the score on 5 June 1975. The synopsis is heavily scored out, has pencil notes added by Serge Diaghilev and is headed "*Prier* Evans d'arranger le synopsis SD." Some markings in the score are by Nijinska.

The previous owner of the manuscript, Anton Dolin, stated that Diaghilev sat at rehearsal marking the changes as Cocteau devised them.

37. Grigoriev mentions how difficult it was to talk to La Nijinska, p. 203.

38. Sokolova, p. 221.

39. Michael de Cossart, *The Food of Love: Princess Edmond de Polignac and her Salon* (London: Hamish Hamilton, 1978), p. 142. See also Edmonde Charles-Roux, *Chanel and Her World* (London: The Vendome Press, 1981), pp. 186–99.

40. *The Queen*, 3 December 1924, n.p.

41. For the complete cast list, see Appendix 8.

42. Program for the "Diaghilev Ballets Russes" at the London Coliseum Theatre, 24 November 1924, in the author's collection.

43. *Le Ménestrel*, 22 June 1924, p. 29.

44. *Revue de Paris*, 21 July 1924, p. 14.

45. *La Nouvelle revue française*, 22 July 1924, p. 12.

46. Boris Kochno, *Le Ballet* (Paris: Librairie Hachette, 1954), p. 259.

47. *The Bystander*, 3 December 1924, p. 26.

48. *New Statesman*, 6 December 1924, p. 42.

49. *Illustrated London News*, 6 December 1924, n.p.

50. *Musical America*, 12 December 1924, p. 38.

51. *Dancing Times*, January 1924, p. 45.

52. Cyril Beaumont, *The Diaghilev Ballet in London* (London: A. and C. Black, 1940), p. 224.

53. Interview with Anton Dolin.

54. Interview with Anton Dolin. See also Richard Buckle, *Diaghilev* (New York: Atheneum Press, 1979), pp. 430–41 for further details on Lifar's limited technique.

55. Arnold Haskell, *Diaghileff* (New York: Simon and Schuster, 1935), p. 307; Arnold Haskell, *Ballet Russe* (London: Weidenfeld and Nicolson, 1968), p. 101.

56. I am indebted to Selma Jeanne Cohen for pointing out this ballet to me. According to P. W. Manchester in an interview, the ballet *Beach* did not last very long and was considered a relic from Diaghilev's "Chi-Chi period." One would have difficulty talking about "innumerable *popular* sporting ballets" as Haskell does when the pieces he mentions barely last a season or less.

57. Pridden, p. 117: "Une certaine tradition qui pour être crapuleuse n'en est pas moins de race."

58. W. A. Propert, *The Russian Ballet, 1921–1929* (London: The Bodley Head, 1931), p. 30. Propert had an excellent view of the later Diaghilev period, which has a tendency to be disregarded by many dance historians, even today. Being a close supporter of Diaghilev and close to him and the company he saw the inner workings better than most people. In the special edition of this book in the author's possession Propert himself has inscribed it to Anton Dolin "in memory of *Train bleu*, which was so sadly lost before its time."

59. Alexandra Danilova, interview with Edward Villella on PBS, 1 February 1978.

60. Dance Collection, Library for the Performing Arts, New York Public Library at Lincoln Center. The letter is dated 5 January 1929.

61. For an illustration of the set see Cyril Beaumont, *Ballet Design Past and Present* (London: Hasel, Watson and Viney, 1946), p. 135.

62. For an interesting discussion of the Chicago attempt to revive *Le Train bleu* see *Dancing Times*, December 1940, pp. 103–9. The gala with Wayne Sleep at which the author was present had Sleep dancing in an excellent copy of the Chanel bathing suit Dolin had originally worn. If the original choreography was anything near what Mr. Sleep danced that night one can see why the part of Beau Gosse was so incredibly difficult for anyone to do.

Chapter 6

1. Francis Steegmuller, *Cocteau* (New York: Atlantic, Little, Brown, 1970), p. 436.

2. For an illustration of the *pas de deux* see *La Danse* (Paris: Masques, 1947), p. 60.

3. For further information on Charrat, see I. Lidova, "Janine Charrat," *Les Saisons de la danse*, August 1970, pp. 46–48. On Petit, see Lidova's complete list of roles and activities in *Les Saisons de la danse*, Summer 1968.

4. Interview with Charrat in *International HAD*, no. 17, n.d., n.p., courtesy of the Stravinsky-Diaghilev Foundation, New York.

5. Ibid.

6. For an illustration of the Petit-Charrat ballet and Cocteau working on the headgear for Petit, see *La Danse*, n. 3, plate 54.

7. Interview with Charrat.

8. For further and more detailed information on the formation of these concert programs, see Pierre Michaut, *Le Ballet contemporain* (Paris: Librairie Plon, 1950), pp. 300–6, and May Neoma, *Recits sur la danse* (Paris: Grund, 1969), pp. 393–408, with interviews with Lidova and others.

9. This was not a revival of the famous 19th-century ballet by Messager but a totally different work.

10. Michaut, p. 303.

11. Souvenir Programme, Ballets des Champs-Elysées, 1946, in the collection of the author. The English version for the London season included a paragraph on "how happy we are to come to London after Paris, since England and France were the two countries Diaghilev preferred above all others in the world. . . . "

12. See Appendix 1 for full text of the Ballets Russes article, and chapter 2 for further information.

13. *Difficulty of Being*, p. 142.

14. Ibid., p. 143, n. 1. Cocteau mentions that he wanted to later replace the Bach with the Mozart overture from the *Magic Flute* for the American performances. However, this was never done.

15. For an interesting summary of the personalities of both these artists see *La Musique et le ballet*, articles on Babilée, Philippart, and Petit by Alain Vigot, in *La Revue musicale*, December-January 1953.

16. *Difficulty of Being*, p. 144.

17. It should be noted that no English, French or American program gives credit to Bérard for his help on the costumes, though Cocteau specifically mentions he asked Bérard to help Karinska. His help was probably advisory.

18. Souvenir Program, Ballets des Champs-Elysées, 1946, in the author's collection.

19. The English souvenir program for the season the next year in London mentions the Bach as being orchestrated by Goedike. There is no reference to Goedike in any of Cocteau's writing and the English reviews refer to Respighi as the orchestrator. The records for the Adelphi Theatre in London, where they played, also indicate no Goedike reorchestration. This may have been an error in the Souvenir Program as the performance scheduled at the Adelphi refers to Respighi as orchestrator.

20. *Difficulty of Being*, p. 144. Most reviewers noted the use of light and shade; see reviews referred to in notes below.

21. Ibid., p. 145. All future quotations throughout the description of the ballet are from Cocteau's text, unless otherwise indicated by the notes.

22. Cyril Beaumont, *Ballets of Today* (London: Putnam and Co., 1954), p. 178.

23. George Balanchine and Francis Mason, *Balanchine's Complete Book of Ballets*, rev. ed. (New York: Doubleday, 1977), p. 322.

24. Ibid.

25. Ibid.

26. Beaumont, p. 179.

27. Balanchine, p. 323.

28. Ibid.

29. Ibid.

30. *Difficulty of Being*, p. 147.

31. Ibid.

32. Ibid., p. 149.

33. *Dance News*, September 1946, p. 2. Jean Georges Noverre (1727–1810) defended the *ballet d'action* with a unified and coherent plot against the more technical style of the *danse d'école*. Salvatore Viganò (1769–1821) was remembered for his "coreodramma" and the subordination of dance and mime to music.

34. Janet Flanner (Genet), *Paris Journal 1944–1965* (New York: Atheneum, 1977), pp. 61–62. Referred to incorrectly in the index as "La Mort de l'homme."

35. *Ballet Annual* (London: A. and C. Black, 1948), II, p. 80.

36. Beaumont, pp. 181–82.

37. *Dancing Times*, April 1947, p. 40.

38. Ibid.

39. *Dancing Times*, July 1947, p. 41.

40. Ibid.

41. *Difficulty of Being*, pp. 149–50.

42. *Dancing Times*, July 1947, p. 41.

43. *Dance Magazine*, June 1951, p. 58.

44. *Dancing Times*, June 1951, p. 201.

45. *New York Herald Tribune*, 15 April 1951, p. 14.

46. Ibid.

47. *The New York Times*, 15 April 1951, sec. 2, p. 2.

48. Pierre Masson, "Le billet juridique," *Danse et Rythmes*, December 1958, pp. 32–38, and January 1959, pp. 41–46. Masson reported on the court case and quoted both Cocteau's defense and, in part 2, the ruling by the tribunal.

49. Masson, part 2, p. 45.

50. For an interesting photo essay on the making of the film see "Le Jeune homme et la mort," *Nureyev in Paris* (New York: Modernismo Publications, 1975). For a review of the film see Jack Anderson, "A Film not for Viewing," *Dance Magazine*, April 1968, p. 101.

51. Mikhail Baryshnikov, *Baryshnikov at Work* (New York: Alfred A. Knopf, 1976), p. 98.

52. Eric Aschengreen, "On the Other Side of the Footlights," *York Dance Review*, Spring 1978, p. 45.

53. *The New Yorker*, 27 January 1975, p. 99.

54. See *Dance Magazine*, November 1983 pp. 20–26 for a review of the Ballet National de Marseilles. Also Norma McLain Stoop, "Opera Etoile Patrick Dupond," *Dance Magazine*, July 1984, pp. 44–47, which includes two pictures of Dupond in *Le Jeune homme et la mort*.

55. Deirdre Pridden, *The Art of the Dance in French Literature* (London: A. and C. Black, 1952), p. 124.

56. Interview and article by Lemaitre in *Internationale HAD*, n.d., n.p., courtesy of the Stravinsky-Diaghilev Foundation, New York.

57. *Difficulty of Being*, p. 149.

58. *Dance and Dancers*, December 1963, p. 51.

59. Michaut, p. 329.

60. For further information on the legend see Apuleius, *The Golden Ass*, trans. Robert Graves (New York: Farrar, Straus, and Giroux, 1950).

61. Cocteau used sections I, II, III (partially) and IV for the ballet. The two chorus sequences were not used from part III and none of part V. The entire symphonic poem, with no cuts, lasts over an hour.

62. Program, American Ballet Theatre, 1951, in the Dance Collection, New York Public Library at Lincoln Center. The same note was used in the French and English programs for the ballet.

63. Michaut, p. 329.

64. All quotes during the plot synopsis come from the original scenario by Sicard and Louis de Fourcaud for Franck's composition. Much of the poetry is very dramatic and would have been familiar to both Cocteau and Babilée; both considered the piece one of their favorite compositions.

65. Beaumont, *Ballets Past and Present* (London: Putnam and Company, 1955), p. 16.

66. Ibid.

67. Balanchine, p. 18.

68. This was Beaumont's particular interpretation. He gives a detailed word picture of the *pas de deux*. The grappling of the leg by Psyche has counterparts in the legend itself: "He flew off but not before the poor girl had seized a hold of his leg and clung to it until the god shook her off and she fell to earth."

69. Walter Terry, *New York Herald Tribune*, 18 April 1951, p. 36, and John Martin, *The New York Times*, 18 April 1951, p. 57.

70. For a further analysis of the ballet see Pierre Tugal, "Babilée's First Ballet," *Dancing Times*, February 1949; pp. 26–28; and for a review of its first London performance see the same magazine, November 1949, pp. 31–33. Charles Payne tells an amusing story about Babilée on tour with this ballet in Chicago in *American Ballet Theatre* (New York: Alfred A. Knopf, 1978), p. 189. A balloon flew onto the set from the neighboring auditorium and Babilée reacted with fury, suspecting sabotage. The critics, however, thought it was part of the set by Cocteau: "The settings are almost overwhelming, brilliantly modern in style, lavish in their use of color, and saved from pretentiousness by a whimsical balloon that had its own moment of stardom."

Chapter 7

1. There are many books on Lifar and his work, both by himself and by others. For an excellent and unbiased survey of his career at the Paris Opéra, see Ivor Guest, *Le Ballet de l'Opéra de Paris* (Paris: Flammarion, 1976), pp. 171–211.

2. Pierre Michaut, "The Choreography of Serge Lifar," *Ballet Annual*, no. 3, ed. Arnold Haskell (London: A. and C. Black, 1949), pp. 81–87.

3. Ibid., p. 85.

4. Maurice Tassart, "The Serge Lifar Story," *Ballet Annual*, no. 14, ed. Arnold Haskell (London: A. and C. Black, 1960), p. 58.

5. Serge Lifar, *Le Livre de la danse* (Paris: Société Française de Diffusion Musicale et Artistique, 1954), p. 203. The original scenario for Lifar's first draft of "Hippolyte" is printed as an appendix in his 1938 book, *La Danse*, confirming that he did think of the myth as a ballet some years before.

6. Serge Lifar, *Ma Vie*, trans. James Holman Mason (London: Hutchinson, 1970), p. 319.

7. Ibid.

8. Guest, p. 196; also Margaret Crosland, *Cocteau* (New York, Alfred A. Knopf, 1955), p. 131.

9. Pierre Michaut, *Le Ballet contemporain* (Paris: Librairie Plon, 1950), p. 372: ". . . qui allait être traité dans l'atmosphère de menace et de sang où Racine rejoint Euripède et Sophocle."

10. Crosland, p. 131: Guest, p. 196; and numerous others.

11. After 1945 Toumanova remained more or less a "freelance" ballerina and was not associated with any one particular company.

12. Michaut, *Le Ballet contemporain*, p. 372.

13. Jean Laurent and Julie Sazonova, *Serge Lifar, Rénovateur du Ballet français* (Paris: Buchet, Chastel, and Correa, 1960), p. 175. Their analysis was based on conversations with Lifar about his ballets.

14. Program, London, 1954. The original French is found in both the French program for 1950 and 1959 as well as the recent Paris Opéra revival (1977).

15. Cyril Beaumont, *Ballets Past and Present* (London: A. and C. Black, 1955), pp. 103–4.

16. Margaret Crosland, *Cocteau*, p. 153: "The most interesting aspect of Cocteau's work on the costumes and decor [of *Phèdre*] was his use of colour, which gives the ballet a new three-dimensional quality. Not since *Parade* has color been so important in any of Cocteau's ballets. . . . "

17. Irene Lidova, *Dance News*, July 1950, p. 3.

18. Ivor Guest, in *Ballet*, September-October 1950, p. 39.

19. Peter Williams, in *Dance and Dancers*, November 1954, pp. 13–16.

20. Noted by Williams, Lidova, Michaut.

21. David Hunt, in *Dance and Dancers*, November 1954, p. 31.

22. Lifar, *Le Livre de la danse*, p. 204; analyzed further by Laurent and Sazonova, pp. 176–77.

23. Laurent and Sazonova, pp. 174–79.

24. Michaut, *Le Ballet contemporain*, pp. 371–74.

25. Marie-Françoise Christout, in *Dance and Dancers*, February 1978, pp. 34–35. Lifar had also revived and staged the ballet after 1959, and before the 1977 revival, in Buenos Aires in 1964 with Esmeralda Agoglia in the title role.

26. Richard Shead, *Music in the 1920s* (London: Duckworth, 1976), p. 8.

27. Nina Vyroubova, who took over from Toumanova after she left the Paris Opéra was notable in her interpretation of the lead. In the revival presented in 1977 Claire Motte, Ghislaine Thesmar and Ninon Thibon were the interpreters of the female lead while Michael Denard, Patrick Dupond, and Charles Jude alternated as Hippolytus. The critics in Paris thought Thibon the most interesting Phèdre; the present author, who saw two of the casts, thought the ballet could be immeasurably weakened if the dancers were not also excellent actors.

28. Laurent and Sazonova, p. 225.

29. See the analysis and photos by Jean Mauran in *Musica Disques*, January 1959, pp. 45–52. Lifar is quoted on his work and theory about this ballet within the context of this detailed outline and critique.

30. Ibid., p. 51.

31. Ibid.

Chapter 8

1. Quoted by Ned Rorem in "Cocteau and Music," *Jean Cocteau and the French Scene* (New York: Abbeville Press, 1984), p. 144.

2. Elizabeth Sprigge and Jean-Jacques Kihm, *Jean Cocteau: The Man and the Mirror* (New York: Coward McCann, Inc., 1968), p. 202.

3. Ibid.

4. Kevin Grubb, "Dancing with the Nouveau Reich," *Dance Magazine*, March 1984; p. 78. The picture of Mr. Reich with the Anubis mask on p. 77 mistakenly identifies *Oedipus Rex* as being performed in 1954, rather than 1952.

5. Sprigge and Kihm, p. 202, say the uproar took place on the first night and the curtain had to be lowered before peace could be restored. However Vera Stravinsky in her diary, quoted in Vera Stravinsky and Robert Craft, *Stravinsky in Pictures and Documents* (New York: Simon and Schuster, 1978), p. 418, states the insults only came during Cocteau's last speech, and only in the upper part of the house. She also says it continued after the performance but Stravinsky had already left. (Stravinsky was only in the audience; Hans Rosbaud was the conductor.) The recording, released by Columbia Records in the United States as ML 4644, used the speeches of Cocteau but dubbed them into a performance Stravinsky himself conducted some eight months later in Cologne.

6. Walter Eichner, in the *Abendzeitung* (Munich), 2 May 1953.

7. Both G. B. L. Wilson, *A Dictionary of Ballet*, and Horst Koegler, *The Oxford Concise Dictionary of the Ballet*, neglect to mention the Zurich position before the Basle appointment. See the interview with Rosen in the *Abendzeitung*, 2 May 1953, for further details on his Zurich career.

8. Heinz Rosen in the opening night program for *La Dame à la licorne*, Speilzeit 1953, Bayerische Staatstheater, Theater am Gartnerplatz.

9. Ibid.

10. Rudiger Robert Beer, *Unicorn: Myth and Reality* (New York: Mason/Charter, 1977), pp. 151–57.

11. It should also be noted that the "à" of the title can be translated as "with," "of," or even "and." In terms of the Cocteau ballet it is probably best translated as *The Lady with the Unicorn*.

12. Beer, pp. 151–52.

13. Beer notes that the final letter may be read as a "J" and if the arms on the tapestry belong to the le Viste family the initial may signify their possession. See also Maria Lanckorovska, *Wandteppiche für eine Forestin* (Frankfurt, 1965), for an interesting thesis that the lady represents Margaret of York.

14. Pierre Verlet and Francis Salet, *La Dame à la licorne* (Paris: Cluny Museum, 1960), discuss the variations in dress and figure of the six ladies.

15. Scenario, *La Dame à la licorne*. See Appendix 10 for complete text.

16. Beer, pp. 184–86.

17. Ibid., p. 157.

18. Scenario. See Appendix 10.

19. *Le Roman de la Dame à la Lycorne et du Beau Chevalier au Lyons* (Dresden: Gennrich, 1909). See also C. A. J. Armstrong's essay, "The Golden Age of Burgundy," *The Courts of Europe* (New York: McGraw-Hill, 1977), pp. 55–77.

20. Opening night program.

21. Program.

22. Heinz Rosen, *Balletheater* (Munich: n.p., 1963), pp. 12–14. The letter includes a drawing for the placing of the spotlights and their correct settings.

23. *Abendzeitung,* 2 May 1953, p. 12.

24. *Darmstädter Echo,* 20 May 1953, p. 14.

25. *Balletheater,* p. 8.

26. *Frankfurter Allegmeine Zeitung,* 13 May 1953, p. 6.

27. Ibid.

28. *Suddeutsche Zeitung,* 11 May 1953, p. 12.

29. *Münchener Merkur,* 11 May 1953, p. 11.

30. Heinz Rode, unidentified clipping from the Munich Staatstheater, 10 May 1953.

31. *Düsseldorfer Nachrichten,* 14 May 1953, p. 10.

32. *Abendzeitung,* 11 May 1953, p. 11.

33. *Mannheimer Morgen,* 12 May 1953, p. 12.

34. *Aachener Volkszeitung,* 14 May, 1953, p. 9. Also published in the *Westfalische Nachrichten,* 19 May 1953, p. 10, and the *Neue Zurcher Zeitung,* 18 May 1953, p. 7.

35. *Frankfurt Abenpost/Main,* 12 May 1953, p. 8.

36. *Der Mittag,* Düsseldorf, 11 May 1953, p. 13.

37. *Balletheater,* p. 18. The letter is dated 19 May 1953.

38. *Arts,* May 1953, n.p.

39. Ibid.

40. Jean Cocteau, *Lettres à Milorad* (Paris: Editions Saint-Germain-des-Près, 1976), n.p. This letter is dated 12 June 1955: "L'essaierai de voir. Vous ignorez encore le secret de la danse. Elle s'oppose à tout intellectualisme. Un ballet se compose avec les mains, les pieds, l'oeil—la tête entre très peu en ligne de compte."

41. Victoria Garcia Victoria, "Colon Does New Cocteau Ballet," *Dance News,* September 1954, p. 1.

42. *Dance News,* April 1957, p. 4.

43. Radio interview, by James Lyon, with Igor Youskevitch and Dorothy Pierre, 20 April 1957; in the Dance Collection, New York.

44. *Dance Magazine,* June 1957, p. 11.

45. *Dance News,* June 1957, p. 9; the author mistakes the source of the music.

46. *New York Post,* 24 April 1957, p. 15; and *Variety,* 1 May 1957, p. 67.

47. *New York Herald-Tribune,* 23 April 1957, p. 19. Terry's feelings about the choreography were supported by one of the dancers in the production, Rochelle Zide, who thought Rosen "seemed to know little about dance." See Jack Anderson, *The One and Only: The Ballet Russe de Monte Carlo* (New York: Dance Horizons Press, 1981), p. 160.

48. *Dance and Dancers,* August 1963, p. 37; the performance took place 20 June 1963.

49. For further information on the stagehands' dispute and strike see Janet Flanner (Genet), *Paris Journal 1944–1965* (New York: Atheneum, 1977), p. 361.

50. *Lettres à Milorad*, p. 103; from a letter dated 26 January 1959: "Je n'ai pu surveiller ni les lumières de *La Dame* . . . mais tant pis. La beauté aime l'ombre."

51. *Dance and Dancers*, April 1959, p. 51.

52. *La Musique*, March 1959, p. 15.

53. *Musica Disques*, March 1959, pp. 41–43.

54. *Balletheater*, p. 20. Cocteau was then convalescing at Milly-la-Forêt. The letter is dated 17 July 1963. Cocteau said, in the same letter, that his illness had forced him to break with his work. "Am I still at the age when one has courage? This I ask myself." He also thought the convalescence difficult "on account of the poisons that snatch us from death, but also which with so much horror and difficulty, are again eliminated from life."

Chapter 9

1. Marie-Françoise Christout, "Cocteau's Dark Angel," *Dance and Dancers*, October 1972, pp. 50–51.

2. Ibid., p. 51.

3. Letter from Jean Cocteau to Heinz Rosen, 11 December 1962; from the estate of Heinz Rosen, Munich.

4. Christout, p. 51. The ballet was subtitled *Ou l'Enfant change en jeune homme* (Or The Child Became a Young Man). Sets and costumes were by Edouard Dermit after Jean Cocteau.

5. Elizabeth Sprigge and Jean-Jacques Kihm, *Jean Cocteau: The Man and the Mirror* (New York: Coward McCann, 1968), p. 236.

6. "Lettre aux Américains," trans. Margaret Crosland, in *Cocteau's World*, ed. Margaret Crosland (New York: Dodd, Mead, 1972), p. 407.

7. Christout, p. 51.

8. Ibid.

9. Jean Cocteau, *La Machine infernale*, trans. Albert Bermel (New York: New Directions, 1963), p. 51. The description of Tetley's ballet, *The Sphinx*, is based on the author's own viewing during the spring season of American Ballet Theatre at the Metropolitan Opera House, New York, in May 1978.

10. Jill Sykes, "The Sydney Dance Company," *Dance Magazine*, May 1981, p. 52.

11. Julinda Lewis, "Reviews," *Dance Magazine*, December 1981, p. 40.

12. Walter Sorell, "An Appreciation of Jean Cocteau," *Dance Magazine*, February 1964, p. 41.

13. Cocteau, *Beauty Secrets*, in *Cocteau's World*, p. 469.

14. Jean Cocteau, "Danse," *Prestige de la danse*, eds. Jean Gueritte and Monique Lancelot (Paris: Charles Portal, 1953), pp. 25–30; the text is quoted in full in Appendix 11: "J'joute, que dans le babélisme contemporain, la danse représente un esperanto. Elle traverse le mur des idiomes. Elle donne, en outre, la traduction directe d'une poésie que les termes trahissent."

15. There are many books about Cocteau's film work, including his own diary for *La Belle et la bête*. Two of the most interesting analyses are René Gilson, *Jean Cocteau: An Investigation into his Films and Philosophy* (New York: Crown, 1969), and Arthur B. Evans, *Jean Cocteau*

and his Films and Orphic Identity (Philadelphia: The Art Alliance Press, 1977). Both note the dance elements in his film but do not really go into any cinematic details of construction in terms of a possible dance picture. This is one area of Cocteau's work that needs further investigation.

16. Author's personal interviews with Joffrey Ballet dancers, February 1976.

17. Carl Wildman, "Jean Cocteau and the Ballet," *Dancing Times*, October 1973, p. 20.

Appendix

1. This letter does not always correlate with the evidence presented in chapter 3. Explanation is given in that chapter.

2. Cocteau always had a fascination with hands, especially his own, and always wore his sleeves with the cuffs turned up to show his long hands. The solo white spot outlining the hand which points to the mysterious banner is a true Cocteau touch and reminds one of lighting and hand effects in his films *Blood of the Poet, Orpheus,* and *Testament of Orpheus.* The scenario also includes Cocteau's other great fixation: mirrors. The mirror effect can also be found in his plays and films.

Bibliography

A. Published Works by Jean Cocteau

L'Art Décorative de Leon Bakst. Paris: n.p., 1913.
Les Ballets des Champs-Elysées. Souvenir program. Paris: Soirée de Ballets, Editions du Chêne, 1945.
Les Ballets Russes. Souvenir programs. Paris: n.p., 1909–1917, 1924, 1925.
Les Ballets Suédois. Ed. Pierre Tugal. Paris: Editions du Trianon, 1931.
A Call to Order. Trans. Rollo Meyers. London: Faber and Faber, 1926.
Cahiers Jean Cocteau. Paris: Gallimard, 1969.
Cocteau's World. Ed. and trans. Margaret Crosland. New York: Dodd, Mead and Company, 1973.
La Comtesse de Noailles, Oui et Non. Paris: Librairie Academique Perrin, 1963.
Dessins. Paris: Librairie Stock, 1923.
La Difficulté d'Etre. Monaco: Editons du Rocher, 1947. Also trans. Elizabeth Sprigge. London: Peter Owen, 1966.
Du: Lettre à Picasso. Paris: n.p., 1952.
Entretiens avec André Fraigneau. Paris: Michel-Claude Jalard, 1965.
Igor Stravinsky. Bonn: n.p., 1952.
Jean Marais. Paris: Calmann-Levy, 1950.
"Le Jeune homme et la mort." *Art and Style*, Paris, October 1946.
Journal d'un Inconnu. Paris: Grasset, 1953.
The Journals of Jean Cocteau. Ed. and trans. Wallace Fowlie. Bloomington: Indiana University Press, 1964.
Lettre aux Américains. Paris: Grasset, 1949.
Lettre-Plainte. Paris: R. Saucier, 1926.
"Le Luxe spirituel est le Seul qui nous Reste." *Arts* (May 1953).
Maalesh, Journal d'une Tournée de Théâtre. Paris: Gallimard, 1949.
La Machine infernale. Trans. Albert Bermel. New York: New Directions, 1963.
"Les Mariés de la Tour Eiffel." *La Danse* (June 1921).
Le Mot. Ed. Cocteau and Iribe. Paris: n.p., 1914–1915.
My Contemporaries. Trans. Margaret Crosland. London: Peter Owen, 1967.
Nouveau Théâtre de Poche. Paris: Gallimard, 1960.
"The Newlyweds on the Eiffel Tower." *Les Ballets Suédois*. Souvenir Program for European Tour, 1920. Paris: n.p., n.d.
Oeuvres complètes. 11 vols. Lausanne: Marguerat, 1946–1951.
Order Considered as Anarchy. Trans. Margaret Crosland in *Cocteau's World*, New York: Dodd, Mead and Company, 1973.
"Parade Réaliste: in which Four Modernist Artists have a Hand." *Vanity Fair* (September 1917), p. 90.
Poésie critique. 2 vols. Paris: Gallimard, 1960.
Portraits-souvenirs, 1900–1914. Paris: Grasset, 1935.

Prestige de la Danse. Paris: Charles Portal, 1953.
Professional Secrets. Ed. and trans. Richard Phelps and Richard Howard. New York: Farrar, Strauss, Giroux, 1970.
"La Saison Russe." *Comœdia illustré* (1911).
Serge Lifar à l'Opéra. Paris: Champrosay-Thibault, 1943.
Six Dessins à V. Nijinsky. (With Paul Iribe) Paris: n.p., 1911.
"Le Théâtre et la Mode." *Masques, Revue internationale* (March 1945), pp. 10–16.
Le Théâtre de Jean Cocteau. 2 vols. Paris: Grasset, 1953.
Théâtre Serge de Diaghilev: Les Biches. Paris: Editions des Quatre Chemins, 1924.
Théâtre Serge de Diaghilev: Les Fâcheux. Paris: Editions des Quatre Chemins, 1924.

B. Unpublished Works by Jean Cocteau

On *L'Amour et son amour*

Material, reviews, and articles pertaining to the Ballet des Champs-Elysées. Courtesy of Mme. Marina Svetlova, private collection.

On *Les Biches*

Manuscript and notes. Poulenc Collection, Paris.

On *Le Boeuf sur le toit*

The Diaries of Darius Milhaud. Courtesy of a private collection, Paris.
Letters from Cocteau to Misia Sert. Courtesy of the Stravinsky-Diaghilev Foundation, Parmenia Migel Collection, New York.

On *La Dame à la licorne*

Material, reviews, and sketches. Bibliothèque de l'Opéra, Paris.
Material, reviews, sketches, and articles. Courtesy of the Munchen Theaterplaz, Germany.

On *David*

Letters from Cocteau to Stravinsky. Courtesy of the Stravinsky-Diaghilev Foundation, Stravinsky Collection, New York.

On *Le Dieu bleu*

Letters from Cocteau to Gabriel Astruc. Dance Collection, New York Public Library, Lincoln Center.
Letters from Cocteau to Serge de Diaghilev. Dance Collection, New York Public Library, Lincoln Center.
Manuscripts of Ballets Russes articles by Cocteau. Lincoln Kirstein Collection, Dance Collection, New York Public Library, Lincoln Center.

On *Les Fâcheux*

Manuscript and notes. Poulenc Collection, Paris.

On *Le Jeune homme et la mort*

Material, reviews, and articles pertaining to the Ballets des Champs-Elysées. Courtesy of Mme. Marina Svetlova, private collection.

On *Parade*

Drawings and photographs. Courtesy of Lady Maynard Keynes (Lydia Lopokova) and Dr. Milo Keynes, F.R.M.S.

Letters from Cocteau to Serge de Diaghilev. Dance Collection, New York Public Library, Lincoln Center.

Letters from Cocteau to Picasso. Dance Collection, New York Public Library, Lincoln Center.

Letters from Cocteau to Misia Sert. Courtesy of the Stravinsky-Diaghilev Foundation, Parmenia Migel Collection, New York.

Manuscripts of Ballets Russes articles. Lincoln Kirstein Collection, Dance Collection, New York Public Library, Lincoln Center.

Materials, letters, and sketches. Courtesy of Leonide Massine, personal collection.

On *Phèdre*

Material, reviews, and articles pertaining to the Ballets des Champs-Elysées. Courtesy of Mme. Marina Svetlova, private collection.

Material, reviews, and sketches. Bibliothèque de l'Opéra, Paris.

On *Le Train bleu*

The Diaries of Darius Milhaud. Courtesy of a private collection, Paris.

Letters from Cocteau to Serge de Diaghilev. Dance Collection, New York Public Library, Lincoln Center.

Letters from Cocteau to Misia Sert. Courtesy of the Stravinsky-Diaghilev Foundation, Parmenia Migel Collection, New York.

Materials, letters and sketches. Courtesy of Sir Anton Dolin, esq.

C. Secondary Sources

Anderson, Jack. *The One and Only: The Ballet Russe de Monte Carlo.* New York: Dance Horizons Press, 1981.

Apuleius. *The Golden Age.* Trans. by Robert Graves. New York: Farrar, Straus and Giroux, 1950.

Aschengreen, Eric. "On the Other Side of the Footlights." *York Dance Review,* Canada, no. 7 (Spring, 1978), pp. 43–46.

Astruc, Gabriel. *Le Pavillon des Fantômes.* Paris: Grasset, 1929.

Astruc papers. Dance Collection, New York Public Library, Lincoln Center.

Auric, Georges. "On the Diaghilev Ballet and Jean Cocteau." *The Ballet Annual,* London: A. and C. Black, 1956.

_____. "Chronique sur Parade." *La Nouvelle Revue française* (February 1921).

_____. "Auric Speaks of Then and Now." *New York Sunday Times,* 25 June 1978, sec. 6, p. 2.

Axsom, Richard. *Cubism as Theatre.* New York: Garland Publishers, 1979.

Beaumont, Cyril. *Ballet Design Past and Present.* London: Hasel, Watson and Viney, 1946.

_____. *Ballets of Today.* London: A. and C. Black, 1954.

_____. *The Ballets of Michael Fokine.* London: Beaumont Press, 1933.

_____. *Ballets Past and Present.* London: A. and C. Black, 1955.

_____. *The Diaghilev Ballet in London.* London: A. and C. Black, 1940.

_____. *Michael Fokine and His Ballets.* London: Beaumont Press, 1935.

Balanchine, Georges and Francis Mason. *Balanchine's Complete Stories of the Great Ballets.* New York: Doubleday, 1977.

Baryshnikov, Mikhail. *Baryshnikov at Work.* New York: Alfred A. Knopf, 1976.

Beer, Rudiger Robert. *Unicorns: Myth and Reality.* New York: Mason Charter, 1977.

Benois, Alexandre. *Reminiscences of the Russian Ballet.* London: Putnam and Co., 1941.

Borgal, Clement. *Cocteau, Dieu, la Mort, la Poésie*. Paris: Centurion, 1958.

Brown, Frederick. *An Impersonation of Angels*. New York: Viking Press, 1968.

Buckle, Richard. *Diaghilev*. New York: Atheneum, 1979.

———. *Diaghilev and de Basil Costumes and Curtains*. London: Sotheby, Park-Bernet, 1967.

———. *In Search of Diaghilev*. London: Sidwick and Jackson, 1953.

———. *Nijinsky*. London: Weidenfeld and Nicholson, 1971.

———. "Some Personal Memories of Jean Cocteau." *The Dancing Times* (December 1963), pp. 132–33.

Buckman, Peter. *Let's Dance: A History of Social, Ballroom, and Folk Dance*. New York: Paddington Press, 1978.

Cabanne, Pierre. *Pablo Picasso*. New York: Morrow, 1977.

Carter, Huntley. "Newest Tendencies in the Paris Theatre." *Theatre Arts* (December 1917), pp. 35–43.

Chardans, J. L. "Jean Cocteau et la Musique." *Paris Theatre*, 8, no. 81 (February 1954), pp. 7–14.

Chanel, Pierre. "Exposition Jean Cocteau." Exhibition catalogue, 27 July–6 October 1968. Musée de Luneville.

Charles-Roux, Edmonde. *Chanel and her World*. London: Vendome Press, 1981.

Christout, Marie-Françoise. "Cocteau's Dark Angel." *Dance and Dancers* (October 1972), pp. 50–51.

———. "Jean Cocteau et la Danse." *Les Saisons de la Danse*, May and June 1973.

Clarke, Mary and Clement Crisp. *Design for Ballet*. New York: Hawthorne, 1978.

Cossart, Michael de. *The Food of Love: The Princesse Edmond de Polignac and her Salon*. London: Hamish Hamilton, 1978.

Cooper, Douglas. "Parade, a Report on its Revival by the Joffrey Ballet," in *Dance and Dancers* (June 1973).

———. *Picasso Theatre*. New York: Abrams Press, 1968.

Craft, Robert and Igor Stravinsky. "On Music and Other Matters." *New York Review of Books*, 14 March 1968.

———. "Stravinsky, Diaghilev and Misia Sert." *Ballet Review* 6, no. 4.

Croce, Arlene. *After-Images*. New York: Alfred A. Knopf, 1978.

Crosland, Margaret, ed. *Cocteau's World*. New York: Dodd, Mead and Co., 1973.

———. *Jean Cocteau*. New York: Alfred A. Knopf, 1956.

Devere, John. "The Creation of Le Jeune homme et la mort." In *Nureyev in Paris*. New York: Modernismo Publications, 1975.

Dickens, A. G., ed. *The Courts of Europe*. New York: McGraw-Hill, 1977.

Dolin, Anton. *Autobiography*. London: Oldbourne, 1960.

———. *Divertissement*. London: Sampson, Low, Marston and Co., n.d. [1932–33].

Dubourg, Pierre. *Dramaturgie de Jean Cocteau*. Paris: Bernard Grasset, 1954.

Duncan, Isadora. *My Life*. London: Gollancz, 1928.

Evans, Arthur B. *Jean Cocteau and his Films of Orphic Identity*. Philadelphia: Arts Alliance Press, 1977.

Fay, Bernard. *Les Precieux*. Paris: Librairie Académique Perrin, 1966.

Fermigier, André. *Jean Cocteau entre Picasso et Radiguet*. Paris: Hermann, 1967.

Fifield, William. "Jean Cocteau, an Interview." *Paris Review*, no. 32 (1964), pp. 13–37.

Flanner, Janet (Genet). *Paris Journal 1944–1965*. New York: Atheneum, 1977.

———. *Paris was Yesterday, 1925–1939*. New York: Viking Press, 1972.

Fowlie, Wallace. *Jean Cocteau: The History of a Poet's Age*. Bloomington, Ind.: Indiana University Press, 1966.

Fraigneau, André. *Cocteau*. New York: Grove Press, 1961.

———. *Entretiens avec Jean Cocteau*. Paris: Jalard, 1965.

Fokine, Mikhail. *Memoirs of a Ballet Master*. Trans. Vitale Fokine. London: Constable, 1960.

Gerogel, Pierre. "Jean Cocteau et son Temps, 1889–1963." Exhibition catalogue. Paris: Musée Jacquemart-André, 1965.

Gide, André. *Journal 1889–1939*. Paris: Gallimard-La Pleiade, 1952.

Gilson, René. *Jean Cocteau: An Investigation into his Films and Philosophy*. New York: Crown, 1969.

Gold, Arthur and Fizdale, Robert. *Misia.* New York: Alfred A. Knopf, 1980.
Gosling, Nigel. *The Adventurous World of Paris, 1900-1914.* New York: Morrow, 1978.
Grigoriev, S. L. *The Diaghilev Ballet.* London: Constable, 1953.
Gruen, John. "Paul Haakon," in *Dance Magazine,* November 1977.
Guest, Ivor. *Le Ballet de L'Opéra de Paris.* Paris: Flammarion, 1976.
Hahn, Reynaldo. *Le Dieu bleu.* Piano score. Paris: Hengel et Cie., 1911.
Harding, James. *Eric Satie.* New York: Praeger Publ., 1975.
_____. *Ox on the Roof.* London: MacDonald and Co., 1972.
Haskell, Arnold. *Ballet Russe.* London: Weidenfeld and Nicholson, 1968.
_____. *Diaghileff.* New York: Simon and Schuster, 1935.
Honegger, Arthur. *I am a Composer.* Trans. by W. O. Clough. London: Faber and Faber, 1966.
Hugo, Jean. *Cahiers Jean Cocteau.* Paris: Gallimard, 1975.
Jullian, Philippe. *Prince of Aesthetes.* New York: Viking Press, 1968.
Karsavina, Tamara. *Theatre Street.* New York: E. P. Dutton, 1931.
Kirby, Michael. *Futurist Performance.* New York: E. P. Dutton, 1971.
Kochno, Boris. *Diaghlev and the Ballets Russes.* New York: Harper and Row, 1970.
_____. *Le Ballet.* Paris: Librairie Hachette, 1954.
Koegler, Horst. *Concise Oxford Dictionary of Ballet.* London: Oxford University Press, 1977; 2nd ed., 1982.
Laloy, Louis. *La Musique retrouvée.* Paris: Plon, 1928.
Lanckorovska, Maria. *Wandteppiche für eine Forestin.* Frankfurt, 1965 (Dissertation).
La Rochefoucauld, Edmée de. *Anne de Noailles.* Paris: Editions universitaires, 1956.
Laurent, Jean and Julie Sazonova. *Serge Lifar, Renovateur du Ballet française.* Paris: Buchet, Chastel, Correa, 1960.
Lederman, Minna. *Stravinsky in the Theatre.* New York: Farrar, Strauss, Giroux, 1949.
Levinson, André. *La Danse d'Aujourd'hui.* Paris: Editions Duchartre et Van Buggenhaudt, 1929.
Lido, Serge. *Panorama de la Danse.* Paris: La Société française de Livre, n.d.
Lidova, I. "Janine Charrat," *Les Saison de la danse,* August 1970.
Lieven, Prince Peter. *The Birth of the Ballets Russes.* London: Allen and Unwin, 1936.
Lifar, Serge. *Le Livre de la Danse.* Paris: Société française de Diffusion musicale et artistique, 1954.
_____. *Ma Vie.* Trans. by J. H. Mason. London: Hutchinson, 1970.
_____. *Serge de Diaghilev.* New York: Putnam, 1940.
MacDonald, Nesta. *Diaghilev Observed.* New York: Dance Horizons, 1975.
Mallarmé, Stéphane. *Oeuvres Complètes.* Paris: Mondor et Jean Aubrey, 1945.
Marais, Jean. *Mes Quatres Verités.* Paris: Editions de Paris, 1957.
Martin, Marianne. "The Ballet *Parade*: A Dialogue Between Cubism and Futurism," in *Art Quarterly,* n.s., Spring 1978.
Massine, Leonide. *My Life in Ballet.* London: MacMillan, 1968.
Masson, Pierre. "Le Billet Juridique." *Danse et Rythmes* (December 1958), pp. 32-38, and January 1959, pp. 41-46.
Mauriac, Claude. *Jean Cocteau, ou La Verité du Mensonge.* Paris: Odette Lieutier, 1945.
Mayer, Charles S. "The Influence of Leon Bakst on Choreography." *Dance Chronicle* 1, no. 2, pp. 4-8.
Michaut, Pierre. *Le Ballet contemporain.* Paris: Plon, 1950.
_____. "The Choreography of Serge Lifar." *Ballet Annual #3.* London: A. and C. Black, 1949.
Migel, Parmenia. *The Ballerinas.* New York: MacMillan, 1972.
Milhaud, Darius. *Diary.* Unpublished.
_____. *Notes without Music.* New York: Alfred A. Knopf, 1953.
[Miskovitch], Milorad. *Lettres à Milorad.* Paris: Editions St. Germain-des-Près, 1976.
Morand, Paul. *Journal d'un Attaché d'Ambassade.* Paris: Gallimard, 1953.
Myers, Rollo. *Eric Satie.* London: D. Dodson, 1948.
Nabokov, Nicolas. *Bagazh.* New York: Atheneum Press, 1975.

Nadelhoffer, Hans. *Cartier, Jewelers Extraordinary.* New York: Harry N. Abrams, 1984.

Neoma, May. *Recits sur la danse.* Paris: Grund, 1969.

Nicolson, Harold. *Diaries and Letters.* London: Collins, 1967.

Nijinska, Bronislava. *Early Memoires.* New York: Holt, Rinehart, Winston, 1981.

Nijinsky, Romola. *Nijinsky.* New York: Putnam, 1934.

Nijinsky, Vaslav. *The Diary of Vaslav Nijinsky.* Ed. Romola Nijinsky. London: Gollancz, 1937.

Noailles, Marie-Laure de. "J'étais la Lolita de Jean Cocteau." *Figaro littéraire,* 17 June 1966, pp. 12–18.

Oxenhandler, Neal. *Scandal and Parade.* New Brunswick: Rutgers University Press, 1957.

Painter, George D. *Proust, A Biography.* 2 volumes. Boston: Atlantic, Little, Brown, 1965.

Payne, Charles. *American Ballet Theatre.* New York: Alfred A. Knopf, 1978.

Peters, Arthur King. *Jean Cocteau and André Gide: An Abrasive Friendship.* New Brunswick: Rutgers University Press, 1973.

_____. *Jean Cocteau and the French Scene.* New York: Abbeville Press, 1984.

Peyrefitte, Roger. "Jean Cocteau." *Arts,* no. 999 (31 March–6 April).

Phelps, Robert. *Professional Secrets.* Trans. by Richard Howard. New York: Farrar, Straus and Giroux, 1970.

Porel, Jacques. *Fils de Rejune: Souvenirs.* 2 vols. Paris: Plon, 1951–1952.

Poulenc, Francis. *Correspondence 1915–1963.* Paris: Editions du Seuil, 1967.

_____. *Moi et mes Amis.* Paris, Geneva: La Palatine, 1963.

Pridden, Deirdre. *The Art of the Dance in French Literature.* London: A. and C. Black, 1952.

Propert, W. A. *The Russian Ballet, 1909–1920.* London: Bodley Head, 1921.

_____. *The Russian Ballet, 1921–1929.* London: Bodley Head, 1931.

_____. *The Russian Ballet in Western Europe.* New York: John Lane Company, 1921.

Proust, Marcel. *Lettres à Reynaldo Hahn.* Paris: Gallimard, 1956.

_____. *Remembrance of Things Past.* 7 vols. Trans. C. K. Scott Moncrieff. New York: Random House, 1924.

Radiguet, Raymond. *Oeuvres complètes.* Paris: Club des Librairies de France, 1959.

Reverdy, Pierre. *Self-Defense: Critique-Esthetique.* Paris: Imprimerie littéraire, 1919.

Ries, Frank W. D. "Acrobats, Burlesque, and Cocteau." *Dance Scope* 11, no. 1, pp. 52–68.

_____. "Cocteau's Review of the First Ballets Russes Season." *Dance Scope* 14, no. 1, pp. 7–12.

Robert, Frederic. "Louis Durey, l'Aine des Six." Paris: Les Editeurs français réunis, 1968.

Le Roman de la Dame à la Lycorne et du Beau Chevalier au Lyons. Dresden: Gennrich, 1909.

Rosen, Heinz. *Balletheater.* Munich: n.p., 1963.

Rostand, Maurice. *Confessions d'un Demi-Siècle.* Paris: Jeune Parque, 1948.

Salmon, André. *Souvenirs sans fin.* 3 vols. Paris: Gallimard, 1955–1961.

Sanouillet, Michel. *Dada à Paris.* Paris: Pauvert, 1965.

Severini, Gino. "Tempo de l'Effort Moderne." In *La vita d'un pittore,* vol. 2. Ed. Piero Pacini. Florence: 1968.

Sert, Misia. *Two or Three Muses.* London: Museum Press Limited, 1953.

Shattuck, Roger. *The Banquet Years.* New York: Random House, 1955, 1968.

Shead, Richard. *Music in the 1920s.* London: Duckworth, 1976.

Silver, Kenneth E. "Jean Cocteau and the Image d'Epinal," in *Jean Cocteau and the French Scene.* New York: Abbeville Press, 1984.

Slonimsky, Yuri, et al. *Marius Petipa Materiali Wospominanija Stati.* Leningrad: Verlag Iskusstwo, 1971.

Sokolova, Lydia. *Dancing for Diaghilev* Ed. Richard Buckle. London: Murray, 1960.

Sotheby and Co. *Ballet and Theatre Material* (Sales catalogue). London: Sotheby and Co., 1975.

Spencer, Charles. *Leon Bakst.* London: Academy Press, 1973.

Sprigge, Elizabeth and Jean-Jacques Kihm. *Jean Cocteau: The Man and the Mirror.* New York: Coward McCann, 1968.

Steegmuller, Francis. *Cocteau: A Biography.* New York: Atlantic, Little, and Brown, 1970.

Stein, Gertrude. *The Autobiography of Alice B. Toklas.* New York: Harcourt, Brace, 1933.
————. *Everybody's Autobiography.* New York: Random House, 1937.
Stravinsky, Igor. *An Autobiography.* New York: Steuer, 1958.
————. "On Music and Other Matters." In *New York Review of Books*, 14 March 1968.
————, with Robert Craft. *Memories and Commentaries.* London: Faber and Faber, 1960.
Stravinsky, Vera and Robert Craft. *Stravinsky in Pictures and Documents.* New York: Simon and Schuster, 1978.
Sorell, Walter. "An Appreciation of Jean Cocteau." *Dance Magazine* (February 1964), pp. 38–41.
Stegen, Ina. "Kubismus und Theater." *Neue Zuricher Zeitung*, 5 March 1967.
Templier, Pierre-Daniel. *Eric Satie.* Trans. E. and D. French. Cambridge: M.I.T. Press, 1969.
Terry, Walter. *I Was There.* New York: Marcel Dekker, 1978.
Tugal, Pierre. "Ballet in Paris, 1946–47." *The Ballet Annual* 2 (1948), pp. 80–89.
————, et al. *Les Ballets Suédois.* Paris: Trianon Press, 1931.
Valéry, Paul. "Philosophy of the Dance." *Salmagundi*, nos. 33–34 (1976), pp. 65–76.
Verlet, Pierre and Frances Salet. *La Dame à la licorne.* Paris: Cluny Museum, 1960.
Vigot, Alain. *La Revue Musicale.* December-January 1953.
Vlad, Roman. *Stravinsky.* Oxford: Oxford University Press, 1960.
Wharton, Edith. *A Backward Glance.* New York: Century Appleton, 1934.
White, Eric Walter. *Stravinsky.* Berkeley: University of California Press, 1966.
Wildman, Carl. "Jean Cocteau and the Ballet." *Dancing Times* (October 1973), pp. 18–20.
Wilson, Edmund Jr. "The Aesthetic Upheaval in France: The Influence of Jazz in Paris and the Americanization of French Literature and Art." *Vanity Fair*, February 1922.
Wilson, G. B. L. *A Dictionary of Ballet.* 3rd ed. London: Adam & Charles Black, Ltd., 1974.

D. Newspapers and Periodicals Consulted

France:

Arts
Comoedia illustré
La Danse
Danse et Rythmes
Le Figaro
International HAD
Le Journal
Masques
Le Ménestrel

Mercure de France
Musica Disques
La Nouvelle revue française
Paris-Midi
La Revue musicale
Revue de Paris
Le Théâtre
Les Saisons de la danse

United Kingdom:

Ballet
Ballet Annual
The Bystander
Daily Mail
Daily Telegraph
Dance and Dancers
Dancing Times
Illustrated London News

Matinee
Musical Standard
New Statesman
Observer
The Queen
Sackbut
The Stage
The Times

Germany and Switzerland:

Abendzeitung
Aachener Volkszeitung
Darmstädter Echo
Düsseldorfer Nachrichten
Frankfurt Abendpost Main
Frankfurter Allegmeine Zeitung
Der Mittag

Mannheimer Morgen
Münchener Merkur
Neue Zurcher Nachrichten
Neue Zurcher Zeitung
Suddeutsche Zeitung
Westfalische Nachrichten

United States and Canada:

Ballet Review
Chicago Tribune
Dance Chronical
Dance Index
Dance Magazine
Dance News
Dance Perspectives
Dance Scope
Musical America
New York Herald Tribune

The New Yorker
New York Post
The New York Times
Saturday Review
Theatre Arts
Variety
Vanity Fair
The World
York Dance Review

Index